THE TAFSĪR OF
SŪRAH YŪSUF

A COMMENTARY OF SŪRAH YŪSUF
THE 12ᵀᴴ CHAPTER OF THE GLORIOUS QUR'ĀN

SHAYKH ABDUL RAHEEM LIMBADA

HAFIZAHULLĀH

Tafseer-Raheemi Publications 2018
info@tafseer-raheemi.com

The Tafsīr of Sūrah Yūsuf
ISBN: 978-1-912301-04-1
First Edition: July 2002
Second Edition: Muharram 1440 / October 2018

Author	*Shaykh* Abdul Raheem Limbādā *Hafizahullāh* (www.tafseer-raheemi.com)
Editing	*Shaykh* Abdul Raheem Limbādā, *Maulānā* Abdullāh Patel, *Maulānā* Abdus Subhan Dalvi, *Maulānā* Omer Anwar
Cover Design	*Mufti* Abdul-Rahmān Mangera
Typesetting	Belal Isakjee
Printed by	Mega Printers, Istanbul (mega.com.tr)

Other available titles in this series:

The Tafsīr of Sūrah Fātiha
The Tafsīr of Sūrah Maryam
The Tafsīr of Sūrah Nūh

Available to purchase from www.tafseer-raheemi.com/shop

CONTENTS

PREFACE

In the name of Allāh, the Most Compassionate, the Most Merciful.

The dearest Maulānā Abdul Raheem Sahib, lecturer of *Hadīth* in *Dārul Uloom*, Bury, [May Allāh ﷻ protect him], requested me to provide a preface for his current work, an exegesis of Sūrah Yūsuf. This *surah* comprises multiple disciplines of study, such as astronomy, geography, mineralogy, and sociology.

The sciences of the Noble Qur'ān are a limitless ocean and a manifestation of the Qur'ānic verse:

$$\text{قُلْ لَّوْ كَانَ الْبَحْرُ مِدَادًا لِّكَلِمٰتِ رَبِّيْ لَنَفِدَ الْبَحْرُ}$$

$$\text{قَبْلَ اَنْ تَنْفَدَ كَلِمٰتُ رَبِّيْ وَلَوْ جِئْنَا بِمِثْلِهٖ مَدَدًا ○}$$

Say: If the ocean were ink [to write out] the words of my Rabb, then surely, the ocean would dry up before the words of my Rabb finished, even if We brought another similar ocean for its aid. [1]

The beginning of the *surah* contains certain phrases which serve as an introduction to the *surah*. The words '*al-kitāb al-mubīn*' [the Manifest Book], provide the name of the Book. The words '*innā anzalnāhū*' [indeed We have revealed it] reveal the source of the Book. The words '*ahsan al-qasas*' [the most beautiful of stories] indicate a specific chapter title. Likewise, the Qur'ānic words '*lā taqsus ru'yāka*' [do not relate your dream] supported by the Hadīth, '*Do not relate a vision except to a boon companion or an intelligent person*' [2] provide guidance in relation to the science of dreams and their interpretation. The words '*fayakīdū laka kaydā* '[otherwise they will concoct a plot against you] substantiate the presence of men of esoteric knowledge unto whom

---

[1] Qur'ān 18:109.
[2] Sunan Abu Dāwūd 5020.

9

information is disclosed and future eventualities become unveiled and that the articulation of such knowledge should not be held as improper. The words 'wa *kadhālika yajtabīka rabbuka*' [and your Lord will choose you] indicate the science of disclosures and character judgement. Effectively, each word seems to unfold a body of knowledge that the reader of this work would become acquainted with.

I supplicate to Allāh ﷻ that He establishes this work as a source of benefit for the author, its readers, and all who assist in the printing and publication of it.

This *sūrah*, as I have previously stated, contains information about situations that both the people of distinction and the masses confront in their worldly lives. It exposes the hidden jealousy of Prophet Yūsuf's ﷺ brothers towards him and his subsequent separation from his father, Prophet Yā'qūb, ﷺ who virtually lost his eye sight, due to a lifetime of yearning and remembrance of his beloved son. The question of the impact this separation had on his mother is also raised. Likewise, how did the late Hadhrat Maulānā Islāmul Haqq Sāhib ﷺ [former *Shaykh-ul-Hadīth* of *Dārul Uloom*, Bury] and his wife, who were also separated from their son, during his infancy, whilst residing amongst a Hindu community in India, live out the remaining thirty five years of their lives? The Prophet Yā'qūb ﷺ however, was eventually reunited with his son, towards the end of his life, whilst the latter was the Governor of Egypt. At this point, he was also informed of the lengthy sequence of events, which characterised his son's life. This includes the period of his son's infancy, enslavement and, of course, the extent to which Zuleikhā and other Egyptian women were infatuated with him, all of which is recorded in great detail in the Qur'ān. This infamous infatuation has produced numerous narratives in various mediums.

My name is also Yūsuf and approximately twenty-five years ago, I had the opportunity to stay in Egypt for a short while. A few months ago, I related to Maulānā Irshād Sāhib, the *Imām* of Howard Street Mosque in Bradford, an anecdote of an Egyptian Zuleikhā, prior to his departure to Egypt for marital purposes. The anecdote is as follows:

"When I was just over twenty-five years of age, I resided in Egypt for a short while. I lived in a flat that was situated on top of a meat shop on Majlis al-Sha'b Street in Cairo. This was between the Laghirigli and the vegetable market. I attended a local Mosque, which was located slightly off the main road on a side street, for the five daily prayers. At the mosque I became acquainted with three people, who would accompany me during their spare time. The three were: Muhammad Yūsuf al-Zafzaf, an extremely courteous person; Midhat, a tall and slim individual; and Mustafā, an exceptional footballer. On one occasion, I arranged their collective names in a verse of poetry and recited it in their presence. They were all exceedingly charmed by the verse and commented that it resembled *Al-Harīrī's Maqamāt*. The verse was:

مَدَحْتُ مُحَمَّدَ نِ الْمُصْطَفَى ـ

I eulogised [madahtu] Muhammad, the chosen one [Al-Mustafā].

All three regularly visited me at my flat after the Asr prayer and occasionally I would call upon them at their residence.

On one occasion, Muhammad invited me to his house for a meal after *Ishā*. I noticed on arrival that extra special attention had been given to prepare the meal. We indulged in conversation in the presence of his parents and other members of his family, in the courtyard of his house. At one point, Muhammad and Midhat took me to a room inside the house where Muhammad's sister, Zuleikhā, was also present. After a short conversation, Midhat pointing towards Zuleikhā and acting in the capacity of her agent informed me, 'I marry her to you.' In a moment of urgency, failing to gather the fortitude within me to make an absolute decision on a matter of paramount importance, I found myself unable to deliver a positive response and considering rejection of the proposal impolite, I remained silent but smiling. On the one hand, both Muhammad and Midhat expressed their anxiety, and on the other, Zuleikhā, despite the open doors, attempted to convince me, هَيْتَ لَكَ 'oh come on' by her desperate eyes, despondent appearance and the lines of her forehead. She was in fact a personification of the verse وَلَقَدْ هَمَّتْ بِهِ 'and indeed she did desire him.' But despite my vibrant youth and the non-existence of religious motive to prevent me, and without witnessing any clear proof [as contained within the *sūrah*] the Qur'ānic verse وَهَمَّ بِهَا 'and he desired her' did not manifest. I did periodically regret this.

11

My *Shaykh*, Hadhrat Shaykh ul-Hadīth Maulānā Muhammad Zakarīyyā [May Allāh ﷺ have mercy upon him] would remark that a *hadīth* instructs us to abstain from wilful want of others possessions and not to reject an offering made without an expression of interest, otherwise that offering could remain elusive even upon request.

I experienced a similar scenario. Zuleikhā and her family extended a marriage proposal with the utmost reverence, courtesy and according to the Islāmic guidelines, but I did not oblige.

As a consequence of leaving Zuleikhā heartbroken, when I intended to remarry at the age of fifty, twenty-five years after the above incident, I continued to hear the echo of her broken heart in the presence of Muhammad and Midhat with two streams of tears flowing freely from her eyes. I would also find myself uttering with distress: يٰحَسْرَتَنَا عَلٰى مَا فَرَّطْنَا فِيهَا 'Oh my loss due to forsaking her' and I would supplicate in favour of Zuleikhā, Muhammad, and Midhat. On occasion, this would be supplemented with the petition of Prophet Yā'qūb ﷺ: وَاللهُ الْمُسْتَعَانُ عَلٰى مَا تَصِفُوْنَ 'Allāh ﷺ is the One whose succour is sought.' Eventually my atonement and continuous supplications overwhelmed the bitterness of Zuleikhā's broken heart and my heart's aspirations were fulfilled.

At present, the invocation of Prophet Yūsuf ﷺ remains on my tongue:

$$رَبِّ قَدْ اٰتَيْتَنِيْ مِنَ الْمُلْكِ وَعَلَّمْتَنِيْ مِنْ تَأْوِيْلِ الْاَحَادِيْثِ ج$$

$$فَاطِرَ السَّمٰوٰتِ وَالْاَرْضِ ۖ اَنْتَ وَلِيّ فِي الدُّنْيَا وَالْاٰخِرَةِ ۝$$

'My Lord! Indeed You have bestowed on me sovereignty and taught me the interpretation of dreams. Oh Creator of the heavens and the earth, You are my Protector in this world and the Hereafter.' [3]

But it fails to continue with the words تَوَفَّنِيْ مُسْلِمًا وَّاَلْحِقْنِيْ بِالصّٰلِحِيْنَ 'Grant me death as one submitting to Your will and let me be from amongst the righteous', due to the infancy of my children, Muhammad and Sulaimān.

[3] Qur'ān 12:101.

My ardent aspiration remains that Muhammad and Sulaimān develop into complete personifications of Prophet Yūsuf, Prophet Yā'qūb 🕮, and their successor Prophet Muhammad, 🕮 and I, in my final moment, utter with ultimate contentment, 'Grant me [Oh Lord!] death as one submitting to Your Will and let me be from amongst the righteous.' *Āmīn!*

Hadhrat Maulānā Yūsuf Motālā *Dāmat Barakātuhum*
Translated by Shaykh Māhmood Chāndia *Hafizahullāh*

FOREWORD

Sūrah Yūsuf is a tale of many contradistinctions of love, longing, and forbearance in the face of loss. It provides a compelling account of the divine reward for patient endurance. This *tafsīr* is a powerful antidote to the modern values of instant gratification that Western Muslims, in particular, aspire towards.

The lessons in Sūrah Yūsuf are inspiring. The excellence of Prophet Yūsuf's ﷺ character shows that lasting contentment comes through obedience to Allāh ﷻ. The trials that Prophet Yūsuf ﷺ experienced, were borne through his dignity and compassion.

Allāh ﷻ grant us the strength to fulfil our devotions by aspiring to the beauty of Prophet Yūsuf ﷺ. May the love that he had for his family visit the reader and inspire him with the greater love for Allāh ﷻ and His Messenger ﷺ.

Allāh ﷻ bestow Maulānā Abdul Raheem with renewed success in similar endeavours and reward him handsomely for enriching the reader with his knowledge.

Āatika Borā
27/04/2002

FOREWORD BY THE AUTHOR

When my Shaykh, Hadhrat Maulānā Yūsuf Motālā Sāhib [May Allāh ﷻ give him a long and prosperous life] initially instructed me to write the Tafsīr of Sūrah Yūsuf for our monthly magazine, *Subulas Salaam*, I was taken aback in surprise and awe, for I considered myself neither qualified, nor worthy of the undertaking. However, since one's parents and teachers are constantly stressing the virtues of respecting the wishes of one's elders, I conceded to the given instruction, and took upon writing the *tafsīr*.

At the inception, the weight of the responsibility dawned upon me. Having to prepare for my lessons throughout the week, as a teacher of *Sahīh Muslim* and *Mishkāt Shareef*, I found time to be a major restraint during the weekdays. So I settled upon the habit of writing the *tafsīr* on Sundays, after *Fajr salāh*.

By the Grace of Allāh, ﷻ and with the *du'ās* of my Shaykh, Allāh ﷻ began to lighten the task, and gradually the 'burden' of the responsibility gave way to the sweetness of research and writing. It is the reason why one may notice that I was unable to write much commentary in the beginning of the *sūrah*, however, in the latter parts, I have tried to cover as many topics as possible.

If I was asked as to the reason why my Hadhrat chose the *tafsīr* of Sūrah Yūsuf in particular, I would not know the answer. However, I may venture to say that Sūrah Yūsuf has many aspects, especially lessons regarding patience [*sabr*], and those regarding dreams and their interpretations. Nowadays, people pay very little attention to dreams. When a person's life is engrossed in sin, he is more apt to see a nightmare than a sweet dream. If someone watches television till the late hours of the night, then falls asleep and neglects his *Fajr salāh*, how can he expect to see a meaningful dream? This is why people have a deep neglect of this science. And if someone does relate a true dream and the interpretation turns out to be correct then many people refuse to accept this, and simply make fun of such people. As the saying goes: الناس اعداء لما جهلوا 'People show hostility towards that which they do not know.'

16

My Hadhrat's name is Yūsuf. Like the Prophet Yūsuf 🕮, Allāh 🕮 has blessed him with the wisdom of dreams and their interpretations. Hadhrat very often sees dreams, which turn out to be as clear as the stroke of dawn.

Recently, just before his departure for South Africa to visit his aged mother, his wife, whilst carrying their youngest son in her arms, slipped down a flight of stairs. Both were injured with the child having to be taken in emergency for treatment. When I heard of the incident, I approached Hadhrat to console him. He smiled and related a dream he saw the night before. He said, "The *dunya* [world] of dreams is *ajeeb* [amazing]. Sometimes, the Angel of dreams comes out and warns us of something which is going to happen." Thereafter, he said, "I saw that the Majlis of Hadhrat Shaykh 🕮 was taking place. Hadhrat beckoned me and I was going towards him. Maulānā Munawwar Hussain Sahib [a great *Khalīfāh* of Hadhrat] met me on the way and started talking to me. I listened to him then I mentioned that Hadhrat was calling me so I had to go. He obliged and we parted. I turned around to see that he started climbing some stairs, and I stood there motionless while he climbed, for he was elderly and I felt he might need some assistance. After climbing a few stairs, he tumbled and fell from step to step into a *hawz* [pond for *wudhū*] that was at the end. I rushed towards him and pulled him out. I thought that he might have been fatally injured. However, he opened his eyes and said, 'I am alright.'"

Once he [Hadhrat] saw that the sun was rising in such a manner that a cross was embedded in it. He felt very grieved and related the dream in a very distressed manner, saying, 'We had hoped for the rise of Islām, and yet I see this?' Then a few days later, he said, 'The dream has been constantly on my mind and I am realising that the cross was more like a plus sign in maths. I feel that the sun should not be interpreted according to its spelling but according to the pronunciation, which would be 'son.' I have a feeling that Allāh 🕮 is about to bless me with a son and perhaps not just one, but more, owing to the plus sign.' The dream came true. First Allāh 🕮 gifted him with Muhammad, and then Sulaimān.

Once he said, "I saw Maulānā Ahmādullāh Sāhib 🕮, the former *Shaykh ul-Hadīth* of Jāmiah Hussainīyah, Rander [One of the most prestigious *Madrasas* in Gujarat, India]. He came to my house at the *Dārul Uloom*, and I was welcoming him.' The next day Maulānā's grandson, Hāfiz Uwais, was brought to the *Dārul Uloom* for admission. Hadhrat said, 'This is the interpretation. Maulānā came to intercede for his grandson's application."

Hadhrat is also gifted with the ability to interpret dreams in a wonderful manner. Maulānā Yūsuf Māmūn Sāhib related that he saw Hadhrat Maulānā Islāmul Haqq Sāhib ﷺ in a dream after his death. He saw him in Nebo Street, Bolton in a very pleasant mood wearing bright white clothes. He had a *tasbīh* in his hand. Maulānā Māmūn asked him, "Hadhrat! Haven't you died?" He replied, "No, I am alive."

Upon hearing this dream, Hadhrat replied, "When a person sees someone after his death as though he is still alive, this means that Allāh ﷻ has given him the rank of a *Shaheed* [a martyr]." Regarding the martyrs, Allāh ﷻ says in the Qur'ān, "They are alive", and Allāh ﷻ gives this rank to whoever He wills.

In one *Hadīth*, the Prophet ﷺ said, "The dream of a true believer is one part of the forty-six parts of *Nubūwwah* [Prophethood]." [4] In another *Hadīth*, the Prophet ﷺ said, "Nothing from *Nubūwwah* is left, except for *Mubashshirāt*." The companions asked, "What are *Mubashshirāt*, O Rasūlullāh?" He replied, "A good dream which a Muslim sees or which someone else sees for him." [5]

Hadhrat Yūsuf ﷺ saw a dream, which turned out to be true. He interpreted the dream of the king as well as the dreams of the two prisoners. The Prophets used to have true dreams, so much so that Ibrāhīm ﷺ on seeing a dream for three consecutive nights, understood it as an instruction to sacrifice his son and acted accordingly. Our Prophet ﷺ used to relate his dreams and would interpret the dreams seen by the Sahābā ﷺ.

The *Ulamā* of this *Ummah* have followed the Prophet ﷺ in every field and consequently, they also see true dreams and give interpretations to them. Among the recent scholars are Hadhrat Maulānā Rashīd Ahmed Gangohī ﷺ and Hadhrat Maulānā Qāsim Nānōtwī ﷺ.

Hadhrat Shaykh ul-Hadīth Maulānā Muhammad Zakarīyā ﷺ was also an expert in this field. He writes in one reply to a letter, 'Your dream of killing snakes is a good dream, as it means 'killing' contemptible, vile habits. It

---

[4] Bukhārī 6983, Muslim 2263.
[5] Abū Dāwūd 876, and others.

would be a great gift of Allāh 🌸 if He killed-off my bad habits as well as those of yours and all my friends.'

In another letter, he writes, 'Do not pay so much attention to dreams. If you see a pleasant dream, thank Allāh 🌸. If you ever see a disturbing dream, recite اعوذ بالله من الشيطان الرجيم then spit to your left. This is what we have been taught in *Hadīth*. Dozens of people see dreams regarding the humble writer. However, I myself see very few dreams. I don't even mention to people that I saw this dream – Your first dream that someone is preaching and the funeral of Rasūlullāh 🌸 is placed there; is quite clear. The *Janāzah* of Rasūlullāh 🌸 denotes the death of his *Sunnah*. That Rasūlullāh 🌸 is running his hands over his face indicates his grief and distress over the situation of the Muslims. Your own grief in the dream shows your feelings over the state of Muslims, which you most often mention. May Allāh 🌸 revive our *deen* and may He give some *sukūn* [tranquillity] to our Prophet 🌸.'

In another letter, he writes, 'To see oneself clean shaven in a dream depends upon the religious inclination of the person having the dream. If he is religious, then it is a glad tiding of forgiveness. 'The dwellers of *Jannah* will be hairless and beardless.' However, if the person is irreligious then this is emulating the *kuffār* [i.e. the person may have a beard in reality but he might be copying the *kuffār* in some other way]. In your case, the second interpretation cannot be taken, therefore the first one is definite.'

To summarise, dreams do have meanings. If a person sees a dream which he thinks could hold some meaning, then he should try to understand its meaning and if need be then enquire about its interpretation from reliable *Ulamā* and seniors.

By the Grace of Almighty Allāh 🌸, the *tafsīr* has been completed. I want to categorically admit that this humble work does not do justice to what Allāh's 🌸 words deserve. It would have been an impossibility for a sinful person like myself to write on the *Paak* and Pure words of the Almighty. If something good has been brought forth, it is through the Grace of Allāh 🌸, and if mistakes have been made, then it is due to my inability – May Allāh 🌸 forgive me.

I am constantly reminded of my Hadhrat's urgings, for many a time, the notion of not continuing had crossed my mind. But my Hadhrat's kind words of encouragement kept me going. May Allāh ﷻ give him a long and healthy life, and may Allāh ﷻ keep His blessed shade over our heads for as long as we live. I remember reading the words of Muftī Mahmūd Sāhib ﷺ in a letter to his Shaykh, Hadhrat Shaykh ul-Hadīth ﷺ. In it, he writes, 'I wish I would die during the lifetime of my Hadhrat because then I could have some hope of dying with *imān*, for the sanctity of my *imān* is also due to your *duās* and your blessed presence. I do not know whether I would be able to safeguard my *imān* after Hadhrat, if Hadhrat were to die before me.'

Furthermore, I would also like to thank the group of students who assisted me throughout the discourses with the typing and type-setting. Most recently, Maulānā Irfān Sidyot, Maulānā Ābid Ghulām Rasūl, Maulānā Sa'īd Mullā, Maulānā Istiāq Vawdā, and Maulānā Yūnus Ravat. Not to forget Maulānā Ismail Gangāt, Sister Āatika Borā and others who took the trouble of proof reading and correcting the earlier drafts.

May Allāh ﷻ accept our humble efforts and make them a source of forgiveness in the hereafter. *Āmīn!*

Shaykh Abdul Raheem Limbādā [*Hafizahullāh*]

July 2002

FOREWORD FOR SECOND EDITION

This *tafsīr* was first published in 2002. The first edition was well received, *Alhamdulillah*. Many friends kept requesting for a copy of the *tafsīr*, however we had run out. My friends urged me and helped me to print a second edition. May Allāh ﷻ reward them all.

My dearest, Maulānā Belal Isakjee pushed it forward. Maulānā Abdullāh Patel of Gloucester and his *Ahliya* went through the whole work again and edited it where required. In fact, they have both given the book a face-lift. They have completely changed the structure of the writings. May Allāh ﷻ reward Maulānā Abdullāh and his *Ahliya Muhtarama* for their time and effort. *Āmīn!*

Maulānā Abdus Subhān Dalvī also deserves such equal thanks as he assisted with the final draft as well and gave some valuable suggestions.

Thereafter, I went through the whole book, and benefited myself too. I had forgotten many of the beautiful subjects included therein, and it was very refreshing for me as well.

May Allāh ﷻ accept and be pleased. May Allāh ﷻ overlook our shortcomings and give us *tawfeeq* to do more. May Allāh ﷻ be pleased with us all. *Āmīn!*

Shaykh Abdul Raheem Limbādā [*Hafizahullāh*]
Dhul Qaa'dā 1438 / August 2017

AUTHOR'S NOTE

I commence the *tafsīr* of Sūrah Yūsuf in the name of Allāh ﷻ, the Most Gracious, the Most Merciful. I seek His refuge from all evils and I very humbly pray for His help in this monumental task ahead of me.

As a beginner with no knowledge and no experience of writing in English, I have nothing but high hopes of assistance from Allāh ﷻ. I have before me various translations of the Holy Qur'ān, from amongst which I give preference to the translation of Pickthall, thereafter *Tafsīr Mājidī* and then various others. I will try to make the commentary as short as possible, giving references for whatever I write.

A BRIEF ACCOUNT OF THE SŪRAH

Sūrah Yūsuf is a Makkan *sūrah* i.e a *sūrah* that was revealed in *Makkah* before *Hijrah*. We do not know the exact date of when this *sūrah* was revealed, but we know roughly that it was revealed around the tenth or eleventh year of the *dā'wah*. It is the twelfth *sūrah* of the Qur'ān, consisting of one hundred and eleven [111] verses and twelve *rūkūs*. It is named Sūrah Yūsuf, because the story of Yūsuf ﷺ is mentioned therein.

In the previous *sūrah* [Sūrah Hūd], the stories of a number of Prophets were related to us. In Sūrah Yūsuf, uniquely, only one Prophet's story is mentioned throughout the whole *sūrah*, without any interruption and in chronological order. Stories of the Prophets are related in different chapters for different reasons, but mainly they serve to console the Holy Prophet ﷺ during the hardships he was enduring. The story of Yūsuf ﷺ is mentioned in one *sūrah* because it was revealed upon the request of people. Likewise, the story of *As'hābe-Kahf* [The People of the cave] and *Zul-Qarnain* is mentioned in only one *sūrah*, [Sūrah Kahf] as it was revealed upon request. [6]

---

[6] Mā'riful Qur'ān of Maulānā Idrīs Khāndelwī.

CAUSE OF REVELATION

Many verses of the Holy Qur'ān are connected to certain incidents in the life of The Messenger ﷺ, which became the cause of their revelation. The *Mufassirūn* ﷺ [exegetes] have written separate books regarding these causes, e.g. Allāmah Suyūtī's ﷺ *'Lubāb an-nuqūl fī asbāb in-nuzūl.'* These incidents are quite important, because quite often, the meaning of a verse cannot be understood without knowing the reason for its revelation.

In the case of Sūrah Yūsuf, two incidents are mentioned, which could serve as the reason for its revelation:

1. Sa'd Ibn Abī Waqqās ﷺ said, "When Allāh ﷻ revealed the Holy Qur'ān, and the Holy Prophet ﷺ had recited it to the *Sahābā* for a period of time, they once requested, 'How wonderful it would be if you also conversed with us', thus Allāh ﷻ revealed the verse:

$$اَللّٰهُ نَزَّلَ اَحْسَنَ الْحَدِيْثِ ۝$$

'Allāh has sent down the best speech.' [7]

Then they said, 'O Prophet of Allāh, tell us a story!' and Allāh ﷻ revealed Sūrah Yūsuf and the verse:

$$نَحْنُ نَقُصُّ عَلَيْكَ اَحْسَنَ الْقَصَصِ ۝$$

'We are relating to you the most beautiful narration.'" [8]

2. Dhahhāk ﷺ narrates from Ibn Abbās ﷺ, "The Jews questioned the Prophet ﷺ regarding the situation of the Prophet Yā'qūb ﷺ and his sons, especially Yūsuf ﷺ. They enquired as to why and how they came to Egypt, when they were originally from Can'ān, Syria.' Thereupon Allāh ﷻ revealed Sūrah Yūsuf." [9]

---

[7] Qur'ān 39:23.
[8] Qur'ān 12:3, Khāzin.
[9] Khāzin.

Maulānā Abdul Mājid Daryābādī ﷺ writes in Tafsīr Mājidī, 'The story of Joseph, as given in the Holy Qur'ān, is similar, but not identical to the Biblical story. The Biblical story is like a folk tale in which morality has no place. Its tendency is to exalt the clever, financially minded Jew against the Egyptian, and to explain certain ethnic and tribal peculiarities in late Jewish history. Joseph is shown as buying up all the cattle and the land of the poor Egyptians for the State under the stress of famine conditions, and making the Isrā'īlites rulers over Pharaoh's cattle. The Qur'ānic story, on the other hand, rather than being a mere narrative, is a highly spiritual reading, explaining the contradictions of life, the enduring nature of virtue in a world full of flux and change, and the marvellous working of Allāh's ﷻ eternal purpose in His plan has unfolded to us on the wide canvas of history. [10]

INTRODUCTION

In order to appreciate the value and the importance of this beautiful *sūrah* and the story contained within it, and the profound lessons we are expected to learn from it, we must understand not just the reason for its revelation, but the deeper context and background in which it was revealed.

As discussed above, the *sūrah* was revealed during the Messenger's ﷺ stay in *Makkah*, after the Year of Grief ['*ām al-huzn*], during the 10th year after Prophethood. The Year of Grief was the most difficult period of the Messenger's ﷺ life, in which he suffered three major personal setbacks.

The first of these was the death of his beloved wife of twenty-five years, his closest confidante and his soul mate, Sayyida Khadījah ﷺ. When the people of *Quraysh*, his own family members, rejected his message, she stood by his side and consoled him, comforted him, and was his first point of call in times of distress. In the traumatic few moments after the original *wahī* was revealed, he had rushed back to Khadījah ﷺ who had helped calm his distress. Khadījah ﷺ was very dear to the Messenger ﷺ due to her unreserved support and selflessness. When a man has that comfort and love inside the house, he is able to face a lot outside. When he is deprived of that, then the

---

[10] Tafsīr Mājidī 356:2.

problems outside become more difficult to bear. Thus, Khadija's ﷠ role wasn't just vital to the Messenger ﷺ on a personal level, but was pivotal to the spreading of Islām.

If that wasn't enough, a few days after her death, he was hit by the death of his uncle, Abū Tālib. Abū Tālib had sacrificed his own reputation and prestige in order to protect the Prophet ﷺ. When the *Quraysh* came to bribe, threaten, and intimidate the Prophet ﷺ, initially Abū Tālib was scared and asked him to stop propagating Islām. The Messenger ﷺ explained his position that he was unable to stop the work of *dāwah*. Abū Tālib realised that his duty as an uncle was to protect his nephew from the enemies. He happily stood by the Messenger's ﷺ side throughout the boycott which was imposed upon the followers and protectors of the Prophet ﷺ, sacrificing his own luxuries for the sake of his nephew. His death opened the doors to relentless persecution at the hands of the *Quraysh*, which proved a great obstacle for the Messenger ﷺ in his mission to spread the word of Allāh ﷻ.

The third calamity to befall the Messenger ﷺ was the tragedy of *Tā'if*. As a result of the persecution at the hands of the *Quraysh* after the death of his uncle Abū Tālib, the Messenger ﷺ travelled to *Tā'if* in order to garner support from their chieftains. Rather than earning their support and protection, he was humiliated and publicly scorned, so much so that the youth of *Tā'if* were sent after him to stone him. This day compounded the sorrow and misery of the previous few months.

It was after these three incidents and heartbreaks that Allāh ﷻ decided to console his beloved ﷺ with the revelation of Sūrah Yūsuf, which contained a similar pattern of heartbreak and misfortune experienced by the Prophet Yūsuf ﷺ. The aim of the *sūrah* was to grant the Messenger peace and consolation, that these tough conditions come upon the most beloved of Allāh's servants too.

A SUMMARY OF THE STORY OF YŪSUF ﷺ

The story of Prophet Yūsuf ﷺ as mentioned in this *sūrah*, the twelfth *sūrah*, is split into twelve parts, in a symmetrical pattern. The first six parts of the story slowly unravel to reveal the final six parts. These twelve parts together provide a summary to the entire *sūrah*.

The first of these twelve parts is the dream Yūsuf 🕊 sees as a child which he then relates to his father. His father is aware of the jealousy of his brothers, and so instructs Yūsuf 🕊 not to mention the dream to them. The second part of the story is based on the brothers eventually finding out about the dream, then plotting to kill Yūsuf 🕊, resulting in them throwing him into a well, alone and abandoned. The third part of the story is centred around the palace of the Minister of Egypt who buys Yūsuf 🕊 as a young slave, and takes good care of him, until his wife Zuleikhā attempts to seduce him against his will, an advance which he resists. The fourth major incident in the story of Yūsuf 🕊 is when he is asked to present himself to the female friends of the minister's wife as they all sit to cut fruit. However, they are so awestruck by his beauty that they mistakenly cut their own fingers. They support the accusations levelled against Yūsuf 🕊 which compounds the case against him, due to which he is made to endure a prison sentence. The fifth development is the [false] imprisonment of Yūsuf 🕊, caused by a spiteful Zuleikhā, due to his rejection and resistance. This is then closely followed by the sixth instalment in this story, when the two prison companions see dreams, which are then interpreted by Yūsuf 🕊. One is destined to be killed, and the other to live on and once again serve the king. The king also then sees a dream that seven fat cows are coming out of a dry river, followed by seven thin ones who swallow the seven fat ones. He also sees seven fine full ears of corn upon which seven dry ones appear enwrapped. This is where the first half of the story of Yūsuf 🕊 ends.

The narrative of Yūsuf 🕊 now begins to resolve. Previously unanswered questions are answered and objections are dealt with. The seventh chapter of the story deals with the dream of the king being interpreted by none other than Yūsuf 🕊. He predicts an increase of produce for seven years, to be followed by seven years of drought. The interpretation of the dream allows for the eighth part of the story to occur: the release of Yūsuf 🕊 from prison. The prison companion who went back into the service of the king forgets about Yūsuf 🕊, but then eventually remembers his expertise in the field of dream interpretations. Once Yūsuf 🕊 interprets the king's dream, he is granted release from prison, only for him to reject the offer, until his innocence is proven. This leads to the ninth part of the story which is based on the confession of the women of Egypt who were besotted with Yūsuf 🕮 and his beauty. They declare his innocence and their confession is soon followed by the confession of the Minister's wife, who finally admits her guilt and acquits him, all of which makes up the tenth episode of his story. The eleventh part of the story is centred on Yūsuf 🕮 being made the treasurer of Egypt and thus responsible for the distribution of provisions during the famine. His brothers arrive from Can'ān seeking provisions only to find their brother, whom they had once thrown into a well, the minister in charge of distributing food. They realise the wrongness of their ways and seek his forgiveness and thereafter the forgiveness of their father, Yā'qūb 🕮. The twelfth and final portion of the narrative is based on the original dream of Yūsuf 🕮 being interpreted, such that his parents and his brothers arrived in Egypt and fall at his feet out of respect and honour.

If you were to take the time to reflect on the beauty of this layout, you would find the miraculous symmetry, with each part of the second half of the *sūrah* relating to the opposite portion in the first half of the *sūrah*. Part one correlates with part twelve, part two with part eleven, part three with part ten, and so on and so forth. In order to help the reader understand this beautiful layout, it is presented below in a simplified form, so one can appreciate the beauty of the Qur'ān:

Part 1	Yūsuf 🕮 sees the dream	Part 12	The dream comes true
Part 2	His brothers plot against him	Part 11	They confess and apologise
Part 3	Zuleikhā seduces him	Part 10	Zuleikhā confesses
Part 4	The ladies try to seduce him	Part 9	The ladies also confess
Part 5	He is wrongly imprisoned	Part 8	He is released from prison
Part 6	The king sees a dream	Part 7	King's dream is interpreted

What makes the above symmetry a literary miracle is the mere fact that the Messenger 🕮 was unlettered, he did not know how to read, nor write. He had no prior knowledge of the story of Yūsuf 🕊, and yet he presented it to the *Sahābā* in such a perfect manner. This could only mean one thing: He 🕊 was divinely inspired, and the Qur'ān was a direct inspiration from a divine being, not from the mind of the Messenger 🕊.

THE TAFSĪR OF SŪRAH YŪSUF

From the brief account of Yūsuf's 🕊 story, we may deduce some similarities between Yūsuf 🕊 and our Holy Prophet 🕊.

The beginning of Yūsuf's 🕊 Prophethood was marked by a true dream. Similarly, *Ummul Mu'minīn* Ā'ishā 🕊 narrates, 'The first signs of revelation to the Holy Prophet 🕊 were through true dreams, whatever he dreamt would occur like the light of dawn.' [11]

Yūsuf 🕊 had dreamt that eleven stars, the sun and the moon were prostrating before him, which meant his parents and his eleven brothers would prostate before him. This interpretation became reality, though after a lengthy period of time.

The brothers of Yūsuf 🕊 were jealous of him, they beat him and tortured him in many ways, and finally did their utmost to slay him. Nevertheless, Yūsuf 🕊 kept patient and steadfast, seeking Allāh's 🕊 help and Allāh 🕊 granted him dignity and victory. However, when the brothers came before him he said to them, 'Let no reproach be on you today, May Allāh forgive you, and He is the Kindest of the kind.' Yūsuf 🕊 never complained nor did he mention their evils, rather he forgave them and bestowed upon them many favours and gifts.

Similarly, the Prophet of Allāh 🕊 was taunted and oppressed in many ways. The *Quraysh* tried to kill him, but he stayed steadfast upon Allāh's 🕊 orders. When they came under his command after the conquest of *Makkah*, he recited the same verse, 'Let no reproach befall you today, may Allāh forgive you for He is the Kindest of the kind. Go! You are the free ones.' He also gave the many converts a great portion of the war booty gained in the Battle of *Hunain*,

---

[11] Bukhārī 3, Tirmīdhī 3565, Muslim 231.

which took place straight after the conquest of *Makkah*. He gave them up to a hundred [100] camels each.

Yūsuf's ﷺ story showed his abstinence and piety. Even though he was in the prime of his youth, with the desire for women and the temptation to commit sin at its peak, he still safeguarded himself, with Allāh's ﷻ help of course. This shows that the Prophets are sinless. They cannot commit a sin because they have gained the special attention of Allāh ﷻ through their good deeds and through constant remembrance of Allāh ﷻ.

I recall here a story of Lūt ﷺ in the Bible, which says that when Allāh's ﷻ wrath descended upon the whole town and as a result, all its inhabitants were killed, only Lūt ﷺ and his two daughters were left behind. The daughters thought to themselves that now that the whole town has perished, we would not exist any longer unless we think of a way of becoming pregnant. They knew that their father would not commit adultery with his own daughters, so they plotted to give him some wine and make him drunk. Accordingly, they made him drunk on the first night and the elder sister slept with him, then on the second night, the younger one did the same. They both got pregnant and the generation which now exists are the offspring of these two girls and their father.

How false is this story! Indeed, it must stem from the additions made in the Bible by some insane people. Who would want to accept that he is an illegitimate child? How can a Prophet of Allāh ﷻ commit such a grave sin? The baselessness of the story is self-evident.

Moreover, I was mentioning that Yūsuf ﷺ safeguarded himself against the offer of a beautiful, young virgin. Similarly, such offers were made to our Noble Prophet ﷺ in his early Prophethood, when the people of *Makkah* offered to marry him to their prettiest daughters in return for him forsaking his mission. The Holy Prophet ﷺ however remained steadfast. [12]

---

[12] Mā'riful Qur'ān of Maulānā Idrīs Khāndelwī ﷺ.

VERSE 1

الٓرٰ ۟ تِلْكَ اٰيٰتُ الْكِتٰبِ الْمُبِيْنِ ﴿١﴾

"Alif Laam Raa, these are the verses of the Manifest Book."

"Alif Lām Raa..." These are abbreviated letters, *Al-Hurūf ul-Muqatta'āt*. Much has been written about its meanings. Some commentators say that they are the names of Allāh ﷻ. Some say that they are the names of the *sūrahs* in which they are mentioned. This can be understood in Sūrah *Yaseen*, *Tā-Hā*, *Sād*, *Qāf* and *Nūn* and others. The majority of *Mufassirūn* say that they are a secret code between the Revealer and to whom they were revealed [i.e Allāh ﷻ and His Prophet ﷺ].

Abū Bakr Siddīq ؓ used to say, 'In every book there are some secrets and Allāh's ﷻ secrets in the Qur'ān are the letters in the beginning of the *sūrahs*.'[13]

Ali ؓ used to say, 'In every book there are some special words, the special words of this book are the *Hurūf ul-Tahajjī*.'[14]

Umar Ibn Khattāb, Uthmān Ghanī, and Abdullāh Ibn Mas'ūd ؓ all state that 'The *Muqatta'āt* are from those mysteries which cannot be explained.'

In other words, between each writer and to whom a letter is written, there are some signs which can only be understood by the two. Similarly, there are some indications in these letters, which only Allāh ﷻ and His Holy Prophet ﷺ understand. We have been ordered to believe them, and for each letter we recite, we shall receive ten *hasanah* [rewards], so for *Alif Lām Raa*, we gain thirty *hasanah*.[15]

Qādhī Baidhāwī ؒ has given a remarkable verdict here regarding the *Muqatta'āt*. He says, 'What has been narrated from the *Khulafā-e-Rāshidīn* [the four rightly guided Caliphs: Abū Bakr, Umar, Uthmān and Alī ؓ] and other Sahābā ؓ could mean that their explanation is not intended, but at the same time, they could be indicating towards the miraculous nature of the Qur'ān. This could be explained in two ways:

---

[13] Sūrah Baqara - Tafsīr Baghawī, 58:1.
[14] Ibid.
[15] Tirmidhī, 2910.

1. The Arabic alphabet from 'Alif' up to 'Yā' consists of twenty-nine [29] letters. The Muqatta'āt are also from the same twenty-nine [29]. The Holy Qur'ān is also compiled from the same twenty-nine [29] letters. The kuffār [disbelievers] who challenged the Holy Qur'ān also converse through the same letters. The Qur'ān challenged the disbelievers in numerous verses to bring forward a work like the Qur'ān. Nobody was able to do so and they admitted their failure. So with these letters, Allāh ﷻ reminds them that this book is not prepared with the Chinese alphabet, rather it is with the same alphabet which you use, and you should be able to tackle it. If you cannot do so, then this means that this book is not Muhammad's ﷺ book – It is from a very high source i.e. the Master of Muhammad ﷺ and the Lord of the Universe. Thus, the miraculous nature of the Holy Qur'ān becomes manifest.

2. To read the alphabetical letters correctly with their original pronunciation is the work of a person who has been to the Madrasah and learnt under the guidance of an Ustādh [teacher]. My daughter Ā'ishā can fluently talk in her mother tongue; Gujarati. However, if she was asked to read the Gujarati alphabet, she would never be able to do so, because she has not learnt them.

It is said that there were only three learned persons in the whole of Makkah who could read out letters and write their reply for the Makkans.

A person who has never visited a Madrasah in his whole life cannot read or pronounce the alphabet. For such a person [i.e Muhammad ﷺ] to pronounce these letters correctly is quite impossible, especially when he mentions them in a remarkable manner which was without precedent in Arabia at that time.

So the Muqatta'āt shed some light on the miracle of the Qur'ān through the Sāhib-e-Qur'ān [the one who brought it to us]. Wallāhu ā'alam

"These verses are of a manifest book..." A manifest book means, one whose divine character is explicit and the commands, constitutions, sermons, and instructions are bright and clear. [16]

---

[16] Uthmānī 1040:2.

The Arabic language is described by the words 'manifest' and 'clear' in many other verses of the Qur'ān, "And indeed this Qur'ān is a revelation of the Rabb of the Worlds. The faithful spirit [Angel Jibra'īl] came down with it. Upon thy heart that thou should be one of the warners. In plain Arabic language." [i.e the revelation is in plain Arabic language]. [17]

'Language of that one to whom they refer is non-Arabic, whereas this [the Qur'ān's language] is very clear Arabic.' [18]

The Holy Prophet 🌸 has urged his followers to speak Arabic. He once said:

'Love the Arabs for three reasons:
1. I am an Arab.
2. The words of the Qur'ān are in Arabic.
3. The conversation of the people of Jannah shall be in Arabic.' [19] [20]

Sayyidunā Umar Ibn Khattāb 🌸 used to say, 'Learn Arabic, because it is part of your *Deen*.' [21]

Arabic is the oldest language on earth. In *Tafsīr Rūh ul-Ma'ānī*, it is stated that when Ādam 🌸 was created, he was taught Arabic, and he used to converse in Arabic. When he made the mistake of eating from the prohibited tree, he was sent to the earth and Arabic was taken away from him. He was then taught another language called *Suryani*. After accepting his repentance, Allāh 🌸 returned Arabic to him. As time went on, and his children spread, they invented other languages.

Arabic has many qualities. It is so vast that for expressing one meaning, you can find plenty of words, and for one word, there are several meanings. For example, 'lion' has five hundred [500] words, 'sword' has one thousand [1000]

---

[17] Qur'ān 26:92-195.

[18] 16:103.

[19] Tabarāni, Mu'jam al-Kabir 122:3; Hākim, Mustadrak 'alas-Sahīhain 87:4.
Note: The authenticity of this narration is highly disputed, but due to supporting narrations, I do not consider it to be fabricated, without denying the chain of narrators being weak, although the message of the narration is correct.

[20] http://www.darulfatwa.org.au/ar/تخريج-حديث-أحبوا-العرب-لثلاث

[21] Bahyaqī, Shuab al-Imān, 257:2.

words, 'calamity' has four thousand [4000] words, and for 'snake', there are two hundred [200] words.

Verse 2

اِنَّآ اَنْزَلْنٰهُ قُرْءٰنًا عَرَبِيًّا لَّعَلَّكُمْ تَعْقِلُوْنَ ۝٢

"We have revealed it, a Qur'ān in Arabic so that you may understand it."

Arabic is the most versatile, well ordered, wise, and grand language. It has been chosen for the revelation of the Qur'ān. As the Holy Prophet ﷺ himself is an Arab, the first audience of the Qur'ān are also Arabs. So through the Arabs, this light should be spread to all four corners of the earth. The words *'You may understand'* indicate this fact, i.e. one of the reasons for revealing in your language is that you are the nation of the Prophet ﷺ, so first you should taste its knowledge and secrets, then make others taste them – And so it happened.

Ibn Kathīr ؓ writes so beautifully: 'The most honourable book, was revealed in the most honourable words, upon the most honourable Prophet, through the most honourable angel, and this took place in the most honourable part of the earth [*Makkah*]. The beginning of the revelation was in the most honourable month of the year which is *Ramadhān*, so it [The Noble Qur'ān] is perfected from all channels.' [22]

Some scholars say that the Jews taught the polytheists of *Makkah* how to test the Holy Prophet ﷺ by questioning him about the story of Jacob and Joseph. This story existed in Hebrew – which the Arabs did not understand – so Allāh ﷻ revealed this *sūrah* and narrated the story in Arabic so that the Arabs could understand it. [23]

With regards to there being non-Arabic words in the Qur'ān, there is a difference of opinion:

---

[22] Uthmānī 1040:2.
[23] Khāzin.

1. Abū Ubaydah ﷺ is of the opinion that there is not a single non-Arabic word in the Holy Qur'ān. He supports his view through the verse before it, i.e. 'A Qur'ān in Arabic.'

2. Ibn Abbās ﷺ, Mujāhid ﷺ and Ikrimah ﷺ are of the opinion that there are some non-Arabic words in the Qur'ān, e.g 'qistās' and 'sijjīl'. 'Qistaas' is a Roman word meaning 'justice', and 'Sijjīl' is a Persian word meaning 'Stones of gravel.'

Khāzin ﷺ says, 'Both opinions are correct; in the sense that the words mentioned are originally non-Arabic, but when the Arabs used them in their conversation, they became Arabic and are now regarded as Arabic words, though originally derived from another language.' [24]

Verse 3

نَحْنُ نَقُصُّ عَلَيْكَ اَحْسَنَ الْقَصَصِ بِمَا اَوْحَيْنَا اِلَيْكَ

هٰذَا الْقُرْآنَ ۙ وَاِنْ كُنْتَ مِنْ قَبْلِهٖ لَمِنَ الْغٰفِلِيْنَ ﴿٣﴾

"We narrate unto you the most beautiful of stories, in that We have inspired in you this Qur'ān, while before [its narration] you were of the unaware."

"We narrate..." It is customary of the Almighty Lord that He uses the pronoun of plural in many verses of the Holy Qur'ān. Even though He is the One and Only God, He has no partners, nor any children. He uses it to show His Pride and Dignity. Indeed, He alone is worthy of all Pride and Dignity that prevails within the universe. The Holy Prophet ﷺ narrates a saying of Allāh ﷻ, 'Pride is my upper sheet and dignity is my lower sheet, whosoever attempts to snatch them away from me, I shall throw him in the fire.' [25]

He also said, 'In comparison to Allāh ﷻ there is none who loves being praised so much.' [26]

---

[24] Khāzin.
[25] Muslim, 6349.
[26] Bukhārī, 500.

It is only He who is worthy of all lofty ranks. He is the Lord, the Majestic, the Creator, and the Sustainer, and only He is worthy of all praises. This is why He uses the majestic pronoun.

I clarified this matter because it so happened that once a group of Christian missionaries, pretending to be attracted to Islām, entered the *Jāmi' Masjid* in Preston, and started showering questions on the *imām*. Their main question was what I have indicated above, i.e. If Allāh ﷻ is One, then why does He say, 'We have done this? We have created this?' Insinuating that the word 'We' points towards the Christian belief of trinity.

The answer is very clear from what I have said above, that the use of 'We' is solely to show His Pride and Dignity. That's why it's called '*The majestic noun.*' Do they not see that the Queen uses the pronoun 'We' in her address to the nation on Christmas Day!

It is also vital to look at the Qur'ān in a more comprehensive manner. Allāh ﷻ only uses the plural pronoun 'We' when addressing Himself in first person. When Allāh ﷻ addresses Himself in second and third person, He uses the words 'He' and the word 'You', both in singular form. Allāh ﷻ doesn't refer to Himself in the plural form, as 'You All', and neither as 'They'. This shows usage of the word 'We' is not literal, to show plurality, but is used for a different reason.

The same Qur'ān which uses 'We' has rejected any partnership to Allāh ﷻ by saying, '*Surely those disbelieve who say Allāh ﷻ is the third of three*'. The Qur'ān declares the unity of God by saying, '*Say: He is Allāh, the One! Allāh the eternal besought of all. He begotteth not nor was He begotten. And there is none comparable unto Him.*' [27]

The answer is very clear. May the Almighty Allāh ﷻ safeguard our *īmān* and keep us steadfast upon the straight path. Āmīn!

"*The most beautiful of stories...*" This indication is either towards the whole Qur'ān, as the Qur'ān consists of stories of the previous nations to take heed from, or specifically towards the story of Yūsuf ﷺ, because it is full of wisdom and knowledge. It consists of the tales of kings, slaves, and scholars of the time; the machinations and intrigues of noblewomen; patience in the

---

[27] Qur'ān 112.

face of hardships and being put upon by enemies; forgiving them when they come under one's command, and many other benefitting factors of the *sūrah*.

Atā ﷺ says, 'Whichever grieved person recites Sūrah Yūsuf, he will get comfort through it.' [28] (Provided he understands it and ponders over its meanings).

Some *Ulamā* say that this *sūrah* is named the best of narrations because there is no other *sūrah* in the Holy Qur'ān, which consists of so much wisdom and so many lessons as this *sūrah*. The final verse of this *sūrah* verifies this, *'Indeed, in their stories is a lesson for men with understanding.'* [29]

"You were of the unaware..." Hadhrat Maulānā Idrīs Khāndlawī ﷺ writes, 'There are three sources of knowing something; common sense; by listening to someone or reading a book; and by seeing it with one's own eyes.'

The previous stories have no connection with common sense, as the events of the past cannot be known through common sense. The Noble Prophet ﷺ did not hear these stories from any historian. If someone says he heard the stories from a particular Jew or Christian, then he should make the identity of that person known. The Noble Prophet ﷺ was unlettered so it is impossible to say that he may have read those events in a book. Furthermore, which books were available to look through them and in which library were they to be found? Those who object should bring forth names of such libraries. With regards to the third point, it is apparent that these events occurred long before the era of the Holy Prophet ﷺ, so he was not there to observe them. Now there is only one possibility, and that is to know these events through an external source, which is known in the *Sharī'ah* as *Wahī*. Allāh ﷺ through the Angel Jibra'īl ﷺ revealed these histories to him. Thus, his Prophethood becomes evident and the miracle of the Holy Qur'ān comes to light.

Allāma Uthmānī ﷺ says in his commentary, 'Through the revelation sent down upon you in the form of the Qur'ān, we relate to you a very fine story in a very beautiful style. You were not aware of this story as your people were quite ignorant of it up to this time.'

---

[28] Khāzin.
[29] Qurtubī 120:9.

This story was found in the books of history and the Bible, but in the form of fiction. The Holy Qur'ān has described the story in its true form. It's relevant and useful portions are so impressively narrated that it not only points out the mistakes of the People of the Book and the storywriters, but also leads towards more significant and glorious conclusions and principles. Rightly speaking, it opened a new chapter of knowledge and research, and supplied deep directions under its reflective description. Some of the most important facts and lessons are summarised below:

1. The determination of Allāh ﷻ cannot be checked, nor delayed, nor put off by any power, and when Allāh ﷻ wills to bestow His grace upon any individual, no one can deprive him of that blessing. Even the whole world cannot change the will of Allāh ﷻ by its collected efforts.

2. Patience and perseverance is the key to the success of this world and the prosperity of the next world.

3. The result of malice and envy is loss and degradation.

4. Human wisdom is a very noble element. By wisdom, man overcomes many difficulties and makes his life successful in both worlds.

5. Moral virtue and piety make a man honourable, even in the eyes of enemies and malevolent people, though it may be after a long run.

These and other innumerable secrets and facts are described in this, the most beautiful of stories.

Commentators have described several traditions about the origin of its revelation. The substance of all these traditions is that once the Jews questioned the Holy Prophet ﷺ, through the Makkan idolaters, about the settlement of the *Banū Isrā'īl* in Egypt. They asked how it was that they settled in Egypt [where they had to face Pharaoh] when Hadhrat Ibrāhīm ﷺ and Hadhrat Is'hāq ﷺ and their children originally belonged to *Shām*. The Muslims were also curious to know the real story with all its facts and insights. Moreover, the events and incidents which were elaborated in the *sūrah*, had a parallel with those occurring in the time of the Holy Prophet ﷺ. The revelation was, as such, a great source of peace and consolation for the Holy Prophet ﷺ. On the other side, it was a great lesson to open the eyes of the Makkan people, who had at last compelled the Holy Prophet ﷺ to vacate his native land, but failed in their plans to bring about the downfall of the Holy Prophet ﷺ. The Jews, whose questions were characterised by a malicious test to disprove his Prophethood, got a satisfactory answer to their query but still resisted believing in his Prophethood. However, the main cause for the *Banū Isrā'īl* settling in Egypt originates from the story of Hadhrat Yūsuf ﷺ.

Yūsuf ﷺ was brought from Palestine and was sold in the markets, and then sent to Prison. He eventually became the ruler of Egypt. He called his whole family over, so his father, all his brothers and all their children came to Egypt. They were seventy-two persons at the time, but they spread very quickly. As time passed, their respect faded away from the hearts of the natives and the natives began to abuse them. Fir'awn became the King and he enslaved *Banī Isra'il*. After a good few centuries, Hadhrat Mūsā ﷺ was sent to emancipate them, to return them to glory, and take them back to Palestine.

Verse 4

اِذْ قَالَ يُوسُفُ لِاَبِيْهِ يَاَبَتِ اِنِّيْ رَاَيْتُ اَحَدَ عَشَرَ
كَوْكَبًا وَّالشَّمْسَ وَالْقَمَرَ رَاَيْتُهُمْ لِيْ سٰجِدِيْنَ ﴿٤﴾

"When Yūsuf said to his father, 'O Father! I saw in a dream eleven stars and the sun and moon, I saw them prostrating before me.'"

Yūsuf ﷺ was the son of Ya'qūb ﷺ as is stated in a *Hadīth* in *Bukhārī*: '*The noble son of the noble son of the noble son of a noble one was Yūsuf, son of Ya'qūb, son of Is'hāq, son of Ibrāhīm.*' [30]

---

[30] Bukhārī, 3202

Another *Hadīth* in the *Sahīh* says: '*The Prophet* 🌸 *was questioned, 'Who is the most noble of all?' He replied, 'The noblest of people is he who is best in conduct.' They said, 'We do not ask about this.' He exclaimed, 'Then the noblest of people is Yūsuf, Prophet of Allāh, son of a Prophet of Allāh, son of a Prophet of Allāh, son of Khalīlullāh.' They said, 'We do not ask about this.' He questioned, 'Then you ask me about the mines of the Arabs.'* [i.e. *Just as the mines throw out gold, silver, copper, steal, coal etc, the Arabs are of different types*]. *They replied in the affirmative. He said, 'Then he who was the best of people during Jāhiliyyah* [period of ignorance before the advent of Islām] *is the best in Islām, provided he attains the understanding of religion.'* [31]*

There are two opinions with regards to the name Yūsuf:

1. It is a Hebrew name, i.e. non Arabic.
2. It is an Arabic name.

Khāzin has related from Abul Hasan Al-Aqta' 🌸, '*Asaf* literally means grief at its highest level, whereas *Aseef* means slave. Both meanings prevailed in Yūsuf thus he was named Yūsuf.' [32]

Yūsuf 🌸 was a cause of grief for his father and he remained enslaved for some time.

Yūsuf 🌸 was the most handsome child of Ya'qūb 🌸. Although his eleven brothers were also very handsome, Yūsuf's 🌸 beauty was outstanding. In *Sahīh Bukhārī* we read, [*In the night of Me'rāj*], '*I passed by Yūsuf* 🌸, *I realised that he was given half a portion of the beauty of mankind.*' [33]

According to one opinion, he was seventeen years old when he saw the dream. His father loved him so much that he couldn't bear his separation, and for this reason, he cried so much that he eventually lost his eyesight.

Qādhī Sayyid Sulaimān Mansūrpūrī 🌸 writes, 'He stayed in the well for three days, then he served the ruler of Egypt for six years, and then he spent seven years in jail. At the age of thirty [30], he became the governor of Egypt. He was reunited with his parents at forty [40] and departed from this world

[31] Bukhārī 3104, Muslim 4383, Abū Dāwūd 4229, Musnad Ahmad 7183, Muwatta Mālik 1573 – Ibn Kathīr.
[32] Khāzin.
[33] Muslim 234, Musnad Ahmad 12047.

at one hundred and ten [110]. He was was buried in Egypt. He made a will that when the *Banū Isrā'īl* leave Egypt, they should take his coffin with them and bury him near *Bait al-Maqdis* [in the vicinity of Masjid al-Aqsā]. When Mūsā 🕮 left Egypt with the *Banū Isrā'īl*, it became impossible for the caravan to proceed. Mūsā 🕮 remembered the will of Yūsuf 🕮, so he dug the coffin out and took it with him to *Bait al-Maqdis*, where it was buried in the graveyard of Ibrāhīm Khalīl-Allāh 🕮, along with his ancestors.

"I saw eleven stars, the sun and the moon..." Khāzin 🕮 says, 'Yūsuf 🕮 saw that the stars descended from the sky along with the sun and the moon, and prostrated before him. He saw this dream on a Friday night [the night preceding Friday] which was also *Lailat al-Qadr*. The interpretation was that the eleven stars were his eleven brothers who were to be a source of guidance like the stars, the sun his father, and the moon his mother, according to the opinion of Qatāda 🕮.'

Suddī 🕮 says that the moon is his aunt because his real mother Raheel [Rachael] had died. [It was the custom to call the father's second wife as mother especially when she is the mother's sister].

"I saw them prostrating before me..." Khāzin 🕮 says that this could have two meanings:

1. By prostrating, it is meant that they would come under his rule. [This happened when they settled down in Egypt and Yūsuf 🕮 was its ruler].

2. The literal meaning i.e. putting the forehead on the earth can also be taken into account, because in those times it was a form of greeting. Our *Sharī'ah* has now forbidden this.

In *Sunan Ibn Mājah* we read, 'When Mu'āz 🕮 returned from Syria, he prostrated before the Holy Prophet 🕮. The Prophet 🕮 exclaimed, 'O Mu'āz! What is this?' He replied, 'When I went to Syria, I saw the Christians prostrating before their religious leaders and their generals. So I thought to myself that we should do the same to you.' The Prophet of Allāh 🕮 said, 'Do not do this! If I were to order someone to prostrate in front of anyone other than Allāh 🕮, I would order the wife to prostrate before her* *husband [due to the rights he has over her]. By He who holds my soul! A woman cannot fulfil the rights of her Lord [Allāh ﷻ] until she has fulfilled the rights of her husband.'* [34]

In *Mishkāt*, we read on the authority of Imām Ahmad ﷺ, Ā'isha ﷺ says, *'The Prophet ﷺ was seated between the Muhājirīn and Ansār, when a camel came forward and prostrated before the Prophet ﷺ. The Sahāba ﷺ said, 'O Prophet of Allāh! Even the animals and the trees prostrate before you, you have more rights over us and therefore we should prostrate before you.' He replied, 'Worship your Lord and respect your brother.' [i.e. He called himself their brother due to humbleness and in order to draw their attention to the fact that he was a human being who was not worthy of worship]. Then he used similar words to those mentioned in the above Hadīth.* [35]

In *Abū Dāwūd*, we find the same request from Qays Ibn Sa'ad ﷺ to which the Prophet ﷺ said, *'If you were to pass by my grave, would you prostrate to it?'* He said, *'No.'* The Prophet ﷺ replied, *'Then don't [prostrate before me while I am alive and in front of you].* [36]

Allāma Tībī ﷺ explains, 'Prostration is the right of only He who is eternal, who is alive and does not die, and to whose sovereignty there is no end.' In other words, the Prophet ﷺ said, 'You might bow down before me due to respect while I am in front of you, but when I go beneath the soil, you would dislike doing the same to me.' It concludes that you would only prostrate before someone who is alive and that is only Allāh, so you should prostrate before Him alone.' [37]

Shāh Abdul Ghanī ﷺ writes in the commentary of *Sunan Ibn Mājah*, 'Prostrating before someone or something for <u>worship</u> is *kufr* and prostrating for <u>greeting</u>, although not regarded as *kufr*, is nevertheless *harām* [forbidden], because the Prophet ﷺ forbade the Sahāba ﷺ from doing so.'

Qādhī Sulaimān ﷺ writes, 'Yūsuf's ﷺ dream is amazing due to three reasons:

[34] Ibn Majah 1843.
[35] Musnad Ahmad 23331.
[36] Abū Dāwūd 1828.
[37] Mishkāt.

1. Seeing eleven stars with the existence of the sun is amazing because the stars fade away at the light of dawn. It is impossible to see the sun and the stars together.

2. What is the reason behind seeing just eleven among thousands?

3. He saw them prostrating which is also astonishing, as stars cannot prostrate before anything.

These are the reasons why Yūsuf 🕊 related the dream to his beloved father.

Verse 5

قَالَ يٰبُنَيَّ لَا تَقْصُصْ رُءْيَاكَ عَلٰى اِخْوَتِكَ فَيَكِيْدُوْا

لَكَ كَيْدًا ط اِنَّ الشَّيْطٰنَ لِلْاِنْسَانِ عَدُوٌّ مُّبِيْنٌ ﴿٥﴾

He said, 'O my dear son! Do not relate your dream to your brothers, lest they devise secretly a plot against you. Indeed, Shaytān is to man an open enemy.'

Allāma Uthmānī 🕊 writes, 'Hadhrat Ya'qūb 🕊 said to Yūsuf 🕊, 'Do not disclose this dream to your brothers. Shaytān is always lying in ambush for man. He may instigate your brothers against you, because the interpretation of the dream is very clear.'

It was not a difficult thing for the brothers of Yūsuf 🕊 to understand the meaning of the dream. They were the sons of a great Prophet and therefore Yā'qūb's 🕊 apprehension was justified. Perhaps he might have also felt beforehand that the stepbrothers of Yūsuf 🕊 were jealous of Yūsuf 🕊 because of the attention and love their father reserved for him. So Hadhrat Ya'qūb 🕊 thought that if his brothers heard the dream, they would surely do something harmful to Yūsuf 🕊 and thus degrade themselves and make their end disastrous. Shaytān would play his most active role in this drama because the matter belonged to no less than a Prophet and his family. This was the reason why Yā'qūb 🕊 forbade him from disclosing his vision to his stepbrothers. As for his real brother Binyāmīn, although there was no fear of him harming Yūsuf 🕊, it was very likely that Binyāmīn might disclose it before other people, as he was a boy younger than Yūsuf 🕮, and thus the news might reach the ears of the stepbrothers. [38]

Ru'yaa literally means a dream. Dreams are of three types:

1. Hadith al-Nafs or Adhghāthū Ahlām: The conversation of the heart. When a person engages himself in a task throughout the day, he may see that particular task in his dreams at night, e.g. a person in love shall see his beloved one, one who is engrossed in the election sees the assembly halls, and a student worrying about exams sees exam related scenes etc.

2. Takhweef Minash Shaytaan: Disturbing dreams. Dreams seen through the instigation of Shaytān. These are sometimes terrifying, sometimes worrying and sometimes exciting; wet dreams also come under this category.

These two types do not hold any interpretation. A person affected by satanic attacks should recite Āyah al-Kursī before retiring to bed. In a Hadīth in Sahīh Bukhārī, the Prophet 🕮 has said that if you recite Āyah al-Kursī before retiring to bed, Allāh 🕮 will command an angel to stand by your bedside, and Shaytān will not be able to come close to you. The angel stays there until you wake up.

3. Ru'ya Sāliha: Just and pious dreams. Dreams that are free from self-indulgence and satanic attacks.

The Ulamā say that this is a sort of spiritual sighting. When a person sleeps and his external senses are out of function, the spirit observes and listens to the matters of the unseen world. The spirit sometimes listens to the sayings of Allāh 🕮, His angels, sometimes it sees the original forms of worldly things and sometimes their identical/similar appearances, which indicate towards future events, e.g. Yūsuf's 🕮 dream of eleven stars, the sun and the moon bowing down before him which indicates future events. These are the true dreams and they require interpretations from an expert in this field. In the Hadīth, these dreams are said to be the forty-sixth part of Prophethood,

---

[38] Uthmānī 1043:2.

meaning that the Prophets were first bestowed with true dreams, and then with Prophethood.

Since the Prophets are free from self-deceit as well as from the instigations of *Shaytān*, their dreams are also *Wahī*. *Shaytān* can never overpower them; thus whatever they dream is a revelation from Allāh 󠀀. Ibrāhīm 󠀀 dreamt that he was slaughtering Ismā'īl 󠀀, his only son at the time, and he acted accordingly.

The *Awliyā* [friends of Allāh] are not *mā'sūm* [innocent from sin] and thus their dreams cannot be regarded as *Wahī*. Their dreams are called '*Ilhām*'. The dreams of a saint will be according to his virtues and piety, i.e. the more piety, the more truthful his dreams. The average Muslim's dream is sometimes true and sometimes false.

Note: Sometimes a *fāsiq* or even a *kāfir* also sees true dreams. Like in our story, the ruler of Egypt, a *kāfir*, saw seven cows and seven green ears of corn and it was interpreted by Yūsuf 󠀀.

Note: Some philosophers deny the concept of dreams. Their main argument is that during sleep or a state of unconsciousness, the senses of a human being are out of function, and thus they cannot see nor hear or feel anything.

One may ask, 'Did these philosophers never see a dream during their lifetime?' Certainly, they must have dreamt something at some stage. Our answer to their objection is that the senses are merely a creation of Allāh 󠀀. He is capable of showing us something without the aid of the senses.

The definition of dreams according to Imām Nawawī 󠀀 and Imām Māzrī 󠀀 is, 'Allāh 󠀀 creates within the heart of a sleeper some observations in the same manner as He creates within the heart of the one awake. He can do whatever He wishes. Neither sleep nor being awake can stop Him from fulfilling His desire.' [39]

---

[39] Ma'āriful Qur'ān Khāndlawī, Khāzin.

TA'BĪR

[INTERPRETATIONS OF DREAMS]

Every layman cannot conduct an interpretation of dreams. It needs a detailed study of the rules of interpretation. One should fully know the language in which the dream was seen, he should know the *Qur'ān* and *Sunnah*, he should have in mind the interpretations given by the Prophet ﷺ and by the pious followers among the *Ummah*. Otherwise, mistakes will occur and interpretations will be incorrect. Once a person narrated his dream to the Prophet ﷺ. Abū Bakr Siddīq ﷺ requested permission and gave the interpretation. The Prophet ﷺ said, 'You got some of it right, and you faltered in some.'

Muhammad Ibn Sirīn ﷺ, who is the *Imām* of dream interpretation, was approached by a person who said, 'I dreamt myself giving Adhān.' He said, 'You shall be blessed with a journey for *Hajj*.' Another person came and related the same dream. He said, 'I fear that you shall be engaged in a robbery.' His students were amazed at the different interpretations of one dream. He said, 'The first person looked religious, and I took interpretation from the verse, 'And call unto mankind for *Hajj*'. [40] The other person was of a different state and I took the interpretation from the verse, 'Then a herald called out, 'O caravans, you are thieves.' [41] His interpretations proved to be true.

Abū Mūsā ﷺ narrates, *'The Prophet ﷺ once said, 'I saw in a dream that I am migrating from Makkah to a town of palm trees. My thought was drawn towards Yamāmah or Hajar, then it turned out to be Yathrib [an earlier name of Madīnah], and I once dreamt that I shook my sword and it broke from the centre, this was the tragedy that befell the Muslims in the battle of Uhud. Then I saw that I shook it once more, and it returned to the best of forms, and this was the conquest of Makkah and the unity of Muslims which Allāh ﷻ generated for us.'* [42]

---

[40] Qur'ān 22:27.
[41] Qur'ān 12:70.
[42] Bukhārī 6514/6519, Muslim 4217, Ibn Mājah 3911.

Abū Hurairah ﷺ narrated that the Prophet ﷺ said, *'While I was sleeping, the treasures of the earth were brought before me, then two golden bangles were put on my fists. They became a burden for me. I was ordered to blow them, I blew and they disappeared. I took the interpretation that they are the two impostors surrounding me; Aswad Anasī of Sana and Musaylama of Yamāmah.'* [43]

Note: Ibn Umar ﷺ narrated, 'It is from the greatest forgeries that a person shows his eyes what they have not seen.' [i.e. one says that I saw such and such a dream when he has not seen it in reality. It is regarded as the greatest lie, because it is lying on Allāh ﷺ, that Allāh ﷺ showed me such and such a dream whereas Allāh ﷺ never did]. [44]

Note: Abū Sa'īd ﷺ narrates from the Prophet ﷺ, *'The most correct dreams are those seen in the early hours of the morning.'* [Since the body has completed its rest, the stomach is empty and therefore there is less possibility of a dream caused by the filling up of the intestines. Also, this is the time the angels descend, and the time of acceptance of *duās*]. [45]

'Indeed Shaytān is to man an open enemy...' Another verse in *Sūrah Faatir* says, *'Verily, Shaytān is an enemy to you so treat him as an enemy. He only invites his adherents that they might become the companions of the blazing fire.'* [46]
His enmity with man started when he was ordered to prostrate before Ādam ﷺ and he rejected, objecting in a very jealous manner by saying, *'I have been created from fire and he from clay. (And fire is superior to clay. So the superior must not be ordered to prostrate before the inferior).'* He was then expelled from Jannah [paradise] and he vowed, *'Then by Thy power I shall lead them all astray.'* [47]
He also said, *'Surely I shall take an appointed portion from Thy bondsmen. And surely I will mislead them, and surely I will create false desires in them, and surely I will command them to slit the ears of the cattle, and surely I will command them and they will change Allāh's ﷺ creation [deface the nature].'* [Allāh ﷺ says] *'And*

---

[43] Bukhārī 6513, Muslim 4218, Tirmidhī 2216, Musnad Ahmad 7901.
[44] Bukhārī.
[45] Tirmidhī 2200, Musnad Ahmad 10810, Dārimī 2053.
[46] Qur'ān 48:6.
[47] Qur'ān 38:82.

whosoever chooses Shaytān for a friend instead of Allāh, has surely suffered a loss that is manifest. Shaytān promises them and creates in them false hopes, but Shaytān's promises are nothing but deception.' [48]

Verse 6

وَكَذٰلِكَ يَجْتَبِيْكَ رَبُّكَ وَيُعَلِّمُكَ مِنْ تَأْوِيْلِ الْاَحَادِيْثِ وَيُتِمُّ نِعْمَتَه
عَلَيْكَ وَعَلٰى اٰلِ يَعْقُوْبَ كَمَاۤ اَتَمَّهَا عَلٰى اَبَوَيْكَ مِنْ قَبْلُ اِبْرٰهِيْمَ
وَاِسْحٰقَ ۚ اِنَّ رَبَّكَ عَلِيْمٌ حَكِيْمٌ ﴿٦﴾

And thus does your Lord choose you and teach you the reality of events and complete his favours upon you and upon the family of Yā'qūb, just as he completed them upon your two fathers, Ibrāhīm and Is'hāq formerly. Verily your Lord is knowing, wise.

Tafsīr Mājidī comments, 'And as thou hast seen in thy dream, thy Lord will choose thee for his apostleship, and as a further gift, He will teach thee the interpretation of discourses, and will fulfil His favours upon the house of Yā'qūb.'

"Choose you...." The *Sūfis* [pious saints who focus on removing spiritual ailments] say that there are two types of people among those associated with Allāh ﷻ:

1. Those who are chosen by Allāh ﷻ.
2. Those who draw themselves closer to Allāh ﷻ and attain His pleasure.

Allāh ﷻ says, 'Allāh ﷻ chooses for himself whom He wills, and guides unto Himself who turns [to Him].' [49]
The Prophets are definitely from the first category, as Prophethood cannot be achieved by abundance in worship or any other way. Nevertheless, among

---

[48] Qur'ān 4:118-120.
[49] Qur'ān 26:13.

the Prophets of Allāh ﷻ, there are some who seem to be distinguished in this respect, for example, our Prophet Muhammad ﷺ is so beloved to Allāh ﷻ, that Allāh ﷻ has never addressed him by his name. We study the Qur'ān and realise that on some occasions Allāh ﷻ addresses him with the words, '*O You, wrapped in clothes*', on some occasions, He says, '*O You, wrapped in mantle*', '*O Prophet*', and '*O Messenger*'.

In the same way Allāh ﷻ has shown this special love to Mūsā ﷺ and Ibrāhīm ﷺ. When we read the above verse, we understand that Yūsuf ﷺ is also among those who are specially chosen by Allāh ﷻ and most beloved to Allāh ﷻ.

"*And teaches you the reality of events...*" The words '*realities of events*' are very meaningful. They include the sharpness and alertness to solve the most complicated matters with ease, the ability to see events before their occurrence, and the interpretations of dreams. All of these qualities can be found in Yūsuf ﷺ.

Yūsuf ﷺ specialised in interpretations of dreams. Some scholars have said that he is the founder of this science. From the Muslim *Ummah*, the great scholar, Imām Muhammad Ibn Sīrīn is said to be the *Imām* of this field.

"*Complete his favours...*" The Arabic word '*Ni'mah*' is literally used for circumstances in which a person gains pleasure. In the Holy Qur'ān, the word has been used for internal, external, religious and worldly pleasures alike:

"*And hath loaded you with His favours both visible and hidden.*"[50] (*i.e. favours that are perceived by one's senses and those perceived by the intellect*).

"*And if you would count the bounty of Allah, ye cannot reckon it.*"[51]

"*The path of those whom Thou hast favoured.*"[52]

---

[50] Qur'ān 31:20.
[51] Qur'ān 14:34.
[52] Qur'ān 43:59.

"He [Jesus] is nothing but a servant of Allāh on whom we bestowed favour." [53]

Taking these verses into account, we learn that the favours bestowed upon Yūsuf ﷺ were of all kinds and the greatest favour amongst them was apostleship.

"Thy Lord is knowing, wise..." By ending the verse with these attributes, there is an indication towards the reason for the preference of Yūsuf ﷺ, i.e. since Allāh ﷻ says in another verse: '*Allāh ﷻ knows best with whom to place His message.*' There is also an indication that the knowledge and wisdom which Yūsuf ﷺ is going to receive is from none but the All-Knowing and Wise Creator Himself.

With these two *sifaat*, Allāh ﷻ has also prepared the reader who will be exposed to the hardships of Yūsuf ﷺ as if to say: 'Don't be alarmed by the ups and downs of his story, for I am aware of his situation and understand the wisdoms behind each stage of his life.'

Verse 7

لَقَدْ كَانَ فِيْ يُوْسُفَ وَاِخْوَتِهِ اٰيٰتٌ لِّلسَّآئِلِيْنَ ﴿٧﴾

"Verily in Yūsuf and his brethren there are signs
[of Allāh's sovereignty] for the seekers [of truth]."

Tafsīr Uthmānī comments, 'For those who want to learn a lesson from such stories, there are ample signs of guidance and lessons in the story of Yūsuf ﷺ and his brethren.' Hearing this story, a mark of the mighty power and glory of Allāh ﷻ is inscribed on the heart. The proof of the truthfulness of the Holy Prophet ﷺ is obtained in that he has divulged the historical facts so thoroughly and clearly, even though he is '*Ummi*' [unschooled] and has not learnt from any mortal. No explanation to this fact can be given except that divine revelation had taught him and informed him about the historical details of the past. For the *Quraish*, who had enquired about this story at the incitement of the Jews, there is a great lesson in the brothers of Yūsuf ﷺ,

---

[53] Qur'ān 43:59.

THE TAFSĪR OF SŪRAH YŪSUF

who drove him out of the house, plotted his murder and expulsion, and degraded him immensely, but then at last a day came in which they were forced to come to him remorsefully, in utter destitution. Allāh ﷻ raised Yūsuf ﷺ to the high ranks of spiritual and material wealth and glory, and he in return turned a blind eye to the faults of his brothers and forgave them with an open heart. Similarly, the brethren of the Holy Prophet ﷺ made unholy schemes against him, troubled him mercilessly, attacked his innocence and prestige, and finally compelled him to leave his home. Soon the day came when the sun of his glory shone, and after a few years, the historical day of the Makkan victory came when the Holy Prophet ﷺ forgave his country brothers of their past faults, saying the same words which Hadhrat Yūsuf ﷺ said to his brethren.

"And his brethren..." Yūsuf ﷺ had one real brother; Binyāmīn, and ten half-brothers. The names are as follows:

1. Reuben.
2. Sham'ūn.
3. Lāwi.
4. Yahūzā.
5. Ashkār.
6. Zabhan. These six are from the wife 'Leah'.
7. Jādd.
8. Ashar. These two are from the slave girl 'Zulfa'.
9. Naftāli [and]
10. Dān, are from the slave girl 'Balhā'. [54]

As mentioned before, it must be kept in mind that Yūsuf's ﷺ brothers were not Prophets. There is neither any Islāmic narration nor any Isrā'īli narration regarding their Prophethood. This is the opinion of Ibn Hazm, Hāfidh Ibn Kathīr, Hāfidh Ibn Taymīyah and Allāma Uthmānī ﷺ.

Some scholars held the opinion of their Prophethood. Their main reasoning is through the verse, '*We revealed upon Ibrāhīm and Ismā'īl and Is'hāq and Yā'qūb*

---

[54] Qazi.

and the tribes...'. The indication of tribes is thought to be towards the sons of Yā'qūb 🕊.

However, Ḥāfidh Ibn Kathīr 🕊 is of the opinion that the said meaning is merely one possible interpretation. The other meaning which is much stronger is that since the Prophets of *Banū Isrā'īl* were from the progeny of Yā'qūb 🕊, the indication is towards those prophets and not towards the sons of Yā'qūb 🕊. Allāh 🕊 knows best.

Note: Yūsuf 🕊 had ten brothers who plotted against him and in the end, Yūsuf 🕊 was victorious. Similarly, there were ten tribes of *Quraish* who were the most active in hurting our beloved Prophet 🕊. Namely:

1. Banū Makhzūm, 2. Banu Adī, 3. Banū Tamīm, 4. Banū Asad, 5. Banū Umayyah, 6. Banū Sahīm, 7. Banū Hanīfah, 8. Banū Abd ad-dār, 9. Banū Ka'b and 10. Banū Nawfal. They embraced Islām in the end. [55]

Verse 8

اِذْ قَالُوْا لَيُوْسُفُ وَاَخُوْهُ اَحَبُّ اِلٰٓى اَبِيْنَا مِنَّا

وَنَحْنُ عُصْبَةٌ ۚ اِنَّ اَبَانَا لَفِىْ ضَلٰلٍ مُّبِيْنٍ ﴿٨﴾

Recall, when they said, 'Surely Yūsuf and his brother [Binyāmīn] are dearer to our father than we, whereas we are more powerful than they, and indeed our father is in a clear mistake.

Here Tafsīr Mājidī relates the verses of the Bible, which are quite similar to the Qur'ānic verses.

The Bible says: 'Now Israel loved Joseph more than all his children, because he was the son of his old age.' [56] 'His father loved him above the rest of his sons, both because of his physical beauty and the virtues of his mind, for he

---

[55] Qazi p.45.
[56] Genesis (The first book of Moses) 37:3 – Tafsīr Mājidī.

excelled the rest in prudence.' [57] 'Upon Joseph centred the love of his father.' [58]

Allāma Uthmānī ⬥ writes: 'Hadhrat Yā'qūb ⬥ loved Yūsuf ⬥ and his real brother, Binyāmīn very much because they were younger than their stepbrothers. Their mother had died so they required more care and love. Moreover, Hadhrat Yā'qūb ⬥, through divine revelation, had understood that the future of Yūsuf ⬥ was bright. Besides that, the extraordinary beauty of his face and his character attracted the attention of Hadhrat Yā'qūb ⬥. His stepbrothers were dissatisfied with this behaviour. They thought that it was they who stood in the time of need, being a powerful band and were the prop of his old age, while Yūsuf ⬥ and Binyāmīn were only children without expectations. With these ideas in mind, they said, 'our father was in a great mistake regarding that affair, and he did not evaluate his profit and loss.'

A question may present itself to the reader, that why did Yā'qūb ⬥ give preference to Yūsuf ⬥ and Binyāmīn whereas a father should treat his children equally?

We read in one *Hadīth*, a *Sahābī* came to our beloved Prophet ⬥ and requested him to be the witness of a gift, which he wanted to give to his son Nu'mān. The Prophet ⬥ enquired, 'Do you have any other children?' He replied, 'Yes.' The Prophet ⬥ then enquired, 'Have you given a similar gift to all of them?' He said, 'No.' The Prophet ⬥ then said, 'Get someone else to be your witness. Does it not please you that they be equal to you in obedience?' He said, 'Of course.' The Prophet ⬥ said, 'Then do not do this.'

It is quite clear that being a Prophet, Hadhrat Yā'qūb ⬥ must have treated them equally with regards to worldly affairs, e.g. food, clothing and shelter amongst other responsibilities that the father must bear for his children. The matter of love is beyond one's control. The heart is not in one's control; it can be attached or attracted towards one child more than the other. There will be no questioning regarding this. One will only be questioned if he acts accordingly in outward matters by preferring one to the other. The Holy

---

[57] Antiquities of the Jews: 11.2.1 – Tafsīr Mājidī.
[58] The book of Jeremiah 246:7 – Tafsīr Mājidī.

Prophet ﷺ had nine wives at one time. He would treat them equally, but his love for Ā'ishā ﵂ was naturally more than his love for the others. This is why he was kind and just with all of them, however, he would supplicate in the following words, "O Allāh! This is my sharing of what is in my control [food, shelter and allowance], so do not reckon me for what is beyond my control [attraction and attachment of the heart]". Similar is the case with children.

Note: It is permissible to give more attention to one child, if there are special reasons for that, e.g. he or she is disabled, or poorer than others, or he or she is engaged in studying and needs more help. In these cases, one is allowed to pay more attention to that particular child, based on mitigating factors.

Verse 9

اقْتُلُوْا يُوْسُفَ اَوِ اطْرَحُوْهُ اَرْضًا يَّخْلُ لَكُمْ وَجْهُ
اَبِيْكُمْ وَتَكُوْنُوْا مِنْۢ بَعْدِهٖ قَوْمًا صٰلِحِيْنَ ﴿٩﴾

[One said] "Kill Yūsuf or cast him away to some land, your father's favour will then be free for you, and you will thereafter become good fellows."

The fire of malice was burning in their hearts. At last, they counselled that in the presence of Yūsuf ﵟ, it was not possible to draw the special attention of their father, so Yūsuf ﵟ should be finished. Either they should kill him or cast him away in some far distant land from where he could have no return. The word used in this passage is *itrahūhu*, from the root word *taraha - yatrahu*, meaning to throw away something of no value, similar to throwing away rubbish, which every person considers an inconvenience.

When Yūsuf ﵟ would be separated from Ya'qūb ﵟ, naturally they will become the centre of attention for their father. Binyāmīn very probably was not significant in their eyes. His position, they might have thought, was supplementary to Yūsuf ﵟ. Afterwards, they thought they would repent of their sin, be pardoned, and become pious men.

Some commentators have said that, 'And thereafter become good fellows', means that after removing Yūsuf ﵟ from their way, all their affairs would be set right, as the attention of their father would turn towards them, because Yusuf ﷺ would no longer be there.

They said the above due to jealousy. How damaging is this bad habit? See what jealousy has done to the household of a great Prophet of Allāh ﷻ. Hurting the person in connection can never satisfy anyone except the jealous person. This is why Ameer Muāwiya ؓ once said, 'I can please all persons, except for the jealous one. Nothing can please him except the destruction of the favours or bounties that I might be enjoying.'

Our Hadhrat [May Allāh prolong his shadow over us] once said in a gathering after *tarawīh salāh*, that jealousy in essence is objecting to the decree and decision making of Allāh, as if we are saying to Allāh, 'Why did you choose to give this blessing to this person and deprive me of the same?' This is why Allāh ﷻ and our beloved Prophet ﷺ have warned us with regards to jealousy and to seek protection from the the evil of those who are jealous. Allāh ﷻ has especially taught us to seek refuge from the jealousy of the jealous. We read in Sūrah Falaq: 'And [we seek refuge] from the evil of the jealous when he shows jealousy.'

"You will thereafter become good fellows..." *Shaytān* is our greatest enemy and the greatest traitor. Here he casts in their minds the thought of committing a major sin on the possibility of becoming virtuous afterwards through repentance. This is exactly how *Shaytān* tricks us into committing sins. He makes the sin seem trivial before we commit it, and incites us, making us believe that we will repent and be forgiven after the sin, then once we have committed the sin, he convinces us that there is now no path to repentance for us. Our condition should be the opposite: before we commit the sin, we must consider it to be the worst possible deed and try to avoid it at all costs, but like the weak servants we are, if we commit the wrong, we must have hope that Allāh ﷻ forgives us and has mercy on us.

There is no question regarding the forgiveness of Allāh ﷻ, but two things should be borne in mind. First, the sin of killing is a major sin. The Qur'ān states that killing a *Mu'min* is a major sin leading to eternal punishment in hell. The *Hadīth* also states that after *shirk* [associating partners with Allāh], murder is the gravest sin.

Secondly, repentance is originally from sins which are committed through forgetfulness, being unmindful and unaware of the consequences of the sin. The Holy Qur'ān says, 'Accepting repentance is only incumbent on Allāh ﷻ for those who do evil in ignorance [and] then turn quickly [in repentance] to Allāh ﷻ. These are they towards whom Allāh ﷻ relenteth. Allāh ﷻ is Ever All-Knower, All-Wise.' [59]

There are two conditions for accepting repentance mentioned here:

1. 'Do an evil deed in ignorance' – not through deliberation and knowing the grave punishment for that particular sin.

2. 'Repent quickly' – if repentance is not done quickly enough, it could have harsh effects on that person. Furthermore, it is not a *Mu'min's* habit to commit sins in the hope of forgiveness. Therefore, the thought of killing Yūsuf ﷺ and then repenting afterwards is very misleading. May Allāh ﷻ safeguard us all from the evil thoughts whispered into our minds by the accursed *Shaytān*, and may He make us aware of the evil tricks of *Shaytān*, and may He safeguard us from falling into his traps. *Āmīn.*

Verse 10

قَالَ قَائِلٌ مِّنْهُمْ لَا تَقْتُلُوا يُوسُفَ وَأَلْقُوهُ فِي غَيَبَتِ الْجُبِّ يَلْتَقِطْهُ بَعْضُ السَّيَّارَةِ إِنْ كُنْتُمْ فَعِلِينَ ﴿١٠﴾

"One speaker from among them said, 'Do not kill Yūsuf, but, if you must be doing, then fling him into the bottom of a pit; some traveller may pick him up.'"

The *Mufassirūn* have written that the speaker was the eldest brother Judah [Yahūzā], who said that killing was a severe thing and they could achieve their objective without it. If they wanted to remove him from their lives, it was advisable that they cast him in some unknown well, far away from their home. Abū Hayyān has quoted some linguists stating that 'Gayābat al-Jubb' is a cabin made in the wall of a well just above the surface of the water. In short,

[59] Qur'ān 4:17.

they refused to bear the sin of the intentional murder. In that case, some caravan passing or someone temporarily residing there might take him out of the well, and thus their hands would be innocent of bloodshed; the snake shall die and the stick will not break.

Hāfiz Ibn Kathīr ؛ quotes Muhammad Ibn Is'hāq ؛ from a report narrated by Ibn Abī Hatim ؛, 'They agreed to a particularly vicious crime that involved cutting the relation of the womb, undutiful treatment of parents, and harshness towards the young, helpless, and sinless. It was also harsh towards the old and weak who have the rights of being respected, honoured, and appreciated as well as being honoured with Allāh ؛ and having parental rights on their offspring. They sought to separate the beloved father, who had reached old age and whose bones had become weak, yet had a high status with Allāh ؛, from his beloved young son, in spite of his weakness, tender age, and his need of his father's compassion and kindness. May Allāh ؛ forgive them, and indeed, He is the Most Merciful among those who have mercy, for they intended to carry out a 'grave error.'" [60]

Verse 11

قَالُوْا يَآ اَبَانَا مَالَكَ لَا تَأْمَنَّا عَلٰى يُوْسُفَ وَاِنَّا لَهٗ لَنٰصِحُوْنَ ﴿۱۱﴾

They said: 'O father! Why is it that you do not trust us with
Yūsuf, whereas we are indeed his sincere well-wishers?"

Having formed the plot, the brothers proceeded and started to put it into execution. The verse indicates that they had also made such requests before, but Hadhrat Yā'qūb ؛ was not satisfied and refused to let Yūsuf ؛ go with them.

Verse 12

اَرْسِلْهُ مَعَنَا غَدًا يَّرْتَعْ وَيَلْعَبْ وَاِنَّا لَهٗ لَحٰفِظُوْنَ ﴿۱۲﴾

"Send him with us tomorrow so that he may refresh himself
[with fruits] and play. Lo! We will definitely take good care of him."

---

[60] Ibn Kathīr, Tafsīr, Sūrah 12:11

Allāma Uthmānī ﷦ writes, 'They relentlessly persued their father to send Yūsuf ﷦ with them to play. They said that Yūsuf ﷦ would become dull at home, and his health would be spoiled if he was not permitted to go out to the fields to run, play, and enjoy the climate of the open land. In the open forest atmosphere, Yūsuf ﷦ would play freely and eat jungle fruits and would be hale and hearty. It is said that generally, their games and means of enjoyment in the jungles were archery and racing.'

Abū Hayyān has said that playing within limits is a source of pleasure and exercise for children, and the brothers made vehement requests and promised full protection. Thus, Hadhrat Yā'qūb ﷦ was pressured to send Yūsuf ﷦ with them. Commentators have written that they had also enticed Yūsuf ﷦ separately, prior to convincing their father.

Verse 13

$$ قَالَ اِنِّيْ لَيَحْزُنُنِيْ اَنْ تَذْهَبُوْا بِهٖ وَاَخَافُ $$

$$ اَنْ يَّأْكُلَهُ الذِّئْبُ وَاَنْتُمْ عَنْهُ غٰفِلُوْنَ ﴿١٣﴾ $$

He said, "Verily it grieves me that you should take him away and
I fear that a wolf may eat him while you are heedless of him."

Hadhrat Yā'qūb ﷦ said to them that the very idea of his separation from Yūsuf ﷦ grieved him. Besides, Yūsuf ﷦ was a boy and the fear of a dangerous beast like a wolf was painful. It is said wolves were frequently found in that jungle. [61]

Maulānā Abdul Mājid Daryābādī ﷦ writes, 'Though now comparatively rare, in ancient Palestine, wolves were amongst the most prominent wild animals.'

There are two words used in this passage which have a similar meaning, but are used in different contexts. The first is huzn, which literally means sadness or grief, and the second is khawf, which means fear. Sadness occurs on past events, and fear grips a person about future eventualities. However, in this āyah, Yā'qūb ﷦ has expressed his sadness [huzn] about something which

---

[61] Uthmānī 1049:2.

hasn't occurred yet. This isn't an error on his part, rather, it is an example of his profound eloquence. He knew that the brothers taking him was an inevitability, but he had hope that they wouldn't go ahead with their evil plot, so that was a fear about the future.

Muftī Muhammad Shafī Sāhib ؒ states, 'Yā'qūb ؑ had seen a dream that he himself was on a mountain and Yūsuf ؑ was in the valley. Suddenly, ten wolves surrounded Yūsuf ؑ and tried to attack him. One of the wolves defended Yūsuf ؑ and saved him. Thereafter, Yūsuf ؑ disappeared into the earth – the interpretation came to be that the ten wolves were the ten brothers and the wolf that defended him was Yahūzā, the eldest brother, and being thrown in the well was the disappearance.'

Ibn Abbās ؓ has said that due to the dream, Yā'qūb ؑ feared from his sons, but did not disclose the full interpretation.

Yā'qūb ؑ had his fears, but how could he put them off from their intentions? If they are driven to open hostility, they may cause even more harm. He must deal with his sons wisely and cautiously. Consequently, he pleaded that he was an old man and due to his immense love for Yūsuf ؑ he would surely miss him and be sad without him.

Yūsuf ؑ was a small boy of less than ten years. He was not at an age to play with them. They would be busy in their game which would leave an opportunity for a wolf to attack Yūsuf ؑ. In saying this, Yā'qūb ؑ unwillingly gave them a clue and they used the same excuse. In other words, that which was to happen passed through his heart beforehand.

Maulānā Idrīs Kāndhlawī ؒ writes, 'Since the hearts of the Prophets are sound, they can smell the falsehood from what is being said to them. The *Hadīth* says, *"Truth is a cause for contentment, whereas lies create doubt."* [62] Upon hearing their request, Yā'qūb ؑ instantly realised the jealousy and wickedness of their plot.'

The *Sūfīs* derive from here that *Taqdeer* is, after all, victorious over *Tadbeer*. The strong feeling of Yā'qūb ؑ and both his excuses were unable to stop the separation of Yūsuf ؑ. Yā'qūb ؑ was compelled to let Yūsuf ؑ go against all his wishes. The Sūfīs say, 'What value does the will of a servant hold in relation to the will of the Lord?'

---

[62] Tirmīdhī, Hasan Sahīh, Hakim 7128.

Verse 14

$$\text{قَالُوْا لَئِنْ اَكَلَهُ الذِّئْبُ وَنَحْنُ عُصْبَةٌ اِنَّاۤ اِذًا لَّخٰسِرُوْنَ ﴿١٤﴾}$$

They said, "If the wolf were to devour him while we are a strong group,
then surely we are the losers."

They said, 'How is it possible that in the presence of such a powerful band
like us, a wolf may devour our young brother?' It would mean we are nothing
and we have lost everything of our character as a strong and powerful group.
[63]

Ya'qūb ﷺ had mentioned two reasons for not letting Yūsuf ﷺ go with
them:

1. His love for Yūsuf ﷺ was such that he would not be able to bear the
separation.

2. He had fear that some wolf may eat him. The brothers rebutted the
second objection but not the first, because that was the cause of their
jealousy.

Verse 15

$$\text{فَلَمَّا ذَهَبُوْا بِهٖ وَاَجْمَعُوْۤا اَنْ يَّجْعَلُوْهُ فِيْ غَيٰبَتِ الْجُبِّ ج}$$

$$\text{وَاَوْحَيْنَاۤ اِلَيْهِ لَتُنَبِّئَنَّهُمْ بِاَمْرِهِمْ هٰذَا وَهُمْ لَا يَشْعُرُوْنَ ﴿١٥﴾}$$

So when they did take him away and they resolved to throw him down to the
bottom of the dark well; We hinted to him, 'You shall surely tell them of this
their affair, while they perceive not.'

Commentators have related heartrending and poignant stories from the time
when Yūsuf ﷺ and his brothers went out of sight from Hadhrat Ya'qūb ﷺ up
to the moment when they cast him into the well. Only Allāh ﷻ knows up to
what extent they are correct. The Holy Qur'ān, from the viewpoint of its own

---

[63] Uthmānī 1049:2.

aim, does not attach much importance to such sentimental details, as they do not serve any sublime motive except emotional presentation to excite the human passion of the reader. The excitement of human passions may be the principle theme of dramas and novels, but it is certainly not the main theme of the divine book. The worldly stories written by the worldly writers generally excite, and move the readers to tears. The Holy Qur'ān aims to create a sensitivity and tender-heartedness in the audience and readers, the sources of which are īmān [belief] and 'irfān [recognition of the Master].

Here in this story, the Holy Qur'ān has described, omitting the middle events, that the brethren of Yūsuf 🕮, with all possible ploys, took away Yūsuf 🕮, from their father and decided to throw him in the well according to their prearranged plan. At the time Allāh 🕮 had hinted to Yūsuf 🕮 without the others being conscious of this, not to worry; one day he would tell them of all their activities and treatment, and that he would be of such high rank at that time, that his brothers would not know him, or due to the lapse of time, it would be difficult for them to even recognise him.

How this divine hint or indication came to Yūsuf 🕮 – either in a dream, or when awake, or through inspiration, or through an angel – is a subject which is absent from the Qur'ān. It is said of course, observing the word Awhaynā that revelation [wahī] is not confined to the age of forty years and above, because Hadhrat Yūsuf 🕮 was a boy at the time. [64]

Hāfiz Ibn Kathīr 🕮 writes under this āyah, 'This part of the āyah magnifies their crime, in that it mentions that they all agreed to throw him to the bottom of the well. This was their intent, yet when they took him from his father, they pretended otherwise, so that his father sends him with a good heart and feeling at ease and comfortable with his decision. It was reported that Yā'qūb 🕮, embraced Yūsuf 🕮, kissed him and supplicated to Allāh 🕮 for him when he sent him with his brothers.'

Allāh 🕮 was with Yūsuf 🕮 in all his difficulties, sorrows, and sufferings, as He is with all His servants who put their trust in Him. His brothers betrayed him and left the poor boy, perhaps to die, or to be sold into slavery. But he was undaunted. His courage never failed him.

---

[64] Uthmānī 1050:2.

This is the habit of Allāh ﷻ with His pious servants whom He tests and puts through trials; He consoles them and becalms them, knowing their human instinct of fear and trepidation. Consider the case of the mother of Mūsā ﷺ, who was instructed to place her only son into a straw basket and leave it to flow in a river. Allāh ﷻ describes her heart as *fārighā*, free from all concerns except that of her baby son. Allāh ﷻ then consoled her, telling her that he will be returned to her and he would be from amongst the Messengers of Allāh ﷻ.

Similar is the case with Mūsā ﷺ himself, whose human instinct of fear took over when he was asked to strike the staff, causing a huge snake to appear. Allāh ﷻ ordered him not to be afraid. We see how Allāh ﷻ helps those who are dear to him through trials and tribulations, which is evident in the story of Yūsuf ﷺ.

I recall here a story of Hadhrat Maulānā Rashīd Ahmad Gangōhī ﷺ [d. 1323A.H]. When he was only five years old, he created a habit of performing his *salāh* in the masjid. One day he was late, so *salāh* had already started. He had to draw water out of the well to perform *wudhū*. As he pulled the bucket, he accidentally slipped and fell inside. On hearing the noise, people broke their *salāh* and ran towards the well. They were really scared. However, Hadhrat shouted from inside, 'Do not worry, I am safe. I have seated myself inside the bucket.' It is this courage that made Hadhrat what he was. One should try and read the biography of Hadhrat Gangōhī ﷺ, named '*Tazkiratur-Rashīd*'.

The Sūfīs say:

1. 'The plot which was planned to ruin the future of Yūsuf ﷺ proved to be the first step towards the rise of Yūsuf ﷺ.'

2. Mujāhid ﷺ says that the hint made to Yūsuf ﷺ is called '*Ilhām*' [divine inspiration given to non-Prophets, or to Prophets prior to Prophethood]. Allāh ﷻ consoles the hearts of His beloved ones through '*Ilhām*'.

3. Ibn Kathīr ﷺ has narrated here that when Yūsuf's ﷺ brothers came to him in Egypt, he recognised them, but they did not recognise him. He called for a pot, put it on his palm and knocked on it. He heard some noise and

said, 'This pot is telling me that you had a half-brother named Yūsuf, you took him away from his father and threw him in a well.' Then he knocked on it again, put it to his ears and said, 'It is telling me that you then put false blood on his shirt and showed it to your father, saying a wolf had eaten him.' The brothers were stunned and they said to each other, 'This pot has surely disclosed the truth to the king.' This is what was revealed to him in the well that one day you shall inform them and they will not know.

The lesson taken from here is that a *sālik* [a person treading the path to self-rectification] should put the matters of his enemies into the hands of his Rabb. [And not take any steps towards degrading them]. It is Allāh ﷻ who will grant him victory, no matter what happens. *'Allāh has control and power over His affairs, but most among mankind know not.'*

Verse 16

وَجَآءُوْ اَبَاهُمْ عِشَآءً يَّبْكُوْنَ ﴿١٦﴾

"And they came to their father at night fall, weeping."

Allāma Uthmānī ﷻ writes, 'Either it was night when they reached home, or they had intentionally delayed their return, because in daylight, it was rather difficult to show their shameless faces to their father. The darkness of night could conceal, to a certain extent, their shamelessness, hardheartedness, false lamentation and crying.'

A'amash has rightly said, 'After hearing the sighing and weeping of the brothers of Yūsuf ﷺ, we cannot believe in the truthfulness of someone only by their tearful eyes and their sobbing.'

Qurtubi ﷻ says: 'Some people are very good at acting, others are not so good.'

Verse 17

قَالُوْا يٰٓاَبَانَآ اِنَّا ذَهَبْنَا نَسْتَبِقُ وَتَرَكْنَا يُوْسُفَ عِنْدَ مَتَاعِنَا

فَاَكَلَهُ الذِّئْبُ ۚ وَمَآ اَنْتَ بِمُؤْمِنٍ لَّنَا وَلَوْ كُنَّا صٰدِقِيْنَ ﴿١٧﴾

They said, "Father! We went off competing and left Yūsuf by our stuff, and a wolf devoured him, but Thou will never believe us even though we are the truth tellers."

"...*We went competing...*" Imām Qurtubī 🌸 narrates that this competing was either in archery, or horse-riding or in sprinting. The aim of sprinting is to train oneself for the battlefield and for fending of wolves from sheep.

Ibn ul-Arabi writes that Rasūlullāh 🌸 raced with Ā'ishā 🌸. She won, but after some time they raced again, and he won. He said, 'This is for that.'

Salama ibn-ul-Akwa 🌸 was a very swift runner. One person was boasting over his sprinting. Salama agreed to compete with him. Salama gave him a head start, but then he ran so fast that he caught up with him, patted him on his back, and then reached Madīnah well before him. He did this to teach him not to boast.

Rasūlullāh 🌸 would conduct races between horse riders. He would reward the winners. He said, 'Competing is not good except in horses, camels, and in archery.' [65]

Imām Shāfi'ī 🌸 said: 'Any other form of racing is gambling (Qimār).'

The *fuqahā* of *Hijāz* and Iraq also say the same. Therefore, other types of racing such as greyhound racing will not be *jā'iz*. Similarly, where horse racing is for no other purpose but gambling, then that will also not be *jā'iz*.

Allāma Uthmānī 🌸 writes, 'The brothers of Yūsuf 🌸 said to their father, "We had not fallen short in giving protection to Yūsuf 🌸. We had seated him near our belongings, then we began racing. To our surprise, no sooner were we out of sight, that some wolf ate him. During such a short time we could not imagine that a wolf would prey on him. You would not believe us as you already have a false impression regarding our conduct with Yūsuf 🌸, even though we may be quite true in your eyes, yet you can never believe us in this particular matter."'

Verse 18

$$ وَجَآءُوْ عَلٰى قَمِيْصِهٖ بِدَمٍ كَذِبٍ ط قَالَ بَلْ سَوَّلَتْ لَكُمْ $$

---

[65] Nasa'ī, Mishkāt.

اَنْفُسُكُمْ اَمْرًا ط فَصَبْرٌ جَمِيْلٌ ط وَاللهُ الْمُسْتَعَانُ عَلٰى مَا تَصِفُوْنَ ﴿١٨﴾

And they bought his shirt with false blood on it, He said, 'Nay but your minds
have made up a tale, so patience is better for me, and it is Allāh only whose help
can be sought on what you express.'

Allāma Uthmānī ﷺ writes, 'The brothers of Yūsuf ﷺ had blotted the shirt of
Yūsuf ﷺ with the blood of a deer or a goat killed for this purpose. They
showed this blotted shirt to Hadhrat Yā'qūb ﷺ as an evidence for their false
statement.'

Tafsīr Mājidī comments, 'And they took Yūsuf's ﷺ coat, killed a kid and
dipped the coat in its blood.' [66]

Some commentators mention that they blotted the shirt with a goat's
blood, because its blood resembles human blood.

Indeed, one lie creates a hundred lies; and even then, it still cannot create
firm belief, because the liar is himself disbelieving his own statement.

Allāma Māwardi ﷺ has said, 'The shirt of young Yūsuf ﷺ was one of the
wonders of that time.' He narrates that three major events are related to it:

1. The event of blotting it with false blood, which in the end proved their
lies.

2. In the story concerning Zuleikhā [which will be covered later in the
sūrah], it was the shirt of Yūsuf ﷺ which proved his innocence.

3. This shirt of Yūsuf ﷺ was taken to his father and put on his face and this
miraculously resulted in the return of Yā'qūb's ﷺ eyesight.' [67]

Yā'qūb ﷺ realised the statements were false for four reasons:

---

[66] Gibbons, 'The History of the Decline and Fall of the Roman Empire' 37:31 – Tafsīr Mājidī 361.
[67] Rumooz, Qurtubī 149/9.

1. He knew the interpretation of Yūsuf's 🕮 dream, that a time will come when Yā'qūb 🕮 would see his beloved son at a very high rank. This was yet to happen so Yūsuf 🕮 could not be dead, therefore indeed this was a plot.

2. The brethren of Yūsuf 🕮 could not find a reason, except that which their father had feared.

3. The shirt was in its original form, whereas if a wolf had devoured him, it would have been torn.

4. A liar himself is in disbelief and thus he has to express his point with different tactics, and he doubts whether his lie will be accepted or not. This is a form of reverse psychology, in order to make their father accept their lies. That is why they said, 'You will not believe us even though we are truth tellers.'

"So patience is better for me and it is Allāh only whose help can be sought..." In this verse, two fundamentals of īmān and yaqīn have been mentioned. Every Muslim is obliged to tackle problems and calamities with two weapons: 'Sabre Jamīl' [beautiful patience] and, 'Seeking help from Allāh 🕮 only.'

The objective of narrating stories in the Holy Qur'ān is not to merely recall narratives, rather to teach meaningful and valuable lessons throughout its narration. The benefit of this procedure is that the teachings gradually settle down in the depth of the heart. Similarly at this point, the Qur'ān teaches us that Yā'qūb 🕮 had to go through the great burden of losing the coolness of his eyes. Yet, he stays patient and seeks help from Allāh 🕮.

SABR

[PATIENCE AND PERSEVERANCE]

The word 'Sabr' has been mentioned nine-hundred [900] times in the Holy Qur'ān.

Imām Ahmad ﷺ says, 'Sabr is wājib on every Muslim according to ijmā [scholarly consensus].' He also says, 'Half of īmān is sabr [patience], and half is shukr [gratitude].'

The literal meaning of Sabr is to stop someone. In the eyes of the Sharī'ah, sabr is to refrain from showing the effects of grief through complaining by the tongue and shouting. The natural flow of tears and the sorrow of the heart are not contrary to sabr. Sabr is a great asset for a believer. Allāh ﷻ says, 'Seek Allāh's help through sabr and salāh.'

Abdullāh ibn Abbās ﷺ was informed of the death of his brother while he was on a journey. He instantly stopped the camel, descended, performed wudhū and then performed two rak'āts of salāh. When he finished his salāh, he read the above verse and said, 'Allāh ﷻ loves those who endure with sabr and has promised great rewards for such people.' Allāh ﷻ says, 'And We will certainly bestow on those who patiently persevere, their reward according to their actions.' [68] He also says, 'Those who patiently persevere will truly receive a reward without measure.' [69] And again, 'How sweet is the reward for those who do good! Those who persevere in patience and put their trust in their Lord and Cherisher.' [70]

In another place, 'The reward of Allāh for him who believes and does right is better, and only the steadfast will obtain it.' [71] He says, 'And Allāh loves those who are firm and steadfast.' [72]

The Holy Prophet ﷺ says, 'The state of a Mu'min [believer] is amazing; every matter of his is a source of goodness, and this privilege is only for a Mu'min. If he is granted joy and happiness, he is thankful, which is good for him, and if any grief strikes him, he is patient, and that is also good for him.' [73] He also says, 'No one has been gifted with something better and broader than sabr.' Sabr is so broad that it takes all the hammering, and despite experiencing negativity, it dissolves all sorrows. [74]

---

[68] Qur'ān 16:96.

[69] Qur'ān 39:10.

[70] Qur'ān 29:59.

[71] Qur'ān 28:80.

[72] Qur'ān 3:146.

[73] Muslim, Sahīh 2999.

[74] Al Jamal wal Kamal. There is a hadith in Muwatta "Whoever has forbearance, Allah will help him. Whoever tries to be independent, Allah will enrich him. Whoever tries to be patient, Allāh will give him patience. And no one is given a better or vaster gift than patience."

Imām Tirmīdhī 🙵 narrates from Abdullāh ibn Abbās 🙵, that the Prophet 🙵 said, '...*And know that help is with patience, relief is with agony, and with hardship there is ease.*'

Abū Dardā 🙵 says, 'A son of the Prophet Sulaimān 🙵 passed away. He was struck with severe grief. So two angels in the form of humans approached him and requested for a judgement. One said, 'I planted some seeds. I hadn't yet harvested them, and this person passed by the field and destroyed the crops.' He asked the other person, 'Why did you do this?' He replied, 'I took the main street and as I was walking, I came upon the crops. I looked to the right and to the left but could not find any path to walk. Then I realised that the crops have been grown on the walkway, and I had no choice but to walk over them.' Sulaimān 🙵 asked the other, 'Why did you plant on the road? Do you not know that people need a road to walk on?' The angel replied, 'So why are you grieving so much? Do you not know that death is the road to the hereafter?'[75] Sulaimān 🙵 understood and observed patience.

We also understand this and if we were to lose our loved ones, we should try our utmost best to hold onto *sabre jameel* and remain as calm as we possibly can.

Verse 19

$$ وَجَاۤءَتْ سَيَّارَةٌ فَاَرْسَلُوْا وَارِدَهُمْ فَاَدْلٰى دَلْوَهٗ ۚ قَالَ يٰبُشْرٰى هٰذَا غُلٰمٌ ۚ وَاَسَرُّوْهُ بِضَاعَةً ۚ وَاللّٰهُ عَلِيْمٌۢ بِمَا يَعْمَلُوْنَ ﴿١٩﴾ $$

And there came a caravan of travellers, they sent their water-drawer, and he let down his bucket. He said, "Good news! Here is a boy." So they hid him as merchandise, and Allāh was the All-Knower of what they did.

It is said that Yūsuf 🙵 remained in the well for three days. Allāh 🙵 protected him. One of the brothers, Judah, came to the well daily and brought some food. The other brothers also felt that Yūsuf 🙵 should not be killed, and that some foreign travellers would remove him from the well and take him away to a foreign land. At last, a caravan was passing by and in accordance with

---

[75] Tanbīh ul-Ghāfilīn p.259.

their custom, the caravan was headed by advanced parties, in order to search for water and to pitch a camp nearby. The water drawer let down the pail into the well. Yūsuf ☙ was not very heavy; he sat in the bucket and caught hold of the rope. The water-drawer was surprised and taken aback when he found this handsome young boy who looked as innocent as an angel with a face as bright as the sun. He cried out with joy and delight, 'It is a strange boy, he will be sold at a very high price.'

Some commentators say that 'Bushrā', the Arabic word for good news, is a proper noun, i.e. the name of the companion to whom he shouted.

Some commentators have narrated here that the brothers of Yūsuf ☙ saw Yūsuf ☙ being taken out of the well. They rushed towards them and claimed that he was their slave who had absconded. They then sold Yūsuf ☙ to the caravan for a meagre sum of money.

The caravan was travelling from Arabia to Egypt carrying spices, balms and myrrh. Amongst them were merchants, who were known to think of every possible avenue in order to make some money. When they saw this youth of unique beauty, the first thoughts that entered their minds were that if this young man could be sold in the Egyptian slave market to one of the rulers of Egypt, what a price he would fetch!

And they hid him as merchandise..." The caravan assumed, and rightly so, that this child wasn't placed in the well by choice. In order to hide him from potential onlookers and others with evil intentions, they hid him amongst their cargo, ensuring he was hidden from public view.

"But Allāh knows..." To different people, the situation appeared different. A young boy was bewildered, a father had lost his son, and was in the sorrow of losing his most beloved one, the brothers were eager to exile Yūsuf ☙ because his return would disclose their lies, and they would be back to square one. The merchants were gloating over their gain but the horizon of all is limited. Allāh ☙ knew their deeds, their feelings and their motives and He had His own plans. If He had willed, He could have made Yūsuf ☙ a master of Egyptian treasures in an instant, without all these procedures but in His wisdom, He delayed. Therefore, despite knowing all things and seeing all matters, everything was done deliberately. It is said:

$$\text{اَلْأَنَاةُ مِنَ اللهِ وَالْعَجَلَةُ مِنَ الشَّيْطَانِ ـ}$$

'Calmness and patient deliberation is from Allāh and haste is from Satan.'[76]

"And there came a caravan..." Was it a coincidence? No. The Lord who sent a caravan to the desert of Arabia and who put in their minds the thought of staying with Hajrāh and Ismā'īl ﷺ, diverted an Arabian caravan towards this Syrian desert to assist Yūsuf ﷺ.

Muftī Muhammad Shafī Sāhib ﷺ narrates here in his *'Kashkōl'* that once a person fell in a well in a deserted island. There was no way out. He was waiting for his death, when suddenly he heard a bang and a snake appeared. The snake approached the person and began to wrap itself around his body. Then it began to crawl on the walls of the well. In this manner, it climbed the walls of the pit and put the person on the ground, and returned to the inside of the well.

The lesson to be learnt here is that whosoever depends upon Allāh ﷻ and has faith in Him during the hardest times, then surely the Merciful Lord's assistance hastens towards him. *'And whosoever puts his trust in Allāh, He will suffice him. Allāh brings His commands to pass. Indeed, Allāh has set a measure for all things.'*

Verse 20

$$\text{وَشَرَوْهُ بِثَمَنٍ بَخْسٍ دَرَاهِمَ مَعْدُوْدَةٍ ج}$$

$$\text{وَكَانُوْا فِيْهِ مِنَ الزَّاهِدِيْنَ ﴿٢٠﴾}$$

"And they sold him for a mean price! A few counted dirhams;
and they were of those who regarded him insignificant."

When the brothers came to know that a caravan had taken him out of the well, they hastened to get there and claimed Yūsuf ﷺ as their absconding slave who ran away from them habitually. They claimed that due to his bad habit of running away, they did not want to keep him and were ready to sell

---

[76] Tirmidhī.

him. It is said that they sold Yūsuf 🙥 for eighteen dirhams or so. Nine brothers took two dirhams each, Judah did not take his share.

The aforementioned *tafsīr* is narrated from Mujāhid and Ikrimah. Qatāda has given a different interpretation saying that the indication is towards the caravan; i.e. the caravan sold Yūsuf 🙥 for a mean price.

Qāzī Sulaimān Mansūrpūri writes in '*Al Jamal wa'l-Kamal*', 'This second opinion is the correct one because:

1. There is no evidence that the brothers returned to the pit when the caravan pulled Yūsuf 🙥 out.

2. By referring this pronoun to the brothers of Yūsuf 🙥, the flow of the conversation is interrupted. The verses 19 and 20 are both related to the caravan.

3. The caravan had picked up Yūsuf 🙥 from the well and its members attached no substantial value to Yūsuf 🙥 [as is the norm with something found on the street]. 'And thus the most precious of human lives in that time was sold into slavery by the caravan.'

Khāzin says, 'The caravan took Yūsuf 🙥 to Egypt and put him up for sale in the slave market.'

Qitfir, one of the ministers of Egypt and the treasurer for the Egyptian King bought him.

Wahb Ibn Munabbih has said that Yūsuf 🙥 was auctioned in the market, and the bidders raised his price to the extent that he was sold for his equivalent weight of silver, silk, and musk. [77]

Tafsīr Mājidī has narrated here from the Bible, 'And they drew and lifted Joseph out of the pit, and sold Joseph to the Ishmailites for twenty pieces of silver.' [78] 'So they drew Joseph up out of the pit and sold him to the

---

[77] Khāzin 11:3.

[78] Gibbons, 'The History of the Decline and Fall of the Roman Empire' 37:26 – Tafsīr Mājidī 363:2.

merchants for twenty minas.' [79] 'Each took two pieces with which he bought shoes.' [80]

Regarding the Isrā'īli narrations, the Prophet ﷺ has ordered us, 'Do not believe them [as most of them are distorted], yet do not reject them outright.' Thus these narrations may not be suitable for proving something, but they can give some indication.

Ibn Kathīr ؓ has supported the first opinion that the meaning of the verse is that the brothers claimed Yūsuf ؑ to be their slave and sold him to the caravan because the caravan was not abstentious to him, rather they were overjoyed and were happy to make a fortune out of Yūsuf ؑ. [81]

"And they attached..." This implies that the brethren were not all keen on making a good sum out of Yūsuf ؑ; they were only keen on getting rid of him anyhow.

Ibn Kathīr ؓ says, 'They attached no value to him because they did not realise his status in the eyes of Allāh ﷻ, nor did they know of his Prophethood.'

The Ṣūfīs say, 'External observation cannot lead to apprehension of the Jewel of Wilāyah, let alone the apprehension of Nubuwwat. Without realisation it is hard to fulfil the rights of those closely attached with Allāh ﷻ. Therefore, a Mu'min and especially a Ṣūfī should constantly supplicate, 'O Allāh! Grant us maximum benefit from the pious souls of our time and gift us with their blessings and do not deprive us through disrespecting them.'

Verse 21

وَقَالَ الَّذِى اشْتَرَاهُ مِنْ مِّصْرَ لِامْرَاتِهِ اَكْرِمِىْ مَثْوٰهُ عَسٰى اَنْ يَّنْفَعَنَا اَوْ نَتَّخِذَهٗ وَلَدًا ط وَكَذٰلِكَ مَكَّنَّا لِيُوْسُفَ فِى الْاَرْضِ وَلِنُعَلِّمَهٗ مِنْ تَاْوِيْلِ الْاَحَادِيْثِ ط وَاللهُ غَالِبٌ عَلٰى اَمْرِهٖ وَلٰكِنَّ اَكْثَرَ النَّاسِ لَا يَعْلَمُوْنَ ﴿٢١﴾

---

[79] 11.3:3.
[80] The Jewish Encyclopaedia 249:7 – Tafsīr Mājidī 363:2.
[81] Tafsīr Mājidī 363:2.

And the man in Egypt who purchased him and said to his wife, 'Receive him
honourably, perchance he may prove use to us, or we may adopt him as a son.'
Thus We established Yūsuf in the land that We may teach him the
interpretation of events. And Allāh has all power and control over His affairs.
But most among mankind know it not.

Yūsuf ﷺ was taken to Egypt and was put up for sale. His handsome presence,
his purity, innocence, his intelligence and integrity attracted all eyes to him.
There was the keenest competition to purchase him but every competitor
was outbid by a high court official, 'Azīz' [in verse 30]. Tafsīr Mājidī has
narrated here that his name was 'Potiphar'.

Potiphar literally means eunuch, as well as 'court official', the most
important offices having been in the Ancient Orient in the hands of royal
slaves who were often eunuchs.

SLAVERY IN ISLĀM

Slavery is not something new. It also prevailed in the ancient days. Thus
there is no religion which has condemned slavery. In fact, St. Paul has
strengthened the issue of slavery. He counselled the Ephesian slaves 'to obey
their masters with respect and fear just as they would the Lord.' [82]

The whole credit falls to Islām, which completely changed the form of
slavery. So much so that even those claiming freedom today can take
lessons. Bilāl ﷺ was a black slave, but when Umar the great ﷺ mentioned
him, he would say, 'Abū Bakr ﷺ is our master and he freed our master, i.e.
Bilāl ﷺ.'

Zaid ﷺ used to be a slave, but the Prophet ﷺ married him to his own cousin.
This act alone diminishes all those thoughts which come to mind when
slavery is mentioned. Among the conditions of marriage, Islām has put a
condition that both the bride and the groom should be of equal status [unless
they agree]. Notwithstanding this, the Prophet ﷺ preferred Zaid ﷺ to a
number of lofty persons.

---

[82] Ephesians, 6:5.

It is the effect of this equality that Hasan Basrī ﷺ, Ikrimah ﷺ, Naafī ﷺ, Ibn Sīrīn ﷺ, whose mothers were slave girls, are unanimously agreed authorities of religion.

All the objections made on slavery, refer to the slavery afflicted by the Jews and Christians, whose barbarism can be witnessed in films like 'Roots'. Islām has never ever permitted such slavery. Islām has given equal rights to the slaves.

Here I would like to narrate an article written by a female convert, Dr Daw Ah Kia, a Burmese lady who carefully studied Islām before accepting it as a religion, and thereafter wrote a marvellous book in the form of a series of questions and answers. The book is not published yet. I was given a copy for proof reading by my beloved teacher, Hadhrat Maulānā Bilāl Sāhib Dāmat Barakātuhum. I found it very beneficial for non-Muslims as well as for those Muslims whose minds have fallen prey to Satanic Whispers.

She writes, 'Question: Why is slavery not forbidden in Islām?
Answer: This question needs to be cleared satisfactorily, because not only outsiders, but also many Muslims are gnawed at by this. If only we trust our Lord and search, we can surely unravel any mystery at all. We have our imperishable Holy Qur'ān and the sayings of the Holy Prophet ﷺ for reference and illumination. When these two sources are studied for the subject, we shall come to know that we are totally ignorant of many highly explosive facts. These are:

1. There is not a single word, let alone a sentence in the Holy Qur'ān, which suggests that slaves mentioned in the Book are what we know them today - those who are preyed upon, herded and sold like cattle or like the unfortunate victims of Africa from two centuries ago. The *slaves* mentioned in the Qur'ān are nothing but 'prisoners of wars taken in battle against the oppression of Islām or its transgression'. There is not a single instance in the Holy Qur'ān which suggests another source of slaves.'

The following is the view of a non-Muslim orientalist:

'According to the Qur'ān, no person can be made a slave except after the conclusion of a sanguinary battle [Jihad in the country of infidels who tried to suppress the religion]. Indeed, whenever slaves are mentioned in the Qur'ān, it is as 'he whom our right hands have conquered' or a special equivalent for neck - he whose neck has been spared thus clearly indicating a prisoner of war and made by the action not of one man only, but many...' [83]

2. It is most interesting to note that in the Holy Qur'ān, slavery never bears a commercial nature. This point will be evident when verses about this topic are presented. There, the reader can scrutinise every commandment, at his leisure.

3. Since wars against oppression are bound to occur throughout human existence, their inevitable product – prisoners and their equitable management – cannot be neglected. The Holy Qur'ān provides the solution in a most merciful and wise manner, in fact, Islām is the only religion which gets involved in this subject, with real compassion and fairness.

At this stage, one would come to notice that slavery or handling of captives cannot be ended, as long as there is man and his wars. How can one abolish a matter when its cause cannot be eradicated?

4. Kindness to the prisoners while in captivity and their welfare are thoroughly exhorted both in the Holy Qur'ān and sayings of the Prophet ﷺ.

EXCERPTS

Allāh says in the Qur'ān: '*And serve Allāh. Ascribe nothing as partners unto him. [Show] kindness unto parents, and unto near kindred, and orphans, and the needy, and unto the neighbour who is of kin [unto you] and the neighbour who is not of kin, and of the fellow traveller and wayfarer and [the slaves] whom your right hands possess. Lo! Allāh loveth not such as are proud and boastful.*' [84]

---

[83] Leitner, G. W., '*Mohammedanism*'.
[84] Qur'ān 4:36.

'If a man has a slave girl in his possession and he instructs her in polite accomplishments, and gives her good education, without inflicting any chastisement upon her, and frees her and marries her, he shall be rewarded with a double reward.'
[85]

5. The Holy Book allows that there is a difference of status between a free man and a captive. Only hypocrisy would deny this fact. How could Albert Speer [German architect and Hitler's minister for Armaments, who was freed from Pandau prison after twenty years of captivity and who died some years ago], or Rudolf Hess [Deputy Fuhrer, who committed suicide a year ago while serving his life sentence since he flew to Scotland in 1941] have been taken as equals to General Eisenhower or Field Marshal Montgomery during their captivity, trials, and verdict? But their lot would have fared much better if their captors were real Muslims, and most important of all, they could have been released long ago as an act of righteousness, charity, grace, atonement, spiritual evaluation or ransom. This will soon become obvious and clear in the next few pages.

With the acknowledgement of a simple truth – that the conqueror and the conquered are not of the same class – Islām does not permit man to ill-treat his prisoner nor can he take females as concubines. Even when they commit lewdness, they cannot be subjected to unbridled penalty. On the contrary, they draw only half the penalty of free women. One only has to read the following lines from the *Hadīth* and the Holy Qur'ān to believe the wonderful realities, which sound too good to be true:

'He who beats his slave without fault or slaps him on the face, his atonement for this is freeing him.' [86]

'And who so is not able to afford to marry free, believing women, let them marry from the believing maids whom your right hand possess, so wed them by permission of their folk, and give unto them their portions in kindness, they being honest, not debauched nor of loose conduct. And if, when honourably married, they commit lewdness, they shall incur the half of the punishment prescribed for free women [in that case]. This

---

is for him among you who fear to commit sin. But to have patience would be better for you. Allāh is forgiving, merciful.' [87]

'And marry such of you as are solitary and the pious of your slaves and maid servants. If they be poor, Allāh will enrich them of His bounty. Allāh is of ample means, aware.' [88]

Force not your slave girls to whoredom that ye may seek enjoyment of the life of the world.' [89]

6. Even after thorough safeguarding of the prisoner is enforced, the fact still remains that it is against morality, justice and social upkeep to hold them in permanent bondage. To remedy this, Allāh ﷻ has laid down a law by which all financially able Muslim's are held responsible for their emancipation. This law perpetually urges them [Muslims] to be mindful of this human duty. Allāh ﷻ prods them from all sides to carry out this task.

Thus, a Muslim must liberate them:

1. As a duty of righteousness whose importance is ranked among the foremost teachings of Islām.

Allāh says in the Qur'ān, which we will quote as evidence: *'It is not righteousness that ye turn their faces to the east and the west, but righteous is he who believeth in Allāh and the last day and the angels and the scriptures and the Prophets, and giveth his wealth, for love of Him, to kinsfolk and to orphans and the needy and the wayfarer and to those who ask, and to those who set slaves free, and observeth proper worship and payeth the poor-due. And those who keep their treaty when they make one, and the patient in tribulation and adversity and time of stress. Such are they who are sincere. Such are the God fearing.'* [90]

---

[87] Qur'ān 4:25.
[88] Qur'ān 4:32.
[89] Qur'ān 4:33.
[90] Qur'ān 2:177.

2. When they ask for their freedom, they are not only to be given freedom but also some capital if they prove to be worthy *'And such of your slaves as seek a writing [of emancipation], write it for them if ye are aware of ought of good in them, and bestow upon them of the wealth of Allāh which he hath bestowed upon you.'* [91]

3. As an act of spiritual elevation, *'Ah, what will convey unto thee what the Ascent is! [It is] to free a slave.'* [92]

4. As an act of charity, *'The alms are only for the poor and the needy... and to free the captives.'* as an act of grace. [93]

5. As ransom, *'Now that ye meet in battle with those who disbelieve, it is smiting of the necks until, ye have routed them then making fast bounds and afterwards either grace or ransom till the war lay down its burdens.'* [94]

6. As an act of expiration of an oath [Kaffārah], *'He who hath killed a believer by mistake must set free a believing slave, and pay the blood money to the family of the slain unless they remit as a charity.'* [95]

7. Freed slaves are not disdained as inferior. There is actual Muslim brotherhood. Zaid, a free slave of the Prophet ﷺ, married the Holy Prophet's ﷺ cousin; Zainab. His authority as commanding officer of the Muslim army was never challenged or disobeyed. Dr Leitner writes in his book, *Mohammedanism*: 'The history of Mohammedanism has since shown not only the admission of the converted slave on equal terms into Mohammedan society [circumstances which do not exist to the same extent among Christian Negroes], but also his rise in several Mohammedan countries, including Egypt, to the highest position in the state, whether as an individual or as a member of a whole class of slaves and irrespective of colour. The brotherhood of Mohammedanism is no mere word. All believers are equal

---

[91] Qur'ān 4:33.
[92] Qur'ān 90:12-13.
[93] Qur'ān 9:60.
[94] Qur'ān 47:4.
[95] Qur'ān 4:92.

and their own high priest, Zaid the ex-slave, led Muhammad's troops, the Ghazavide Dynasty was founded by the slave Sabakatgin. The first King of Delhi, Qutbuddīn was a slave. [96]

Another ex-slave from Makkah, Bilāl ﷺ, was highly esteemed and exalted in the annals of Islām for his religiousness and endurance at the hands of the disbelievers.

In one *Hadīth* of *Sahīh Muslim*, our beloved Messenger ﷺ is reported to have said: *"They (your servants and slaves) are your brothers. Allāh has put them in your care, so feed them with what you eat, clothe them with what you wear. And do not burden them beyond their capacities; but if you burden them (with an unbearable burden), then help them (by sharing their extra burden)."*[97]

Consider this *Hadīth* with an objective mind, and wonder at the honour and respect Islām has afforded to the slaves.

Here again, only reality counts and what bliss is there in the serving class in a society, where no one believes in God and his accountability for all his actions in the hereafter? His servants, valets or employees may not be called slaves, but their condition is unspeakably worse than that of the slaves of a real Muslim who believes and fears his Lord, so he dares not insult them even under threat or bribe.

It does not make for pleasant reading what President L. B. Johnson had done to one of his subordinates in the 'Little House'. Below is an account of what happened:

'...On the other hand, he was more than generous to Kennedy appointees; He kept many of them on and gave them a major role in government. But he felt to humiliate others. For Johnson, love too often meant submission, and once a man submitted, Johnson disposed him. Crudity was a favourite weapon. With great glee, L. B. Johnson described 'a delicate Kennedyte' whom he dragged into the bathroom to continue a conversation. 'He found it utterly impossible to look at me while I sat on the toilet.' Johnson badgered him to come closer so that they could talk. 'Then began the most ludicrous scene I had ever witnessed. Instead of simply turning around and walking over to me, he kept his face away from me and walked backward, one rickety step at a time. It certainly made me wonder how that man had made it so far in the world.' [98]

This Kennedyte was not a slave, but what significance is there in his designation, when he is subjected to such humiliation? Even so, LBJ's description only typifies the authoritarian nature of the ruling class. God only knows how many suffer in billions of offices and homes the world over.

With all this, LBJ would have heartily mocked the slavery of Islām; so would Stalin and Hitler under whom untold millions of men, women, and children underwent indescribable cruelties and went missing; so would Howard Hughes and other tycoons who had also gleefully deflowered many innocent virgins in their midst or abused their employees with impunity.

It is the perpetual irony of man to be ignorant of real facts. As a result, he almost always points his finger in the wrong direction. I prefer much to be the slave of a true believer under whose inevitable conscience I would be well protected with a glaring prospect of release than to be an employee or a follower of a non-believer or a false Muslim for whom fairness means a laughable and pitiable stupidity.

By this time, it would be proper to hope that the reader may judge slavery in Islām in a much more proper and deserving manner.' [99]

"Receive him honourably. Do not treat him like a slave. Perchance he may profit us." When he grows up I may be able to take him as an assistant in the affairs of government. The *Azīz* of *Misr* [Egypt] had foreseen the bright future of Yūsuf 🕮, just by his outstanding appearance. Handsome people normally have the advantage of good fortune and thus they are treated with special care. There is a saying, 'Two persons never suffer from hunger: 1. A Wise intelligent person, 2. A handsome person.'

I can recall a quote, which says, 'Good looks and good manners are attached to each other.'

Ibn Mas'ūd 🕮 says, 'The most wise persons of the entire universe are three:

---

[98] Time Magazine, Pg 33, April 19, 1976 – Article on 'Lyndon Johnson and the American Dream' by Doris Kern, associate professor of Government at Harvard.

[99] The Simple Way to Live Islām, Pg. 146-153.

1. The ruler of Egypt who had foreseen the future of Yūsuf 🕮 and ordered his wife to treat him honourably.

2. The daughter of Shu'ayb 🕮 who said to her father regarding Mūsā 🕮, *'Keep him as a labourer. Indeed the best person whom you desire to keep is the one who is strong and trustworthy.'*

3. Abū Bakr Siddīq 🕮 who foresaw the brightness of Umar 🕮 and appointed him as the Khalīfah. [100]

It is interesting to note here that even though Yūsuf 🕮 was bought as a slave, who is expected to work for his master, Allāh 🕮 made it such that the master is telling his wife to look after the slave!

"Or we may adopt him as a son." Adoption is the *'Rasm'* [practice] of the era of *Jāhiliyyah*. The disbelievers brought it about. They thought that adoption is the treatment for not having children. Whereas the matter is somewhat different.

Adoption is indirectly an act of disrespect to the court of Allāh 🕮, the Creator. In other words, 'If you did not give me any children, then so what? I myself have found a child for myself.'

Note that adoption and fostering are two different things. In adoption, the lineage is changed and the real parents are not revealed. Fostering is just looking after a distressed child. This is highly rewarding, especially when the child is an orphan.

In the story of Yūsuf 🕮, we see that Yūsuf 's 🕮 adoptive mother falls in deep love with Yūsuf 🕮. Can a real mother do this to her child? In the case of Mūsā 🕮 who was also adopted by Pharaoh, Mūsā 🕮 himself turns out to be the cause of the destruction of Pharaoh, which shows that many a time adoption ends in misery.

"And so we established Yūsuf 🕮 in that country." Allāma Uthmānī 🕮 says, 'Allāh 🕮 by His unlimited power and meticulous planning brought Yūsuf 🕮 out of hardship and troubles which he bore at the hands of his brothers and established him in the house of the Azīz of Misr. Then Allāh 🕮 cast love and

---

[100] Ibn Kathīr, Tafsīr, 12:21.

affection into the heart of the Azīz of Misr, gave Yūsuf ☼ a respectable place in Egypt, and made him loveable in the eyes of the Egyptians which furthered his future career and became a catalyst for the habitation of the *Banū Isrā'īl* in Egypt. It was also required that he observed the councils of the rulers and governors and understood the secrets and rules of administration. For his future needs, he would also need to obtain the perfect experience, and master the science of setting all things in their apportioned places.'

Tafsīr Mājidī narrates from the Bible, 'And Joseph found grace in his sight and he served him and he made Joseph the overseer over his house, and all that he put in his hand. He had him the greatest honour, and taught him the learning that he become a free man, he entrusted also the care of his house to him.' [101]

"And Allāh ☼ is dominant in His affairs but most among Mankind know not." The *Sūfīs* say that the meditation of this verse [pondering over its meaning] is a tested remedy for all fears, and strengthens the heart of a true believer to a limit where this true *Mu'min* becomes a heavy burden upon Shaytān.

I recently saw an article in *Sirāt-e-Mustaqīm* that a team of psychologists in the USA have established the fact that people with religious belief cope with problems very easily and recover from trauma much quicker than those who have no beliefs. They also avoid many surgeries which other people have to go through. *Subhān-Allāh!*

Verse 22

وَلَمَّا بَلَغَ أَشُدَّهُ آتَيْنَاهُ حُكْمًا وَعِلْمًا ط

وَكَذٰلِكَ نَجْزِى الْمُحْسِنِينَ ﴿٢٢﴾

And when he reached his maturity, we endowed him with judgement [in mundane affairs] and knowledge [of religious truths] and thus we recompense the well doers.

---

[101] Tafsīr Mājidī 363:2.

Allāma Uthmānī 🕮 says, 'When Yūsuf 🕮 was fully grown up and all his potential powers reached perfection, he received Allāh's 🕮 mighty inspiration of judgement and knowledge abundantly. He would resolve most complex problems and complicated matters very prudently, give wise judgements in the disputes of the people, and understood the profound secrets of Divine Religion. He was true to his word, he did what he said, was pure from base morals, was proficient in the Divine Constitutions, with the interpretation of dreams being his special science. Those people who create good morals and build up decent character, grappling with the ups and downs patiently, whether by the guidance of nature or in the footsteps of the saints, and by the help of Allāh 🕮, Allāh 🕮 bestows upon them such rewards.'

The word 'Muhsinīn' means well doers. Literally it means 'To beautify'. In the Hadīth of Jibra'īl 🕮, Ihsān has been interpreted as the following, 'That you worship Allāh 🕮 as though you are seeing Him, if you do not see Him, He is definitely watching you.' Both meanings apply in the case of Yūsuf 🕮. He was a doer of good, as well as achieving the grade of constant remembrance of Allāh 🕮.

Verse 23

وَرَاوَدَتْهُ الَّتِيْ هُوَ فِيْ بَيْتِهَا عَنْ نَّفْسِهِ وَغَلَّقَتِ الْأَبْوَابَ وَقَالَتْ هَيْتَ

لَكَ ۚ قَالَ مَعَاذَ اللهِ اِنَّهُ رَبِّيْ اَحْسَنَ مَثْوَايَ ۚ اِنَّهُ لَا يُفْلِحُ الظَّالِمُوْنَ

﴿٢٣﴾

And she in whose house he was, sought to seduce him. She fastened the doors and said, 'Now come.' He said, 'Allāh forbid! Truly He is my lord! He has made me a good dwelling. Verily the wrong doers do not prosper.'

Allāma Uthmānī 🕮 writes: 'On one hand, Allāh's Subtle Grace was nurturing Yūsuf 🕮 in an amazing manner. But on the other hand, the wife of the minister put him through a grave test, which was a very slippery slope. Zuleikhā fell in love with him due to his extraordinary beauty and grace. She tried presenting all possible fascinating charms to overcome him and to cause his heart to lose composure. It was a delicate moment for Yūsuf 🕮. All items of luxury and enjoyment were presented to him, with full freedom to satisfy the sexual passions, her loving and admiring behaviour, the expressions of earnest desire from the side of the woman herself while being alone with him. The doors would be closed so no one could interfere. Yūsuf ﷺ was also young and unmarried, full of power and passion; enough factors to test the piety of any god-fearing person. But whom Allāh ﷻ called *Muhsin* and gave him wisdom and knowledge, and raised him to the sublime height of Prophetic *Ismat* (being protected from sins), could never be overpowered by the Shaytān. He called out, 'مَعَاذَ الله *Shelter of Allāh!*' And all *Shaytānī* nets were broken. How can one who takes refuge in Allāh be subdued by any satanic power?

Yūsuf ﷺ said, 'Allāh forbid! How can I commit this abhorrent act? Azīz is my master who has kept me in comfort and treated me with kindness. Should I attack the honour of my Master? Then I would be hugely unjust. Ungrateful and unjust people can never see the face of success and prosperity. When we are so indebted to the mortal benefactor, how much should we be obliged to the Real Benefactor – the Cherisher of the whole universe, Almighty Allāh? We should feel ashamed of Him who cherished us and appointed His servants to serve us.

Some *Mufassirīn* have said that إِنَّهُ رَبِّي refers to Allāh ﷻ. He has been very kind to me and I feel ashamed of Him. [102]

Tafsīr Mājidī narrates, 'And it came to pass after these things that his master's wife cast her eyes upon Joseph, and she said, *'Lie with me.'* However, as she spoke to Joseph day by day, he hearkened not unto her, to lie by her, or to be with her. And it came to pass about this time that Joseph went into the house to do his business; and there was none of men of the house there within. And she caught him by his garment, saying *'Lie with me'.* [103]

Yūsuf ﷺ strongly rejected her proposal. In the Egyptian culture, premarital immorality was no big deal, whereas misconduct with a married woman was condemnable.

---

[102] Tafsīr Uthmānī p.1056.
[103] Tafsīr Mājidī 364:2.

"*He said: Allāh forbid!*" The *Sūfīs* derive from here that the constant remembrance of Allāh 🕮 is the root of safeguarding from all sins. [104]

Qāzī says, 'Allāh 🕮 did not mention the name of the wife of Azīz. Rather he used the words, 'She in whose house Yūsuf 🕮 was.' This is to indicate that Yūsuf 🕮 was under her total command, and in such a situation it is hard to refrain from sin.

Here it would be worth mentioning the following *Hadīth*: The Holy Prophet 🕮 says: '*There are seven persons whom Allāh 🕮 will grant shelter on the day when there will be no shelter, save the shelter of Allāh:*

1. A just leader,

2. A youth who grew up in the worship of Allāh 🕮,

3. A person whose heart is attached to the Masjid; when he comes out of the masjid until he returns,

4. Those two persons who befriended one another for the sake of Allāh 🕮; for Allāh 🕮 they gathered, and for Him they separated,

5. A person who donated some amount [but with so much sincerity that] his left hand did not know what his right hand has spent,

6. A person whom a lady with great beauty and great attraction called, yet he said, 'I fear Allāh 🕮',

7. A person who remembered Allāh 🕮 secretly and his tears began to flow.' [105]

From the above qualities, the second, sixth and the seventh prevail in the case of Yūsuf 🕮.

---

[104] Rumooz.
[105] Bukhārī 629, Muslim 2248.

"The wrong doers do not prosper." In this sentence, Yūsuf ﷺ is indicating that an adulterer does wrong not only to himself, but also to his wealth, his family, the woman, her family, her husband, the illegitimate child born from the act and to the whole nation.

ZINĀ

harām [forbidden], Allāh ﷻ says:

$$\text{وَلَا تَقْرَبُوا الزِّنٰىٓ اِنَّهُ كَانَ فَاحِشَةً ۗ وَسَآءَ سَبِيْلًا ۟}$$

"Do not go near fornication; it is a grave sin and it is an evil road to take." [106]

And:

$$\text{وَحُرِّمَ ذٰلِكَ عَلَى الْمُؤْمِنِيْنَ ۟}$$

"...And it has been prohibited upon the faithful." [107]

He also says:

$$\text{وَلَا تَقْرَبُوا الْفَوَاحِشَ مَا ظَهَرَ مِنْهَا وَمَا بَطَنَ ۟}$$

"Do not go near indecent deeds, open or secret." [108]

He also says, *'Say to the believing men that they should lower their gazes and guard their modesty: that will make for greater purity for them: And Allāh ﷻ is well acquainted with all that they do. And say to the believing women that they should lower their gaze and guard their modesty...'*

We notice that Allāh ﷻ did not just prohibit *Zinā*. He also prohibited the channels that lead to *Zinā*, i.e. staring, idle talking with a non-*Mahram*, touching, hugging, kissing, etc.

Not only has *Zinā* been forbidden in the Qur'ān, it was also forbidden in the *Tawrāh* and *Injīl* [Bible], because it is one of the greatest sins. It destroys families, demolishes self-respect as well as the respect of fellow human

---

[106] Qur'ān 17:32.
[107] Qur'ān 24:3.
[108] Qur'ān 6:151.

beings. It mixes up the lineages by bringing one person's child to another person's family. It is a cause of the destruction of the whole society.

Huzaifah Ibn Yamān 🕮 narrates from the Prophet 🕮, who said:

'Refrain from *Zinā* because it has six disadvantages; three in the *dunyā* and three in the hereafter. The three in the *dunyā* are:

1. Reduction of *Rizq* [sustenance].
2. Shortening of life.
3. Extinction of beauty.

The three in the hereafter are:

1. The wrath of the Almighty.
2. Severe reckoning.
3. Dwelling in the hellfire.' [109]

Anas Ibn Mālik 🕮 narrates that the Prophet 🕮 says:
'The one who is constantly engaged in
Zinā is like the one who worships idols.' [110]

Once the Holy Prophet 🕮 was shown some strange scenes in a dream. One of the scenes was that he saw a huge *tannūr* [cauldron type oven]. Fire was burning in it and there were many naked men and women inside. When the flames would rise, they would also rise up to the opening of the *tannūr*, and when the flames would go down, they would also go down. They are unable to come out of the *tannūr*. He asked Jibra'īl 🕮 regarding them, who replied that they are the adulterers.

Zinā with a neighbour's wife is the most horrendous. The Prophet 🕮 counted three major sins, he said: '*The gravest of all major sins are: 1. To assign a partner to Allāh 🕮, 2. To murder a faithful soul which Allāh 🕮 has granted respect, without any valid reason, and, 3. Zinā with the wife of your neighbour.*'

---

[109] Ibn Al Jawzī pg.137.
[110] Ibn Al Jawzi pg.137.

Imām Muhammad Ibn Idrīs Al-Shāfi'ī says:

عِفُّوا تَعِفَّ نِسَاؤُكُمْ فِى الْمُحْرَمِ ۞ وَتَجَنَّبُوا مَا لَا يَلِيقُ بِمُسْلِمِ

Be chaste and the ladies in your household will stay chaste –
Refrain from that which does not suit a Muslim.

اِنَّ الزِّنَا دَيْنٌ فَاِنْ اَقْرَضْتَهُ ۞ كَانَ الْوَفَا مِنْ اَهْلِ بَيْتِكَ فَاعْلَمِ

Zinā is a loan - if you give it to someone,
then remember it will be repaid to you from within your family.

يَا هَاتِكًا حُرَمَ الرِّجَالِ وَقَاطِعًا ۞ سُبُلَ الْمَوَدَّةِ عِشْتَ غَيْرَ مُكَرَّمِ

Oh you who severs the dignity of noble people, and devours the
paths of love and harmony, may you live void of any respect.

لَوْ كُنْتَ حُرًّا مِنْ سُلَالَةِ مَاجِدٍ ۞ مَا كُنْتَ هَتَّاكًا لِحُرْمَةِ مُسْلِمِ

If you were a noble person from a respected family,
you would not cause any disgrace to your fellow Muslim.

مَنْ يَزْنِ يُزْنَ بِهِ وَلَوْ بِجِدَارِهِ ۞ اِنْ كُنْتَ يَا هٰذَا لَبِيبًا فَافْهَمِ

Remember! Whosoever fornicates will have to suffer the same, even if the act
was to be repeated with the wall of his house. If you are a man of
understanding, then take heed.

May Allāh ﷻ save the nation from this indecent act. *Āmīn*

Verses 24-29

وَلَقَدْ هَمَّتْ بِهِ ۚ وَهَمَّ بِهَا لَوْلَا اَنْ رَّاٰ بُرْهَانَ رَبِّهِ ۚ كَذٰلِكَ لِنَصْرِفَ عَنْهُ السُّوْءَ وَالْفَحْشَاءَ ۚ اِنَّهُ مِنْ عِبَادِنَا الْمُخْلَصِيْنَ ﴿٢٤﴾ وَاسْتَبَقَا الْبَابَ

وَقَدَّتْ قَمِيْصَهٗ مِنْ دُبُرٍ وَّاَلْفَيَا سَيِّدَهَا لَدَا الْبَابِ ۚ قَالَتْ مَا جَزَآءُ مَنْ
اَرَادَ بِاَهْلِكَ سُوْءًا اِلَّاۤ اَنْ يُّسْجَنَ اَوْ عَذَابٌ اَلِيْمٌ ﴿٢٥﴾ قَالَ هِيَ
رَاوَدَتْنِيْ عَنْ نَّفْسِيْ وَشَهِدَ شَاهِدٌ مِّنْ اَهْلِهَا ۚ اِنْ كَانَ قَمِيْصُهٗ قُدَّ مِنْ
قُبُلٍ فَصَدَقَتْ وَهُوَ مِنَ الْكٰذِبِيْنَ ﴿٢٦﴾ وَاِنْ كَانَ قَمِيْصُهٗ قُدَّ مِنْ دُبُرٍ
فَكَذَبَتْ وَهُوَ مِنَ الصّٰدِقِيْنَ ﴿٢٧﴾ فَلَمَّا رَاٰ قَمِيْصَهٗ قُدَّ مِنْ دُبُرٍ قَالَ اِنَّهٗ
مِنْ كَيْدِكُنَّ ۚ اِنَّ كَيْدَكُنَّ عَظِيْمٌ ﴿٢٨﴾ يُوْسُفُ اَعْرِضْ عَنْ هٰذَا
وَاسْتَغْفِرِيْ لِذَنْۢبِكِ ۚ اِنَّكِ كُنْتِ مِنَ الْخٰطِئِيْنَ ﴿٢٩﴾

"And surely she desired him and he would have desired her, were it not that he had seen the argument of his Lord. Thus we did in order that we might avert from him all evil and indecency. Verily Yūsuf was a single-hearted bondsman of ours. And the two raced to the door, and she tore his shirt from behind. And the two met her master at the door. She said, 'What is the punishment of he who intended evil towards thy household, except that he be imprisoned or [given] an afflictive chastisement?' Yūsuf said, 'It is she who solicited me,' - and a witness from her own household bore witness: If his shirt is torn in front, she speaks the truth, and he is a liar! But if his shirt is torn from behind, she lies and he is a true teller!' So when he saw his shirt, torn from behind; he said, 'Verily, it is the guile of you women! The guile of you women is mighty!' Yūsuf! Turn away from there and thou woman! Ask for forgiveness for thy sin. Verily, thou has been guilty.'

In both the above verses, the name of the woman has been omitted. Maybe because of her lewdness. How could the Glorious Qur'ān mention the name of such a seductive woman? It is a fact that the Holy Qur'ān has not mentioned the names of any woman, except for Maryam 🙶.

The *Mufassirūn* say that within the Arab culture, mentioning the wife's name in a gathering was regarded as contrary to modesty. They would use phrases like 'The mother of Ahmed'. Allāh 🙵 mentioned the name 'Maryam'

THE TAFSĪR OF SŪRAH YŪSUF

in numerous places to show that she is not a wife of Allāh ﷻ, nor is Jesus the son of God.

Abdullāh Yūsuf Alī ﷺ says, 'Zuleikhā was blinded with passion, and his plea had no effect on her. He was human after all, and her passionate love and her beauty placed a great temptation in his path. But he had a sure refuge, his faith in Allāh ﷻ. His spiritual eyes saw something that her eyes, blinded with passion, did not see. She thought no one saw when the doors were closed. He knew that God was there and everywhere. That made him strong, and proof against temptation.'

"And she surely desired him..." The desire of Zuleikhā was strong. Her advances were very clear. Maulānā Abdul Mājid Daryābādī ﷺ narrates: 'She attired herself in the richest garments, and was more ardent then ever in her appeals to Joseph; and to escape them, he turned and fled abruptly from her presence.' [111]

"And he would surely have..." One interpretation here is that Yūsuf ﷺ never felt the slightest desire towards her. "We averted the evil from him. He saw the clear proof from his Lord."
What was this proof?

1. He saw a vision of his father, Ya'qūb ﷺ biting his finger,
2. He saw a picture of his master, the king.
3. Ibn Jareer narrates from Muhammad Ibn Ka'ab al Qurazi, 'Yūsuf ﷺ lifted his head towards the roof and saw the following inscribed on the walls, 'Do not go near fornication; Lo! It is an abomination and an evil path. 'Thereafter, Ibn Jareer says, 'It would be more befitting to say that it was some sign from the signs of his Lord Almighty, which halted him from proceeding towards any evil. It could be the face of Ya'qūb ﷺ, it could be the face of the king and it could be the writing on the wall. [112]

2. Some *Mufassirūn* say, 'She desired him and he intended to reprimand her by hitting her.'

---

[111] Polano Oprit 81 – Tafsīr Mājidī 366:2.
[112] Ibn Kathīr 246:2.

3. Maulānā Idrīs Khāndelwī ⚬ narrates from some who say, 'Here the word 'Hamma' does not mean desire. It means to have a thought about something. If one has a thought about evil, but he does not put it into practice, then he will not be questioned about it. It is like the one who is fasting on a hot day and he feels like drinking some icy drink, but he does not do so because he knows Allāh ﷻ is watching him. This person will not be reckoned for this thought that came to his mind. Rather in some cases, he might even get reward for refraining from acting upon his evil thought.

One *Hadīth Qudsī* [Divine statement from Allāh spoken by the Messenger ﷺ] says,

'When my servant intends to do good, write it down for him. Then when he puts it into practice, write it down in ten folds up to seven hundred times more [according to sincerity], and when he intends to commit a sin, do not write it down. If he leaves it, write it as a good deed because he refrained from it due to my fear. However, if he does put it into practice, then write down just one sin.' [113]

In the case of Yūsuf ⚬, even if he did get a thought of evil, he ran away from it, thus he should be rewarded for his piety.

One *Hadīth* says, "The Holy Prophet ﷺ saw a woman, and so he came to his wife, Zainab, as she was tanning a leather. He fulfilled his need with her. He then said to his Companions: '*The woman advances and retires in the shape of a devil* [the devil uses the womenfolk to lure susceptible men], *so when one of you sees a woman, he should come to his wife, for that will repel what he feels in his heart.*'" [114]

Note: Here the words, *"We might avert all evil from him.."* This means that evil was approaching Yūsuf ⚬. Allāh ﷻ stopped it and drove it away from him. Allāh ﷻ did not say here, "We averted Yūsuf ⚬ from the evil," because that would mean that Yūsuf ⚬ approached the evil and we had to stop him. This

---

[113] Bukhāri 6491, Muslim 131.
[114] Mishkāt.

as well as the ending of the verse indicates that the Prophets are *ma'sūm* [innocent from any wrong], sinless, protected by special attention from the Almighty Allāh ﷻ.

Īmām Fakhruddīn Raazī ﵁ has a *Risāla* named عصمة الانبياء. He has given many evidences to prove that Prophets are *mā'sūm*. They are human beings, so desire of sinning could creep in their minds, however, Allāh's special protection does not let them commit that sin. Their condition is like a child who is learning to walk. The father grabs hold of the child's hands and protects him if he is about to fall. Similarly, Prophets are also protected.

We are also instructed to follow in the footsteps of the Prophets. If they were to sin, we would have to follow them in that sin as well. This would create confusion. One act would be *harām* due to it being a sin, but at the same time it would be *wājib* (or at least *Jā'iz*) because the Prophet has done it, whereas one act cannot have conflicting rulings.

Hadhrat Maulānā Qāsim Nānōtwi ﵁ says, 'Just as the *Ambiyā* are *ma'sūm*, the *Awliyā* are *mahfūz* [protected]. Allāh ﷻ takes care of his bondsmen.'

There was a student in Delhi, during the time of Shāh Abdul Azīz Muhaddith Dehlawī ﵁. On his way to the Madrasah, a girl who used to see him pass by daily, fell in love with him. She tried her best to attract him, but he resisted. One day, she made a plot and lured him into her house. She told an old woman to stand at her doorstep and when the student passed, she cried for help. She did so and the student entered the house to assist. The girl locked the door. Then she ordered him to lie with her and fulfil her desire, and threatened to shout loudly and accuse him if he did not obey. He outwardly agreed and requested to go to the toilet first to relieve himself. In those days the toilets were not like our luxurious ones. In the toilets, wooden tubs would be placed, and every few days a *bhangī* [dirt collector] would come and empty the tubs. So the student went to the toilet and took some *najāsat* [stool] and rubbed it on his chest and shoulders. Then he approached her. With utmost disgust, she rebuked him and threw him out. He ran to a nearby river, as he was getting late for the lesson. He washed himself and hastened towards the lesson, which was conducted in the Masjid. Shāh Sāhib suddenly smelt this pleasant fragrance and enquired as to who had applied such pleasant *Itr* [perfume]. The students smelt each other and eventually it came to light that this smell was from the body of this student. Wherever he had rubbed that stool, Allāh ﷻ fragranced it with perfume. The narrator of this story says that this smell prevailed throughout the entire life of that student. *Subhān-Allāh!* How graceful is the Almighty Lord. One step towards His obedience brings such a high reward in this life. How much should we expect in the hereafter? [115]

The story of the three men from the *Banū Isrā'īl* is very famous. They were trapped in a cave and supplicated to Allāh ﷻ through their good deeds. One of them pleaded with the following words, 'O Allāh! You know that I had a cousin sister who was the most beloved person to me. I tried to lure her towards me but she refused. Until one day she, struck with poverty, approached me and begged for help. I worked hard and gathered one hundred [100] Dinārs [gold coins], then I said to her, these are yours if only you let me sleep with you. She agreed. When I sat between her legs, she said: 'Fear Allāh! Do not break the seal without its right.' [Marriage]. I instantly left her with the gold coins. O Allāh! If I did this just for your sake, then remove this rock from the entrance of this cave.' The rock moved and eventually they were able to get out. [116]

"Verily Yūsuf ﷺ was a single hearted bondsman of ours..." Mukhlas means the protected, the chosen one, the gifted one. Allāh ﷻ chooses for delivering his message whoever He wishes. And when He chooses someone, He protects him and guides him. Just as any government of this world would do so for its delegations which are entrusted with the most important of its messages to another neighbouring country.

Yūsuf ﷺ ran onwards to open the door and get away, and Zuleikhā was chasing him to stop. In this struggle, she caught the back of his shirt and pulled it, but Yūsuf ﷺ went on running and the shirt was torn. Even though the doors were closed, Yūsuf ﷺ somehow managed to open the door and run out. Zuleikhā followed, and her husband, the Azīz of Misr, who was near the door and was intending to enter the room, encountered both. Zuleikhā at once fell back and accused Yūsuf ﷺ of evil intention towards herself. She said Yūsuf ﷺ should be punished, but because she loved him, she did not want

---

[115] Narrated by Peer Zul Fiqaar Naqshbandi Sahib in his discourses.
[116] Muslim 2743.

her husband to kill him, so she suggested one of two punishments: either he should be thrown into prison for a few days, or he should be given a few lashes.

Yūsuf 🕮 had to defend himself, and so he disclosed the fact that it was Zuleikhā who desired him and Yūsuf 🕮 was trying to save himself by running out.

This dispute was going on when a witness from Zulekhā's family, her cousin, bore testimony. Some narrations say it was her paternal cousin and some say it was her maternal cousin.

Also, Ibn Jarīr and Al-Baghawī here narrated from Ibn Abbās 🕮, that this witness was a new-born baby who was still being weaned.

One narration states that four babies have spoken in their weaning days:

1. Hadhrat Īsā 🕮 [Jesus peace be upon him].

2. The son of *Māshitah Āl-Firoun* [the lady who was the hairdresser of Firoun's daughter].

3. The baby who testified for Juraij Rāhib [George, the monk].

4. The baby who testified for Yūsuf 🕮. [117]

Some have said that this person was a wise man from the family of Zuleikhā who was at the time coming into the house with the Azīz of Misr.

Anyhow, he gave his observation that if Yūsuf's 🕮 shirt was torn from the front side, then he was at fault because if he approached her, as Zuleikhā was saying, then he must be facing her, and she would be trying to put him off, and in the struggle his shirt could have been torn. Whereas, if Yūsuf 🕮 was right in saying that Zuleikhā was trying to seduce him, and he was trying to escape, then the shirt should be torn from behind. When the Azīz saw the shirt torn from behind, he also agreed that it seemed to be Zuleikhā's fault, so he requested Yūsuf 🕮 to bury the event there and then, and not to make it public, as it would be a cause of much disgrace and humiliation. Turning

---

[117] Abū Hurairah, Hasan Basrī and Sa'īd Ibn Jurair have mentioned this narration. See Ibn Kathīr, Tafsīr 12:29.

towards his wife, he instructed her to ask for forgiveness of her sin from God or he meant that she should apologise to Yūsuf ﷺ.

Allāh ﷻ says here: *"The guile of you women is mighty."*

Qāzī Sanāullā Panipati ﷺ says, 'I do not fear Shaytān, as much as I fear the women." In the Qur'ān, Allāh ﷻ has said, *'The guile of women is mighty'*, whereas in another verse Allāh ﷻ says, *'The guile of Shaytān is weak.'* Also Shaytān, due to fear, makes his plots secretly, whereas a woman openly makes her plots and executes her plan very cleverly.'

Maulānā Abdul Mājid Daryābādī ﷺ writes, under the verse 'Your guile is mighty': Notice that this is not the pronouncement of Islām, but an observation of Portiphar - a view that has found favour with many non-Muslim scholars and writers: 'Nature has not destined them, as the weaker sex, to be dependent on strength, but on cunning; that is why they are instinctively crafty, and have an ineradicable tendency to lie.' [118]

Compare the following Buddhist aphorism: 'Inscrutable as the way of a fish in water is the nature of women, those thieves of many devices with whom truth is hard to find.' [119]

Compare also the observations of modern scientific writers: - 'Everyone is acquainted with instances from life or from history of women whose quick and cunning ruses have saved lover or husband or child. It is inevitable, and results from the constitution of women, acting in the conditions under which they are generally placed.' [120]

'...From folklore and myth, from national proverbs and traditions, and from the text-books of the oldest religions, therefore, we learn that woman is two-faced, or false or treacherous, or disloyal...' [121]

'Woman's tendency to ruse and deception is a constant positive and life promoting instinct.' [122]

---

[118] Schopenhauer, Essays, Pg.66.
[119] Hasting 'Encyclopaedia of Religion and Ethics' 271:4 - Tafsīr Mājidī 367:2.
[120] Havelock Ellis, Man and Woman, Pg.196 - Tafsīr Mājidī 367:2.
[121] Ludovici, The Woman, Pg.304 - Tafsīr Mājidī 367:2.
[122] Pg. 307, n.

'Finally among the great thinkers of Europe who have held the view that women are indifferent to truth, and incapable of rectitude, I would further mention Rousseau, Diderot, La Bruyere, and that great genius Kant.' [123]

Another observer, Mr Ingleby Oddit, London coroner for twenty-seven years, only so recently as December 1939 summed up his age-long experience with regard to the truthfulness of women in the following words:

'I have come to the conclusion that most women are simply born liars and can't help themselves. I have seen them stand up in front of men and give the most detailed and precise information, every word of which has been a lie.' [124]

Islām, on the other hand, has mentioned:

'Paradise lies beneath the feet of mothers.' [125]

'Whoever has three daughters and looks after them properly, they will form a barrier between him and the fire of hell.' [126]

'I have not seen anyone, who has little understanding and little religiousness, yet is well capable of overpowering the wisest man, other than you womenfolk.' [127]

This *Hadīth* seems to criticise women, but at the same time, looking more closely, it indicates the quality of a woman in making her husband fulfil the commands of Allāh ﷻ.

If every Muslim woman were to aid her husband in practicing the *Sharī'ah*, we would have a very different environment surrounding us. May Allāh ﷻ grant us the *Tawfīq, Āmīn*.

In the story, Yūsuf's ﷺ innocence is quite evident. The Azīz of Misr had seen the signs of Yūsuf's ﷺ innocence. Yūsuf ﷺ had stayed in his house for quite some time and he had never experienced anything that would cause doubts. Also, Yūsuf ﷺ was the slave of the woman, and it is not possible for a slave

---

[123] Pg.320 n.
[124] The Sunday Express, London, 17th December 1939 – Tafsīr Mājidī 367:2.
[125] Sunan Nasa'i, 3104
[126] Ibn Mājah 3659, Musnad Ahmad 16762.
[127] Bukhārī 293, Muslim 114.

to try and seduce his master's wife. Thirdly, they had seen that Yūsuf ﷺ was trying to run away, and a desiring person would not run away. Fourthly, they had seen that Zuleikhā was adorned in her best clothes and she had beautified herself to attract Yūsuf ﷺ. So it was Zuleikhā who should be doubted. That is the reason why the Azīz did not show any anger towards Yūsuf ﷺ and instead he reprimanded his wife by ordering her to repent.

Verse 30

وَقَالَ نِسْوَةٌ فِى الْمَدِيْنَةِ امْرَاَتُ الْعَزِيْزِ تُرَاوِدُ فَتٰهَا عَنْ نَّفْسِهٖ ج

قَدْ شَغَفَهَا حُبًّا ط اِنَّا لَنَرٰهَا فِىْ ضَلٰلٍ مُّبِيْنٍ ﴿٣٠﴾

And some ladies in the town said: 'The wife of Azīz is seeking to seduce her slave, verily he has inflamed her with violent love. Truly we see her in a clear error.'

As a matter of common gossip, women in the city began saying that the wife of Azīz has fallen in love with her slave, and she desired him to license himself for her. She has been completely infatuated by him. She has fallen so low as to attach herself to her own slave. It is a shameful thing for the wife of such a respected authority to stoop to the level of her slave. In their words, Zuleikhā had definitely gone astray.

'Shigāf' literally means the outer layer of the heart. When someone is engrossed in the love of someone, they say that the love has pierced into the heart.

Verse 31

فَلَمَّا سَمِعَتْ بِمَكْرِهِنَّ اَرْسَلَتْ اِلَيْهِنَّ وَاَعْتَدَتْ لَهُنَّ مُتَّكَاً وَّاٰتَتْ كُلَّ

وَاحِدَةٍ مِّنْهُنَّ سِكِّيْنًا وَّقَالَتِ اخْرُجْ عَلَيْهِنَّ ج فَلَمَّا رَاَيْنَهٗ اَكْبَرْنَهٗ وَقَطَّعْنَ

اَيْدِيَهُنَّ وَقُلْنَ حَاشَ لِلّٰهِ مَا هٰذَا بَشَرًا ط اِنْ هٰذَا اِلَّا مَلَكٌ كَرِيْمٌ ﴿٣١﴾

Then when she heard of their craft, she sent for them and prepared for them a banquet and she gave to each one of them a knife and said (to Yūsuf), 'Come forth before them.' When they saw him, they were dumbfounded, and cut their hands [in amazement], and said, 'Ḥāshā Lillāh' [how perfect is Allāh], this is not a human being. He is naught but a noble angel.'

Wahb ibn Munabbih says: 'There were forty of them whom she invited for a feast.' The fruit that was placed before them was some citrus fruit. [128]

The women must have been ladies of high rank and fit to dine with the Minister's wife. In the houses of the rich, floors were covered with heavy rugs and luxurious cushions. Stools and chairs with comfortable and beautiful leather seats were also provided. Thus, she invited the ladies and since the Egyptians were familiar with the use of cutlery, she gave them each a knife. Then she ordered Yūsuf 🙶 to come before them.

We can imagine them reclining at ease after the manner of fashionable banquets. When the time for dessert came, and talk flowed freely about the gossip which made their hostess interesting, they were just about to cut their fruit with their knives when Yūsuf 🙶 was suddenly brought before them. Imagine the concentration which his beauty elicited, so much so that it resulted in them cutting their fingers.

With regards to their craft, Allāma Uthmānī 🙶 writes: 'Their conversation among themselves was portrayed with the word 'makr' (plotting), because they were gossiping secretly. By criticising Zuleikhā, they were attempting to portray their piousness and holiness.

In reality, they had heard of the beauty and good looks of Yūsuf 🙶 and they were eager to see him.

It is highly likely that by criticising Zuleikhā, they intended to infuriate her so that she might call them in and allow them to see him. They could have thought that we may create hatred of Yūsuf 🙶 in Zuleikhā's heart and then win him over. It is also possible that Zuleikhā might have informed some of her friends in confidence that she loves Yūsuf 🙶. However, they betrayed her trust and exposed her secret. In short, the plotting of women could have any of the above meanings.

---

[128] Qurtubī.

"They cut their hands..." Mujāhid says: 'They injured their hands.' i.e. they did not fully sever them. Some say, 'They cut their fingertips yet never felt any pain, because their hearts were captivated by the beauty of Yūsuf ﷺ.

'Hāshā lillāh' is a phrase which denotes remoteness from imperfection or being free from it and maybe, *'I ascribe unto God remoteness from every imperfection.'* I marvel at the power of Allāh ﷻ in the creation of a person such as Yūsuf ﷺ who is so innocent and free from all blemishes.

"This is not a human being..." Tafsīr Mājidī states that this indicates towards moral dignity and sublimity of character rather than physical beauty or carnal charms. The highly placed Egyptian ladies are paying tribute to Yūsuf's ﷺ character as a human being.

Rasūlullāh ﷺ says in a *Hadīth* of *Sahīh Muslim*, while describing his trip to the heavens, *"I saw Yūsuf (peace be upon him) who had been given half of the (world's) beauty"*. Umar ﷺ once saw a handsome person and exclaimed, 'I have never seen such a handsome person except for that which has been reported regarding Yūsuf ﷺ.' The Sūfis say that the beauty of Yūsuf ﷺ was transparent, whereas the beauty of our Prophet Mohammad ﷺ was concealed. Only after deep observation would one notice how handsome he was. That is why Sayyidunā Alī *Karamallāhu wajhahū* would say:

$$مَنْ رَآهُ بَدِيهَةً هَابَهُ وَمَنْ خَالَطَهُ مَعْرِفَةً أَحَبَّهُ يَقُولُ نَاعِتُهُ لَمْ أَرَ قَبْلَهُ وَلاَ بَعْدَهُ مِثْلَهُ ـ$$

Whoever saw him for the first time (*Badīhah*) would be awestruck by him, and whoever got to know him, loved him. The one who tried to describe him would have to say: 'I have not seen before him or after him anyone who resembles him (ﷺ)'.[129]

The Ulama say that Yūsuf ﷺ had *'Jamāl'* (beauty). However, our Prophet ﷺ was blessed with *Jamāl* and *Jalāl*, i.e. *Haybat*, awe, inspiration.

[129] Tirmidhī: 3999.

Amr ibn Al-Aas ﷺ said: 'I was never able to fix my gaze on him. (I always looked down in his presence). That is why if someone asked me to describe him, I wouldn't be able to do so. One poet said:

يُغْضِىْ حَيَاءً وَيُغْضَى مِنْ مَهَابَتِهِ

فَمَا يُكَلَّمُ اِلَّا حِيْنَ يَبْتَسِمُ -

'He (my beloved) lowers his gaze due to modesty, while they lower
their gaze due to his awe. So he is not spoken to, except when he is smiling.'

Allāma Uthmānī ﷺ writes: 'It is possible that the modesty, chastity, and innocence which was shining upon Yūsuf's ﷺ face and in his manner of walk gave them the impression that this can't be a human being, this is an Angel.'

Verse 32

قَالَتْ فَذٰلِكُنَّ الَّذِيْ لُمْتُنَّنِيْ فِيْهِ ط وَلَقَدْ رَاوَدْتُّهُ عَنْ نَّفْسِهٖ فَاسْتَعْصَمَ ط

وَلَئِنْ لَّمْ يَفْعَلْ مَآ اٰمُرُهٗ لَيُسْجَنَنَّ وَلَيَكُوْنًا مِّنَ الصّٰغِرِيْنَ ﴿٣٢﴾

She said, 'This is he about whom you blamed me. I did seek to seduce him from
his [true] self, but he abstained [he firmly saved himself]. Yet if he does not do
what I say to him, he is sure to be imprisoned and sure to be humiliated.'

Abdullāh Yūsuf Alī ﷺ writes, 'Her speech is subtle, and shows that any repentance or compunction she may have felt is blotted by the collective crowd mentality into which she has deliberately invited herself to fall. Her speech falls into two parts. In the first part there is a note of triumph, as much to say, 'Now you see! Mine was no vulgar passion! You are just as susceptible! You would have done the same thing! Finding encouragement from their passion and their fellow feeling, she openly avows as a woman amongst women [a sort of freemasonry] what she would have been ashamed to acknowledge to others before. She falls a step lower and boasts of it. A step lower still, and she sneers at Joseph's innocence, his firmness in saving himself guiltless! There is a pause.

The tide of passion rises still higher, and the dreadful second part of her speech begins. It is a sort of joint consultation, though she speaks in monologue. The women all agree that no man has a right to resist their solicitations. Beauty spurned is the highest crime. And so now Zuleikhā rises to the height of tragic guilt and threatens Joseph. She forgets all her finer feeling, her real love, and is overpowered by brute passion. After all, he is a slave and must obey his mistress! Or, there is prison, and the company of the vilest, instead of the caresses of beauty and fashion in high places! Poor, deluded, fallen Zuleikhā! She sank lower than herself, in seeking the support of the crowd around her. What pain and suffering and sorrow can expiate the depth of this crime?'

"But he abstained." Nasafī writes that this is a clear proof that Yūsuf ﷺ never intended to do the evil and those who commented by saying that Yūsuf ﷺ had a slight intention to fulfil the desire, are totally wrong.

Verse 33

قَالَ رَبِّ السِّجْنُ اَحَبُّ اِلَيَّ مِمَّا يَدْعُوْنَنِيْ اِلَيْهِ ج وَاِلَّا تَصْرِفْ
عَنِّيْ كَيْدَهُنَّ اَصْبُ اِلَيْهِنَّ وَاَكُنْ مِّنَ الْجٰهِلِيْنَ ﴿٣٣﴾

He [Yūsuf] said, 'O my Lord! The prison is dearer to me than that to which they invite me; and if Thou does not turn away their snare from me, I shall yearn towards them and join the ranks of the ignorant.'

It seems that these women tried to persuade Yūsuf ﷺ to obey his mistress. Some commentators say that externally they were working for Zuleikhā, but internally they all wanted to draw his attention towards themselves. When he saw himself surrounded, he took refuge in Allāh ﷻ in the most polite manner. He preferred imprisonment to the sin. He did not rely on his *Ismat* [divine innocence]. Rather, he entirely depended on Allāh ﷻ for protection.

"The prison is dearer to me..." Khāzin narrates here that if he did not seek imprisonment for himself, he would not have been tested by being sent to prison. It is better for a person to pray for *Āfiyah* [peace, comfort, goodness].

Hadhrat Shāh Sāhib also states the same. Allāma Uthmānī ﷺ has narrated a *Hadīth* from *Tirmidhī Sharīf* that the Prophet ﷺ overheard a person praying, 'O Allāh! I pray to Thee for sabr!' The Prophet ﷺ said, '*You have asked Allāh ﷻ for calamity, ask Him for security.*' [130] It means that patience presupposes calamity, because patience is carried out when problems and troubles arise. Therefore, a person should ask for security and peace. Yes, when calamity does afflict a person, he should ask for patience.

$$ وَلَمَّا بَرَزُوْا لِجَالُوْتَ وَجُنُوْدِهٖ قَالُوْا رَبَّنَآ اَفْرِغْ عَلَيْنَا صَبْرًا وَّثَبِّتْ اَقْدَامَنَا وَانْصُرْنَا عَلَى الْقَوْمِ الْكٰفِرِيْنَ ۟ $$

'And when they emerged for Jaloot and his army, they supplicated: 'O our Rabb! Pour down sabr upon us and keep our feet firm, and assist us against the Kāfireen people.' [131]

In another Hadīth, the Prophet ﷺ said [in Jihad], '*Do not yearn for the approach of the enemy, but ask Allāh for Aāfiyat.* [Because one does not know and he might be tested and run away from the enemy which would be a major sin]. [132]

Maulānā Hifzur Rahmān Suyuhari ﷺ states in '*Qasasul Qur'ān*' that even though these great commentators are on one side, on the other side is a great Prophet of Allāh ﷻ; Yūsuf ﷺ. Therefore, it cannot be said that he made a wrong supplication. Indeed, the supplication at the time was the best he could have made. He had a choice of sin or prison. The woman had vowed to have him imprisoned unless he fulfilled her desire, and look at the after effects of the imprisonment. Once Yūsuf ﷺ was sent to prison, Zuleikhā totally took him out of her mind. The other ladies also left him alone and Yūsuf ﷺ secured his chastisement. A Prophet's *dua* and its acceptance are both from Allāh ﷻ. Therefore, it would be better to say that Yūsuf's ﷺ *dua* was the best which anyone could have made under such circumstances.

---

[130] Tirmīdhī 3450, Musnad Ahmad 21009.
[131] Qur'ān 2:250.
[132] Bukhārī 2744, Muslim 3276.

"I shall yearn towards them..." Note here that a Prophet who is *ma'sūm* fears from his self-deceit, therefore, the thinking of some *pīrs* [spiritual leaders] that once they reach a certain age, it is their right that the women lift their veils in their presence, and that they no longer have to observe the veil in front of them, is totally wrong. The Prophet ﷺ said, *'Whenever a person sits in privacy with a woman, the third of them is Shaytān.'* [133]

Hadhrat Shaykh [Maulānā Muhammad Zakarīyā Khāndhlawī] ﷺ mentions in *'Aap Beetī'* [his autobiography], that a person saw the Prophet ﷺ in his dream and asked him the above-mentioned question. He replied, 'Even if that man is a great saint like Junaid Baghdādī, and that woman is as pious as Rābiā Basrīyā, still Shaytān will be present with them.'

We see some false *pīrs* who mix with the gatherings of women, some hold their hands when doing *bay'at*, and some have women surrounding them at all times; all this is contrary to the *Sharī'ah* and should be avoided.

Verse 34

$$ فَاسْتَجَابَ لَهُ رَبُّهُ فَصَرَفَ عَنْهُ كَيْدَهُنَّ ۚ $$

$$ اِنَّهُ هُوَ السَّمِيْعُ الْعَلِيْمُ ﴿٣٤﴾ $$

"So his Lord answered him and averted their guile from him.
Verily He! He is the all Hearing, the all Knowing."

Allāh ﷻ heard the prayers of the Prophets before him, so He answered Yūsuf's ﷺ prayer and safeguarded him from the plots of the women.

Verse 35

$$ ثُمَّ بَدَا لَهُمْ مِّنْ بَعْدِ مَا رَاَوُا الْاٰيٰتِ لَيَسْجُنُنَّهُ حَتّٰى حِيْنٍ ﴿٣٥﴾ $$

"Thereafter it occurred to them, even after they had
seen the signs, to imprison him for some time."

---

[133] Tirmidhī 1171.

Allāma Uthmānī ﷺ says, 'Though they had seen many proofs and signs of his innocence, yet they thought it suitable to send him to the jail for some time so that the general public should think that Yūsuf ﷺ was guilty, the woman being defamed for no reason. Thus, the woman accomplished the threat of imprisonment, which she made when attempting to seduce him. Those people might have thought that by sentencing Yūsuf ﷺ to imprisonment, the criticism of the woman can be brought under control and Yūsuf ﷺ would be kept away from her eyes for a while as well. The woman would have thought that under the hardships of the jail, Yūsuf ﷺ would also soften up and she might be able to achieve her goal.

Mājidī states, 'The judges then ordered that the torn garment should be brought to them, and upon examination of the same they pronounced Joseph 'not guilty'. But still, they sent him to prison, that the character of the wife of one as high in the state as Potipher might not suffer.' [134]

'The dungeon into which Joseph was thrown was not an ordinary detention, but a very special prison for dangerous criminals or political offenders... It was in the well-known fortress of Sarū on the borders of the Palestine frontier.' [135]

Verse 36

وَدَخَلَ مَعَهُ السِّجْنَ فَتَيَانِ ۗ قَالَ اَحَدُهُمَآ اِنِّیْۤ اَرٰىنِیْۤ اَعْصِرُ خَمْرًا ۚ وَقَالَ الْاٰخَرُ اِنِّیْۤ اَرٰىنِیْۤ اَحْمِلُ فَوْقَ رَاْسِیْ خُبْزًا تَاْكُلُ الطَّيْرُ مِنْهُ ؕ نَبِّئْنَا بِتَاْوِيْلِهٖ ۚ اِنَّا نَرٰىكَ مِنَ الْمُحْسِنِيْنَ ﴿۳٦﴾

"And there entered with him into the prison two youths. One of them said, "I see myself [in a dream] pressing wine." The other said, "I see myself [in a dream] carrying bread upon my head, and the birds are eating thereof. Tell us its interpretation, we see thee of the good-doers."

---

[134] Polano, Op Cit Pg.82.
[135] Yahudha, Accuracy of the Bible, Pg.5.

Meanwhile two young men were brought to the prison about the same time as Yūsuf ﷺ. They were both officers of the king whose name was Rayyan Ibn Al-Waleed. [136] One of them was a cook for the king, whose duty was to prepare the king's bread, the other was the cup-bearer [the butler or chief steward]. They were both accused of trying to poison the king.

Khāzin states, 'A group of parliamentary leaders plotted to kill the king. They promised great reward to the two youths if they succeeded in poisoning the king. Both of them agreed to the plot. Then the butler felt guilty and refused to accept the bribery, whereas the cook accepted the bribery and put poison in the king's food. When the king's dinner was brought before him, the butler exclaimed, 'Do not eat the food for it has been poisoned.' And the cook suddenly said, 'Do not drink the wine for it has been poisoned.' Now the king ordered the butler to drink the wine, which he did, and ordered the cook to eat from the food, which he refused. The food was given to an animal which died instantly. The king became angry and sent them both to prison.'

In the jail, Yūsuf ﷺ was known as a man of sympathy, honesty, truthfulness, good morals, enormous worship and an expert dream reader. The two prisoners became very close to Yūsuf ﷺ and expressed their love and admiration for him.

Suddī narrates, 'They said to Yūsuf ﷺ, 'By Allāh ﷻ we have great love for you.' Yūsuf ﷺ replied, 'May Allāh ﷻ gift you with barakah and prosperity. Whoever has loved me has brought grief to me through his love. My aunt loved me and I was harmed because of her, my father loved me and I was thrown in the well because of his love, the wife of Azīz loved me and the same happened.' [I have been thrown in prison]. They replied, 'By Allāh ﷻ, we have no control over anything in relation to your love.' [137]

One day they told their dreams to Yūsuf ﷺ and asked for an interpretation. Mājidī says, 'In Egypt [as in Babylon, and indeed in other ancient countries], much importance was attached to dreams.' The butler saw in his dream that he is pressing wine for the king.

Ikrimah states, 'He saw that he planted just one seed of grape which grew and a few bunches came out. Then he pressed them and presented it to the

[136] As mentioned in Tafsīr Uthmānī.
[137] Ibn Kathīr, Tafsīr 12:36.

king.' [138] The other said, 'I saw that I am carrying three baskets upon my head, which contain bread and some other types of food, and the wild birds are eating from it.'

"We see thee of the good-doers." Dhahhāk was questioned, 'What were his good deeds?' He replied, 'When a prisoner would fall ill, he would visit him and treat him. When someone was in hardship, he would help him. When someone was needy, he would gather some money for him, and on top of this, he would engage himself in worship, he would fast during the day and perform *tahajjud* throughout the whole night.' It is also said that the prison officer became so fond of him that he said, 'If it was in my hands, I would release you, but I will be easy with you and do good to you.' Mājidī states that the prison officer made Yūsuf ◉ the chief of all prisoners.

We can understand from here that the effect of good deeds become evident upon one's face, and that one should only rely on pious and wise people, and that dreams should not be narrated to a *fāsiq* [openly sinful] person.

Verse 37

قَالَ لَا يَأْتِيكُمَا طَعَامٌ تُرْزَقَانِهِ اِلَّا نَبَّأْتُكُمَا بِتَأْوِيْلِهِ قَبْلَ اَنْ يَّأْتِيَكُمَا ط

ذٰلِكُمَا مِمَّا عَلَّمَنِيْ رَبِّيْ ط اِنِّيْ تَرَكْتُ مِلَّةَ قَوْمٍ لَّا يُؤْمِنُوْنَ بِاللّٰهِ

وَهُمْ بِالْاٰخِرَةِ هُمْ كٰفِرُوْنَ ﴿٣٧﴾

He said: "Before any food comes to you for your sustenance, I will surely reveal to you the interpretation [of your dreams] before its arrival. That is part of the knowledge, which my Lord has taught me. Indeed I have abandoned the ways of people who do not believe in Allāh and who especially deny the hereafter."

Allāma Uthmānī ◉ comments: 'Hadhrat Yūsuf ◉ first consoled them that they would soon know the interpretation of their dreams. He would finish the interpretation before the daily meals came to them. But more important than the interpretation, was the more beneficial knowledge whereby he

---

[138] Ibn Kathīr, Tafsīr 12:36.

interpreted the dreams. He was not a professional astrologer or astronomer. On the contrary, the source of his knowledge was the Divine Revelation and Divine Inspiration, which Allāh ﷻ bestowed upon him because he always kept away from the creed and religion of the unbelievers and false Ideologists, and followed the religion of his pious and holy fathers [Hadhrat Yā'qūb, Hadhrat Is'hāq, and Hadhrat Ibrāhīm ﷺ], who were great Prophets of Allāh ﷻ and who established the religion of Divine oneness. The oneness of Allāh ﷻ had been the cornerstone of their beliefs. No one in the world should be made His partner, neither in self, nor in attributes, nor in Actions, nor in Lordship, nor in Divinity. Everyone should bow down before Him alone, should love Him alone, and surrender their living and dying to that Lord alone. However, Yūsuf ﷺ invited them to *īmān* and *tawhīd* at the appropriate time, in a very impressive way. It is the business of the Prophets that they do not leave any chance of inviting humanity to truth whenever they find some appropriate occasion. Hadhrat Yūsuf ﷺ thought that they had probably become soft, suffering the hardships of imprisonment; so he should use this opportunity for the benefit of *tablīgh* [spreading the message of Allāh]. First, he should tell them about religion and then tell them the interpretations of their dreams. In the beginning, he had told them that definitely they would know the interpretation, lest they should feel weary of the sermon.

Hadhrat Shāh Sāhib says: 'Allāh ﷻ put this *hikmah* in the imprisonment that his heart broke from the love of the unbelievers, then on his heart shone Allāh's ﷻ knowledge; he desired first to teach them of Religion, afterwards tell them the interpretation of the dreams, so for that he consoled, lest they should be perplexed, that up to the meal time he would also tell it [the interpretation of their dreams].' [139]

Maulānā Idrīs Kāndhlawī ﷺ writes: 'Hadhrat Yūsuf ﷺ knew the interpretations and that one of them is going to die very soon, so he turned towards giving good advice and a call for religious beliefs in order to prevent him from eternal hellfire. It seems that these Egyptian men were steeped in materialism, idolatry and polytheism. So he first mentioned a miracle to prove his Prophethood. Hadhrat Īsā ﷺ was also gifted with a similar miracle.

[139] Mūzih ul-Qur'ān.

"And I declare to you what you eat and what you store." So Yūsuf ﷺ promised to tell them beforehand whatever food is being prepared for them, and the amount of food which they will be served with, and the time it will arrive from their homes.

They may have asked that you are neither an astrologer nor an astronomer, then how could you foretell such a thing. He replied, *'This is part of the Knowledge which Allāh ﷻ has taught me.'* After proving his Prophethood, he moved towards *tawhīd*.

In saying, 'I have abandoned', he does not mean that I was first engaged in that decree and now I have abandoned it, because Prophets are free from all types of sins even before their Prophethood, and *kufr* [disbelief] is something which no prophet can even imagine. So Yūsuf ﷺ is mentioning his purity and proving how distant he is from *kufr*.

Verse 38

وَاتَّبَعْتُ مِلَّةَ اٰبَآءِىْ اِبْرٰهِيْمَ وَاِسْحٰقَ وَيَعْقُوْبَ ۄ مَا كَانَ لَنَآ اَنْ نُّشْرِكَ بِاللهِ مِنْ شَيْءٍ ۄ ذٰلِكَ مِنْ فَضْلِ اللهِ عَلَيْنَا وَعَلَى النَّاسِ وَلٰكِنَّ اَكْثَرَ النَّاسِ لَا يَشْكُرُوْنَ ﴿٣٨﴾

"And I follow the ways of my fathers – Ibrāhīm and Is'hāq and Yā'qūb – and never could we attribute any partners whatever to Allāh. That is of Allāh's grace upon us and upon mankind, yet most of mankind are not grateful."

Allāma Uthmānī ﷺ writes: Hadhrat Yūsuf ﷺ said to the prisoners, 'Our adherence to the pure *tawhīd* and the creed of Ibrāhīm ﷺ is a mercy not only to us but the whole human race, because it is the candle of Ibrāhīm ﷺ whereby the people can light the candles of their hearts. But Alas! They should have followed the path of Divine Unity with the feelings of gratitude. On the contrary, they are following the way of sin and association ungratefully.'

By mentioning the names of his fathers, Yūsuf ﷺ wants to confirm that he is from within the family of Prophets, so that people may listen to his advice attentively and have faith in his teachings of *tawhīd*. All Prophets have been equal in teaching *tawhīd* and refuting *shirk*. Allāh ﷻ says, '*And if they [the Prophets mentioned above, i.e from Ibrāhīm to Lūt] were to join partners [with Allāh], even their good deeds would be abolished.*' [140]

'*And indeed it had already been revealed to you, as it was to those before you, 'If you were to join gods with Allāh, your work will truly be fruitless and you will surely be amongst the losers'* [141]

Behold! Luqmān ؑ said to his son admonishing him, '*O my son, join not in worship with Allāh; for false worship is indeed the highest wrong-doing.*' [142]

"*Yet most of mankind are not grateful.*" '*Shukr*' means appreciating the favour of someone, being grateful. If we take a look at the context in which Yūsuf ؑ is saying these words, speaking about *shukr*, it should teach us all a lesson. He has just been imprisoned, wrongly, for upholding the command of Allāh ﷻ, and rather than blaming Allāh ﷻ for his situation, or lamenting over his fate, he would rather point out that Allāh ﷻ deserves more appreciation and gratitude than mankind give. This is similar to Yā'qūb ؑ's reaction in the face of adversity, telling his sons he will exercise *sabr*, and not any usual type of patience, but '*beautiful patience*'. How strong and firm was their *īmān* and trust in Allāh ﷻ, and how distant are we from such a condition! May Allāh ﷻ also grant us a high level of conviction and faith. *Amīn*

SHUKR

Shukr is among the greatest characteristics of a Muslim. We should always be grateful to Allāh ﷻ for his bounties and blessings which he continues to shower upon us, and also to any people who have done favours for us. Even if a driver gives way to us, it is common courtesy and also the demand of *Sharī'ah* that we acknowledge his favour, in order to thank him.

One *Hadīth* says: '*One who does not thank people, does not thank Allāh.*' [143]

---

[140] Qur'ān 65:88.
[141] Qur'ān 39:65.
[142] Qur'ān 31:13.
[143] Tirmīdhī 1878, Musnad Ahmad 10850.

Allāh ﷻ says in Sūrah Naml, 'Whosoever is thankful, then he himself will benefit from his gratitude, and whosoever is ungrateful, then my Rabb is free of need, Gracious.

Luqmān ﷺ said to his son, 'Be thankful to Allāh! Whosoever is thankful, then he himself will benefit from his gratitude, and whosoever is ungrateful then Allāh is not in need [of anyone's shukr], He is the Praised One.'

One Hadīth says, 'Four things, whosoever gets them has achieved the good of this world and the hereafter: 1. A tongue busy in remembrance [of Allāh], 2. A heart grateful [for the bounties of Allāh], 3. A body, which is patient when any test falls upon it [e.g. illness], and, 4. A wife who is not being unfaithful in one's wealth and nor in her body.' [144]

Verse 39

$$يَٰصَاحِبَيِ السِّجْنِ ءَأَرْبَابٌ مُّتَفَرِّقُوْنَ$$

$$خَيْرٌ اَمِ اللهُ الْوَاحِدُ الْقَهَّارُ ﴿٣٩﴾$$

[The speech of Yūsuf continues:] "Oh my two fellow prisoners! Are Sundry Lords better or Allāh the One, the Subduer?"

Notice here the deep touching form of address. He says, 'Are we not also companions in misfortune? And may I not speak to you on terms of perfect equality as one prisoner to another? Would you not then tell me who is better? Either various gods of different magnitude or one All-Powerful God, He who has absolute power over His creation and He whose authority is unchallengeable and whom the enemies cannot overpower. Knowing all this, decide for yourselves: before whom should we bow down in worship?' [145]

Zaid Ibn 'Amr Ibn Nufail, a Unitarian in the midst of the polytheists of Makkah, said before the advent of Islam, the religion of tawhīd:

$$أَرَبًّا وَاحِدًا أَمْ أَلْفُ رَبٍّ أَدِيْنُ إِذَا تَقَسَّمَتِ الْأُمُوْرُ؟$$

---

[144] Mishkāt.
[145] Tafsīr Uthmānī.

تَرَكْتُ اللَّاتَ وَ الْعُزَّى كَذَلِكَ يَفْعَلُ الرَّجُلُ الْبَصِيرُ

"Should I worship one Rabb or one thousand Rabb? Is it some kind of
religion wherein all matters are distributed [to different deities]? I have
abandoned all the Lāt and Uzzā (names of Idols), a wise person should do this."

Al-Qahaar means the subduer. It means the subduer of His creatures by His
Sovereign Authority and Power, and the Disposer of them as He pleaseth,
with and against their will.' [146]

Verse 40

مَا تَعْبُدُوْنَ مِنْ دُوْنِهِ اِلَّا اَسْمَاءً سَمَّيْتُمُوْهَا اَنْتُمْ وَاٰبَآؤُكُمْ مَّا اَنْزَلَ اللهُ بِهَا
مِنْ سُلْطٰنٍ ط اِنِ الْحُكْمُ اِلَّا لِلّٰهِ ط اَمَرَ اَلَّا تَعْبُدُوْا اِلَّا اِيَّاهُ ط ذٰلِكَ الدِّيْنُ
الْقَيِّمُ وَلٰكِنَّ اَكْثَرَ النَّاسِ لَا يَعْلَمُوْنَ ﴿٤٠﴾

"You do not worship besides Him, but only names which you have forged, you
and your forefathers. Allāh has not sent down for them any authority. The
command is for none but Allāh. He has commanded that ye worship none but
Him; that is the right religion but most of the mankind knows not."

In other words, Yūsuf ﷺ says, 'If you name other gods, they are nothing but
your inventions – names which you and your fathers put forward without
any reality behind them. It is sheer ignorance to bow down before them in
adoration. Who gave you authority to do such a thing? The only authority is
Allāh ﷻ. He is the Sovereign, the only Lawgiver. He has been sending down
his order through the Messengers that none except Him should be
worshipped and no one must be associated with Him in worship. Allāh ﷻ says
in Sūrah Zukhruf, 'And question though [O Muhammad] Our Messengers whom We
sent before thee: 'Did We ever appoint deities other than the Most Gracious [Allāh]
who could be worshipped?" [147]

---

[146] Majidi 2:372.
[147] Qur'ān 43:45.

Mājidī says, 'Science has now established that monotheism, not polytheism was the original religion of mankind.' [148]

Then Yūsuf ﷺ says that this is the right religion and the straight path in which there are no complications, it is not a pathway that zigzags. By walking on it, one can easily reach Allāh ﷻ without any risk or obstacles. Many people, due to foolishness or prejudice do not understand such a clear fact.

Maulana Daryābādī ﷺ writes: 'He alone is all inclusive of Sovereignty. In the theocracy of Islam, God is the only Sovereign, the only law-giver. And this has a direct bearing on the political theory of the Islamic State.' [149]

During one of my travels, one idol worshipper was sitting beside me on the plane. He started a conversation and then started explaining polytheism by saying that we are human beings. We need to see something to worship. The idols are a manifestation of god. We have an image in front of us to worship. I explained monotheism to him that God is only One. He is the Sovereign. If he had allowed us to make such images, we would do so. But he has prohibited us, so we can't make them according to our understanding. When we were getting off the plane, a child was clinging onto a teddy bear. I thought to myself that it is a childish act to have an image for comfort. Men with wisdom don't need images.

Verse 41

يٰصَاحِبَيِ السِّجْنِ اَمَّآ اَحَدُكُمَا فَيَسْقِىْ رَبَّهٗ خَمْرًا ۚ وَاَمَّا الْاٰخَرُ فَيُصْلَبُ فَتَاْكُلُ الطَّيْرُ مِنْ رَّاْسِهٖ ۚ قُضِيَ الْاَمْرُ الَّذِىْ فِيْهِ تَسْتَفْتِيٰنِ ﴿٤١﴾

'Oh my two fellow prisoners! As for one of you, he will pour out wine for his master and as for the other, he will be crucified and the birds will eat off his head. (Thus) is decreed the affair of which you two enquired.

Allāma Uthmānī ﷺ writes: 'After performing the duty of *tablīgh* [spreading the message of Allāh], Hadhrat Yūsuf ﷺ narrates the interpretation of the dreams that the one who pressed grapes in the dream, would bear wine to

---

[148] See Marston, The Bible comes alive, pp 25-250. Tafsir Majidi, Vol 2, pg. 373.
[149] Majidi 2:373.

the King in real life, and the one who saw the birds eating bread on his head would be crucified, and wild birds would eat off his head. This was decided once and for all, the decree has been made, in which there will be no changes. So did it happen – the cupbearer was acquitted of the charge of giving poison to the King, and the cook, after being proven guilty, was sentenced to death. [150]

It is stated in the Bible: 'After three days, there was an annual ceremony of the King. The royal butler was cleared of charges, whereas the royal baker was proven guilty and crucified.' [151]

It seems here that hanging on the cross was an ancient practice of the Pharaohs of Egypt. In the case of Mūsā ﷺ, the Pharaoh of the time also warned the magicians who decided to follow Mūsā ﷺ, that unless they turn back to Pharoah worship, he would hang them on a cross. Hanging on a cross has been one of the most severe punishments. The victim's hands and feet would be nailed in the wood, he would be left bleeding, left to die in hunger, thirst, and pain.

From here we can judge how feeble is the belief that Īsā ﷺ, a great Prophet of Allāh ﷻ, was crucified by members of the Jewish community. They claim that, 'It is we who hanged the accursed Jesus on the cross.' In the Torāh, it is stated that whosoever is hanged on the cross is accursed.

It is amazing that the Christians also accept this theory of the crucifixion and believe that he was crucified due to their sins. First, they take him to a high grade as the son of God, and then bring him down to a state where he had to be crucified for the sins of the sinners. Someone commits the sins and the punishment is inflicted on someone else.

The Qur'ān strictly denies this theory. It says in Sūrah Nisā, [The Jews incurred the Divine displeasure] *'Because they boasted that it is we who killed Masīh, Īsā son of Mary, the Messenger of Allāh ﷺ. But they did not kill him nor crucify him. Only the likeness of that was shown to them. And those who differ therein are full of doubts with no [certain] knowledge. But only conjecture to follow. For surely they did not kill him. Nay, Allāh raised him up unto Himself. And Allāh is Exalted in*

---

[150] Uthmānī 1067:2.
[151] 'Antiquities of the Jews II 5:3' – Tafsīr Mājidī 373:2.

112

Power, the Wise.' [152] So Jesus was not crucified, nor was he accursed. His look alike was crucified, and he was raised high above the heavens.

In the verse, upon which we are commenting, Allāh ﷻ says: *'Decided is the affair of which you two enquired.'* There are two opinions of the *Mufassirūn* regarding this. One is that that two prisoners did see such a dream. The other is that they had never seen any such dreams. They just fabricated one to test the ability of Yūsuf ﷺ.

Abdullāh Ibn Mas'ūd ﷺ says, 'When Yūsuf ﷺ gave the interpretation, they said, 'We have not seen any dream.' Yūsuf ﷺ replied in the above-mentioned words', meaning 'whatever I have said was through revelation, and it will surely come to pass.'

A similar incident is narrated regarding Hadhrat Umar Fārūq ﷺ. Rabī'ah Ibn Umayyah Ibn Khalaf once said to Umar ﷺ, 'I dreamt that I am going through a beautiful garden and I suddenly entered into a desert, I woke up while I was in the desert.' Umar ﷺ replied, 'You will embrace Islām and then reject it to become an apostate.' Rabī'ah replied, 'I never dreamt anything.' Umar ﷺ then said, 'Decided is the affair which you enquired.' And this is exactly what happened. Rabī'ah accepted Islām, but after some time when he saw that Islām prohibits wine, he abandoned it to become a Christian and died in this state. May Allāh ﷻ safeguard our *īmān,* and keep us steadfast to the crystal clear and the straight path. Āmīn.

With regards to the dream, the Prophet ﷺ says, *'The dream is like something hanged to the claws of a flying bird, so long as it is not interpreted. When it is interpreted, it falls to whatever interpretation is given.'* He also said, *'Do not relate a dream except to a close companion or a wise person.'* [153] The reason being that they will give a fair interpretation.

We also learn from this incident that we should not test the godly people, because if something slips out of their tongues, Allāh ﷻ will surely fulfil their sayings. In one *Hadīth,* we read, *'Some servants of Allāh are such that if they swore by Allāh, Allāh would surely fulfil their oath.'* This is for those who have attached themselves to their Lord, through obedience to Him, constant remembrance and never engaging in His displeasure. If a person is not of such a status and

---

[152] Qur'ān 4:157.
[153] Tirmidhī: 2447, 2448; Abū Dāwūd: 5020; Ibn Mājah: 3914.

he swears by Allāh 🕮, then for him is the saying of the Prophet 🕮, 'And whosoever swears by Allāh, Allāh will surely prove him to be a liar.' From this second category are the imposters, false claiimants of Prophethood.

Verse 42

وَقَالَ لِلَّذِيْ ظَنَّ أَنَّهُ نَاجٍ مِّنْهُمَا اذْكُرْنِيْ عِنْدَ رَبِّكَ ۚ فَأَنْسَٰهُ الشَّيْطَٰنُ ذِكْرَ رَبِّهِ فَلَبِثَ فِي السِّجْنِ بِضْعَ سِنِيْنَ ﴿٤٢﴾

And he said to one of them, whom he imagined would be saved, 'Mention me before your master.' But Shaytān caused him to forget to mention him to his Lord. And he stayed in prison for several years.

'When thou art in authority, do not overlook us in this prison, wherein thou wilt leave us, when thou art gone to the place we have foretold; for we are in prison, not for any crime, but for the sake of virtue and sobriety and we were condemned to suffer the penalty of malefactors.' [111]

When the cup-bearer's dream came true and he was being released, we can imagine him taking affectionate leave from Yūsuf 🕮, and even asking him if he could do him any earthly favours, but the divine grace of Allāh was enough for Yūsuf 🕮. However he had great work to do, which could not be carried out from the confines of prison, work for the future of Egypt, her King, and the world at large. If the cup-bearer could mention him to the king, not by way of recommendation, but because the King's own justice was being violated in keeping an innocent man in prison, then perhaps that might help to advance his cause. And so he said, 'Mention me before your master.'

But Shaytān made the released prisoner heedless through whispering in his heart so that he utterly forgot to mention Yūsuf 🕮 to the King, and with that Yūsuf 🕮 had to stay in prison for several more years.

The word 'Bidh' in Arabic signifies a small indefinite number, between three and nine. It is said that Yūsuf 🕮 stayed in prison for seven years.

---

[111] 'Antiquities of the Jews II 5:2' – Tafsīr Mājidī 373:2.

"But Shaytān made him forget..." In the story of Mūsā ﷺ, when he was travelling to meet with Khidhr ﷺ, his disciple forgot to inform him of the miraculous manner in which the cooked fish came to life and made its way inside the sea. After they walked for a long distance and felt hungry, Mūsā ﷺ asked for food. Only then did his disciple recall the incident. He also used the same phrase, *'I did indeed forget [about] the fish, and none but Shaytān made me forget to tell you about it.'* Shaytān whispers into the heart of a human being causing him to forget his duties.

Many times, forgetfulness is due to the whisperings of Shaytaan. This is when trying to recall something, e.g. Dhikr of Allāh or to recite Durud Shareef.

Verse 43-45

وَقَالَ الْمَلِكُ اِنِّىْ اَرٰى سَبْعَ بَقَرٰتٍ سِمَانٍ يَّاْكُلُهُنَّ سَبْعٌ عِجَافٌ وَّسَبْعَ سُنْبُلٰتٍ خُضْرٍ وَّاُخَرَ يٰبِسٰتٍ ۚ يٰٓاَيُّهَا الْمَلَاُ اَفْتُوْنِىْ فِىْ رُؤْيَايَ اِنْ كُنْتُمْ لِلرُّؤْيَا تَعْبُرُوْنَ ﴿٤٣﴾ قَالُوْٓا اَضْغَاثُ اَحْلَامٍ ۚ وَمَا نَحْنُ بِتَاْوِيْلِ الْاَحْلَامِ بِعٰلِمِيْنَ ﴿٤٤﴾ وَقَالَ الَّذِىْ نَجَا مِنْهُمَا وَادَّكَرَ بَعْدَ اُمَّةٍ اَنَا اُنَبِّئُكُمْ بِتَاْوِيْلِهٖ فَاَرْسِلُوْنِ ﴿٤٥﴾

'The King [of Egypt] said: 'I do see [in a vision] seven fat kine, whom seven lean ones devour, and seven green ears of corn, and seven [others] withered. O ye chiefs! Expound to me my vision if it be that you can interpret visions. They said: 'A confused medley of dreams: and we are not skilled in the interpretation of such dreams. But the man who had been released, one of two [who had been in prison] and who now bethought him after [so long] a space of time, Said: 'I will tell you the truth of its interpretation: send me ye [therefore].'

In other words, the King saw in his dream that seven fat cows were coming out of a dry river, followed by seven thin ones, who upon appearance swallowed the seven fat ones.

He also saw seven fine full ears of corn after which seven dry ones appeared and enwrapped them. He held a council and related to them his dream and ordered an interpretation. But either no one knew the interpretation or some of them knew, but did not want to take the responsibility of the interpretation, and so they declined and said that the dream was meaningless.

It was then that the cupbearer remembered Yūsuf 🕊 and requested permission to go out and meet him. He wanted to take the whole credit for himself and this is why he did not call upon Yūsuf 🕊 to attend the meeting. He preferred to go himself to investigate and then inform the King.

He knew the nature of Yūsuf 🕊, and had no fear of being rejected or ridiculed and so he addressed Yūsuf 🕊.

Some commentators say that this jail was far from the King's city and some say it was inside the same city.

Allāma Ālūsī mentions in *Rūḥ al-Maʿānī* that today some people indicate towards a certain prison, eight miles from the River Nile, and say that this was the prison of Yūsuf 🕊. Allāh 🕊 knows best.

Verse 46

يُوسُفُ اَيُّهَا الصِّدِّيْقُ اَفْتِنَا فِيْ سَبْعِ بَقَرَاتٍ سِمَانٍ يَّأْكُلُهُنَّ سَبْعٌ عِجَافٌ وَّسَبْعِ سُنْبُلَاتٍ خُضْرٍ وَّاُخَرَ يٰبِسٰتٍ ۙ لَّعَلِّيْ اَرْجِعُ اِلَى النَّاسِ لَعَلَّهُمْ يَعْلَمُوْنَ ﴿٤٦﴾

"Yūsuf! O man of truth! [Or Saint!] Give an answer to us in regard to seven fat kine which seven lean ones are devouring and seven green corn-ears and seven others dry. Perhaps I may return to the people and that they may know."

The King's butler approached Yūsuf 🕊 in jail. Their conversation must have been much longer, but we are just given the relevant points. He knows that Yūsuf 🕊 knows the meaning of the dream and the truth is shining on his face [as with all the Prophets], so if he is told, he can then return to the council and inform them. It would be rude and disrespectful to mention to Yūsuf 🕊, a Prophet of Allāh 🕮, the bribe of the hope of his release. Notice how smoothly he avoids referring to his own lapse in having forgotten Yūsuf 🕮 for so long and how the magnanimous Yūsuf 🕮 has not a word of reproach, but gets straight on with the interpretation.

Note: In the above verse, the word *siddīq* is mentioned. In Arabic, two words are used, *sādiq* and *siddīq*. (صادق ، صدّيق)

A *sādiq* is a person who is overcome by his truthfulness in such manner that his speech, sayings, actions and intentions are all according to the commands of his Creator. The Qur'ān says: *'O you who believe! Fear Allāh and stay in the company of the Sādiqīn.'*

On the Day of Judgement, the *Sādiqīn* will be questioned about their *sidq* and it is only *sidq* that will be beneficial on that day.

Hadhrat Mālik bin Dinār used to say that, 'When a *sādiq* will be reckoned for his *sidq*, then what will happen to us liars and hypocrites? We say things, which we do not do. There is a huge difference between what we talk and what we do.' May Allāh 🕮 have mercy upon us, *Āmīn*.

Siddīq is of a higher grade; he is absorbed in seeking the pleasure of his Lord. He has no intention of his own; his Lord Almighty makes his intentions. This is the highest status after Prophethood. Allāh 🕮 says, *'Those who obey Allāh 🕮 and his Messenger, they will be with those whom Allāh 🕮 has favoured, from the Prophets and the Siddīqīn and the martyrs and the righteous [who do good]. Ah! How good is their company!'*

In the above verse, in connection to this, Yūsuf 🕮 has been addressed with the good name of *siddīq*. Among this Ummah, Abū Bakr 🕮 achieved this high status. The Qur'ān says: *'And he who brought the truth and he who confirmed [supported] it such are the true men who do right.'* [112]

The indication in *'Who confirmed it'* is towards Abū Bakr 🕮. He was the first to believe in the Prophet 🕮. It was his preaching that converted the likes of Uthmān, Talhā, 'Abd ur-Rahmān Ibn Auf and Abū Ubaydah Ibn Jarrāh 🕮.

Regarding the event of *Mi'rāj*, Abū Bakr 🕮 was the one who confirmed it without any hesitation. Throughout his life, he was the most trusted person

---

[112] Qur'ān 39:33.

amongst the companions of the Holy Prophet ﷺ. Hadhrat Alī ؓ also reached this status as is mentioned in a narration in Sunan Ibn Mājah.

Siddīqs will be born until the Day of Judgement. Allāh ﷻ knows best who is of which status, but there is only one *Siddīq Akbar* [the greatest siddīq], Hadhrat Abū Bakr ؓ.

Verse 47-49

قَالَ تَزْرَعُوْنَ سَبْعَ سِنِيْنَ دَاَبًا ۚ فَمَا حَصَدْتُّمْ فَذَرُوْهُ فِيْ سُنْبُلِهٖ اِلَّا قَلِيْلًا

مِّمَّا تَاْكُلُوْنَ ﴿٤٧﴾ ثُمَّ يَاْتِيْ مِنْۢ بَعْدِ ذٰلِكَ سَبْعٌ شِدَادٌ يَّاْكُلْنَ مَا قَدَّمْتُمْ

لَهُنَّ اِلَّا قَلِيْلًا مِّمَّا تُحْصِنُوْنَ ﴿٤٨﴾ ثُمَّ يَاْتِيْ مِنْۢ بَعْدِ ذٰلِكَ عَامٌ فِيْهِ يُغَاثُ

النَّاسُ وَفِيْهِ يَعْصِرُوْنَ ﴿٤٩﴾

He [Yūsuf] said, 'You shall cultivate seven years persistently, so what you harvest leave it in the year, but a little, which you eat. Then hereafter there shall come upon you seven hard years that shall eat up what you have put for them, but a little which you will withhold for seed. Thereafter another year will come when people will have rain and when they will press [grapes and oil].'

Yūsuf ؑ interpreted the dream and also informed them of the solution. Such is the quality, simplicity, and the nature of Allāh's ﷻ Prophets ؑ. Yūsuf ؑ never mentioned a single word as to why the butler had forgotten him for so many years and how he boldly strode into the prison cell to enquire about the dream.

One may question here that how can a *kāfir's* dream come true, because true dreams have connections with the internal state of the dreamer. If he is purified with *imān* and good deeds, only then is he able to see true dreams. One *Hadīth* says:

وَأَصْدَقُكُمْ رُؤْيَا أَصْدَقُكُمْ حَدِيْثًا ۔

'Among you, the one who speaks the most truth is the one who sees the truest dreams.'[154]

A *kāfir* is a liar on God, therefore, how can he see a true dream?

Shaykh Abdul Azīz Dabbāgh ﷺ answers, 'A *kāfir* may see a true dream if the dream has any connection with other people. The Kings dream had connections with the general public of Egypt.' One of the students enquired, 'Then what of the dreams of the butler and the cup-bearer who were in the prison with Yūsuf ﷺ? Their dreams had no connection with other people and they were still true?' He replied, 'They were connected to Yūsuf ﷺ. Yūsuf's ﷺ greatness in the field of interpretation was made clear through them. In fact, it was the cause of the rise of Yūsuf ﷺ from the prison cell to the throne of Egypt.' [As you will see in the following verse]. Anyhow, sometimes a *kāfir* also sees a true dream in order that he may come closer to *haq* [the truth], and that he may accept it. Many converts saw the Prophet ﷺ in their dreams before they embraced Islām, or saw themselves reading the Qur'ān in their dreams etc.

Verse 50

$$وَقَالَ الْمَلِكُ ائْتُوْنِيْ بِهٖ ۚ فَلَمَّا جَآءَهُ الرَّسُوْلُ قَالَ ارْجِعْ اِلٰى رَبِّكَ فَاسْأَلْهُ مَا بَالُ النِّسْوَةِ الّٰتِيْ قَطَّعْنَ اَيْدِيَهُنَّ ۚ اِنَّ رَبِّيْ بِكَيْدِهِنَّ عَلِيْمٌ ﴿٥٠﴾$$

And the king said, "Bring him unto me." Then, when the messenger came to him, he [Yūsuf] said, "Return to thy Lord, and ask him, what about the women who cut their hands? Verily my Lord is the Knower of their guile."

The King was very impressed by the interpretation given by Yūsuf ﷺ. He ordered that Yūsuf ﷺ be brought before him so that he may appreciate his genius first-hand and pay him a homage which befitted his high position. But when the messenger arrived with the Royal message, Yūsuf ﷺ refused to come out of the prison without clearing his name. If he had hastened in

---

[154] Muslim: 2263a.

coming out, his dignity may have been blotted with doubts in the future and the work of *da'wah* [propagation] and *irshād* [guidance] which Allāh 🕮 has destined to take through him, would have been affected. Someone at some time could have had a chance to plot against him and create some sort of propaganda.

The *ulamā* say it is *wājib* to stay away from doubtful places and to refrain from doubtful actions. *Mirqāt al-Mafātīḥ* narrates a *Ḥadīth* which says, *'Whosoever believes in Allāh and the last day should never stand at a place of doubt.'* [155]

Imām Muslim has narrated that the Prophet 🕮 was in *I'tikāf* when one of his wives came to visit him. Upon her return, he accompanied her to the door of the *masjid*. A passer-by saw them. The Prophet 🕮 said, *'This is my wife.'* He exclaimed, 'O Prophet of Allāh, I could have a bad thought about someone else, but not you.' He replied, *'Shaytān runs through the body of a human being like blood. And I feared that he may instigate something in your heart.'* [113]

Abū'l-Qāsim Zamaksharī had lost one leg. He got written proof from the judges that his foot was not cut due to some crime, but it was the result of some frostbite, which caught him during a journey. Wherever he would travel, he would keep that paper with him and show it to the people so that they wouldn't think bad of him.

Note: In this verse, Yūsuf 🕮 did not mention Zuleikhā's name, but he referred to those women who cut their hands when they saw Yūsuf 🕮. This may be due to respect for the wife of the king or because he feared that Zuleikhā might still be in a whimsical state of mind, and that she might try something else. So, he mentioned those ladies, hoping that they might stick up for him.

---

[155] Mirqāt al-Mafātīḥ 2:795.
[113] Muslim 4040, Musnad Aḥmad 12132.

Verse 51

قَالَ مَا خَطْبُكُنَّ اِذْ رَاوَدْتُّنَّ يُوْسُفَ عَن نَّفْسِهٖ ط قُلْنَ حَاشَ لِلّٰهِ مَا عَلِمْنَا عَلَيْهِ مِنْ سُوْءٍ ط قَالَتِ امْرَاَتُ الْعَزِيْزِ الْاٰنَ حَصْحَصَ الْحَقُّ ز اَنَا رَاوَدْتُّهٗ عَنْ نَّفْسِهٖ وَاِنَّهٗ لَمِنَ الصّٰدِقِيْنَ ﴿٥١﴾

He said, "What was the matter with you when ye solicited Yūsuf against himself?" They replied, "How perfect is God! We know not of any evil against him." The wife of the Azīz said, "Now hath the truth come to light; I, even I, solicited him against himself, and verily he is of the truth tellers."

Note: A *Hadīth* in Muslim states, '*Had I stayed in prison the amount of time Yūsuf* 🕊 *stayed, I would have accepted the caller [and responded to the King's call straight away].*' [156]

Some *Mufassirūn* say that the Prophet 🕊 is clearly praising the patience of Yūsuf 🕊 and on the other hand he has indicated towards his '*Abdiyyah*' [servitude and submission to the will of Allāh].

"*What was your affair...*" The king assumed such a style of enquiring as if he knew the story beforehand, so that they would not dare to tell a lie. Moreover, the patience and perseverance of Yūsuf 🕊 must have impressed him as he did not want to come out of the jail without clearing his name, and he had mentioned their guile, by the words: 'Indeed my Lord is well aware of their snare.' It is also possible that the cupbearer may have narrated some events supporting the innocence of Yūsuf 🕊 to the king, who realised that it is his wife who was at fault.

'*They replied...*' Zuleikhā stood on one side and listened to the replies of the women who acknowledged the innocence and high principles of Yūsuf 🕊.

---

[156] Bukhārī 3192.

When they finished, she began, '*Now the truth has come to light...*' She did not mince her words. Rather she accepted her guilt freely and frankly. She adored Yūsuf ﷺ in every sense, in words and deed and she wanted the truth to be proclaimed in the open court, before all. So what had happened to her then? She had learnt a lot in sorrow, pain and humiliation. She had learnt the embarassment of carnal love. Yūsuf ﷺ, true of heart, calm in every turn of fortune, had taught her to question herself whether, in spite of all her sins since, she could yet be worthy of him. Perhaps when her husband was dead, and she was a widow. However, she must see whether she could understand love in the sense in which Yūsuf ﷺ would have her understand it, that pure surrender of the self, which is not tainted by earthly matters.

اَبَى الْحُبُّ اَنْ يَخْفَى وَكَمْ قَدْ كَتَمْتُهُ

فَاَصْبَحَ عِنْدِىْ قَدْ اَنَاخَ وَطَنَّبَا ـ

A poet says: 'Love refuses to hide, although I have tried to conceal it countless times. It just returns and settles itself in my courtyard.'

اِذِ اشْتَدَّ شَوْقِىْ هَامَ قَلْبِىْ بِذِكْرِهِ

فَاِنْ رُمْتُ قُرْباً مِنْ حَبِيبِىْ تَقَرَّباً ـ

'When my yearning intensifies, my heart revolves around his remembrance. Then when I want to get closer to my beloved, he himself draws closer to me.'

Ibn Aḥmar says: 'While I was making circumambulation [*tawāf*] of the Ka'bā, my eyes fell upon a lady in her hijab, she was reciting the couplets:

'Allāh will never accept any deed from the beloved, when her lover is furious and has been abandoned [by her]. She will not be rewarded for murdering her lover, whereas he will be rewarded for in this circumstance [this is because he stayed within the boundaries of the Sharī'ah and did not do anything silly upon his beloved's abandondment].' I said to her: 'Are you saying such couplets in such a place? In front of the Ka'bā?' She replied, 'Have you ever been in love?' I said, 'No, I don't know what love is?' she said: 'By Allāh! Love can never hide [it is evident from the face and the action of the one in love]. It may be concealed in the heart but it cannot be seen with the naked eye. It is like the fire in the stone, if you strike the stone, sparks will appear, but if you leave it, the fire will hide.' [157]

Ibn al-Qayyim narrates from Rajā Ibn Amr Al-Nakha'ī, who says: 'There was a young man in Kūfā, who was very handsome, but at the same time was engaged in immense worship. He had gone pale due to his efforts. He came to live in the tribe of Nakh'a. His eyes fell upon a girl from the tribe. She also loved him and became mad about him. The young man sent a proposal, but her father refused saying she was already engaged to her cousin. The girl's love increased and she sent a message to him saying that either you come to me or I shall make a plan to come to you. He replied saying, 'None of the options are possible, because the Qur'ān says: 'Say: If I were to disobey my Lord, then I fear the punishment of the great day.' [158] She said to herself: 'Inspite of his love he has so much fear of Allāh! By Allāh, no one but he is going to have me.' Thereafter, she left all her luxuries and she also engaged herself in worship. Inspite of her immense love, she did not commit any act which would be against Sharī'ah. Eventually, she died. The youth would then go to her grave and weep. One day he was crying near her grave, when he saw her in a dream. He questioned her, 'How are you?' She replied, 'O my desired one! How nice is your love. A true love which dragged me towards virtues and good deeds.' He asked her, 'What have you received in return for this love?' She replied, 'I was taken to such luxuries which are never going to fade, in the everlasting garden which will never perish.' He said to her, 'Remember me over there, because I never forget you.' She replied, 'By Allāh! I also never forget you. I even requested my master and your master to let us stay together [in these luxuries] so help me by working hard [i.e. help my plea by making a lot of sacrifice in worship]. He asked, 'When will I be seeing you?' She replied, 'You will be joining us very soon.' After this dream, the youth did not live more than seven days. [159]

---

[157] Rawdhat ul-Muhibbīn pg. 460.
[158] Qur'ān 39:13.
[159] Rawdhat ul-Muhibbīn Pg.230.

Verse 52

$$ذٰلِكَ لِيَعْلَمَ اَنِّىْ لَمْ اَخُنْهُ بِالْغَيْبِ وَاَنَّ اللهَ لَا يَهْدِىْ كَيْدَ الْخَآئِنِيْنَ ﴿٥٢﴾$$

"This [I say], in order that he [the Azīz] may know that I have never betrayed
him in his absence and that Allāh does not guide the guile of the treacherous."

The majority of the *Mufassirūn* relate the following conversation of Yūsuf ﷺ.
Yūsuf ﷺ said that, I requested for this investigation and research so that a
Prophet's innocence and integrity may come to light, and so that the people
may know the plots of the treacherous do not succeed. The guile of the
women failed and the truth prevailed.

Verse 53

$$وَمَآ اُبَرِّئُ نَفْسِىْ ۚ اِنَّ النَّفْسَ لَاَمَّارَةٌۢ بِالسُّوْءِ اِلَّا$$

$$مَا رَحِمَ رَبِّىْ ؕ اِنَّ رَبِّىْ غَفُوْرٌ رَّحِيْمٌ ﴿٥٣﴾$$

"Yet I do not say myself holy [pure]. No doubt, self [nafs] teaches evil, unless
if my Lord shows His mercy. No doubt my Lord is All-Forgiving, All-Kind."

This is the saying of Yūsuf ﷺ. He says that I don't make my *nafs* [self] appear
to be pure of sins. It is nothing but the mercy of my Lord that He saved me
from evil.

The *nafs* constantly orders one to practice evil. It is the mercy of Allāh ﷻ
which safeguards a person. We have read earlier in this sūrah, 'It is we who
diverted the evil away from Yūsuf ﷺ. Indeed, he [Yūsuf ﷺ] is from Our sincere
bondsmen.'

Allāh ﷻ says in another verse, 'Do not hold yourself purified [Do not consider
yourself to be pure and innocent].' [160]

So, Yūsuf ﷺ is displaying his humility and his submission to the will of God
by saying it is only the Mercy of Allāh ﷻ that safeguarded me.

Mufassirūn comment here on the three statuses of the *nafs*:

---

[160] Qur'ān 53:32.

1. Al-Nafs al-Ammārah,
2. Al-Nafs al-Lawwāmah, and
3. Al-Nafs al-Mutma'innah.

Generally, when the *nafs* of a human being instigates evil thoughts in his mind and lures him towards sin, this is called *Ammārah*. If the Muslim seeks refuge in Allāh ﷻ and supplicates for His divine help by which he can control the *nafs* and save himself from the sin, then his *nafs* begins to reprimand him, this is called *Lawwāmah*.

When a nafs easily obeys the commands of Allāh ﷻ and progresses in attaining nearness to Allāh ﷻ, then it gains peace and tranquillity. The *nafs* does not have any difficulty in fulfilling the commands of Allāh ﷻ and this is called *al-Nafs al-Mutma'innah*. This is the status of the prophets, the *awliyā* [friends] of Allāh, the *kāmilīn* [those who seek perfection in *dīn*], and those who purified their souls through the guidance of a Shaykh.

The first type is mentioned here in Sūrah Yūsuf, the second in Sūrah Qiyāmah, and the third in Sūrah Fajr.

My friend Maulānā Mahmood Chāndia, who is also one of my dearest students, once delivered a speech in Zakarīyā Mosque, Bolton. He explained therein the condition of the *nafs* in a very beautiful manner. I would like to put forward an extract of that speech:

'Shaykh Alī Muttaqī of India, a person of great merit and a very big scholar of Islām, wrote a very voluminous book on *Hadīth*. A compilation of *Hadith* that he organised according to the subjects of jurisprudence [Islāmic law]. Consequently, it became very easy for students to use this work. It is known as '*Kanz ul-Ummāl*'. He has also written over a hundred books. He lived in the sixteenth century between 1485 and 1567. One of his works is the '*Jawami'ul-Kalim Fi'l-Mawā'iz Wa'l-Hikam*'. It is a collection of 3000 wise sayings. In one chapter, he puts forward an analysis [his view], as he was an expert in this field of animal nature and human nature within mankind, which I will disclose very briefly.

He states that the human being is attacked by Shaytān. He himself has a team working with him in the heart, where the faith is preserved and he has four attackers altogether [And I don't mean attackers like Shearer, Salas, or Ronaldo]. These attackers are very dangerous. In the front, mankind is always confronted by what he refers to as 'The Dunya'. This could be translated as materialism, the love of the world, and the need for more. In front of man, especially the Mu'min, Shaytān puts the world. He glorifies the world in front of him, he convinces the person that this world should be aspired to: 'I must have the world, I have must have its pleasures'. This is the message, the continuous message.

On the right hand side, on the right wing, he has what is known as the 'Nafs'. The Sūfīs categorise the stages of the 'nafs', the inner soul, the outer soul. The nafs also has a team working under him. This is the soul and it is the job of this soul, this nafs, to attack the heart with all kinds of things, being proud, haughty, miserly, not eating halāl, not wanting good for another person, etc.'

On the left wing, Shaykh Alī Muttaqī describes in his analysis that there is what we call Hawā, 'I want this, I want that', similar to when children approach you and demand something. This creates in the human being a desire: 'I want'.

And behind, substituting the back four is 'Shaytān' himself. He is orchestrating, choreographing all of the moves. He is the one saying 'yes, do this, do that'. Therefore, from all four sides the believer is attacked.

Shaykh Alī Muttaqī ﷺ says that it is very necessary for this believer to have in opposition to these four attackers, four of his own players; four features of himself, four of his own characteristics.

For example, if the material world is put in front of you, it is necessary that we have the quality of zuhd (abstinence from the dunyā) within ourselves. No matter how much the dunyā will come in front of you, zuhd will combat it for as long as it has been developed.

On the right wing, I said there was nafs. For that Shaykh Alī Muttaqī proves that one MUST acquire knowledge to fight the nafs. In order to fight against the enemy, you must know the ploys of the enemy.

On the left wing, we have hawā. It is very necessary for the human being, especially the believer, to create and develop within himself an intellect, an intelligence, a capacity to think: my desires are afflicting me and swaying my aim, leading me astray from what I should be doing.

At the back, Shaytān himself. Shaykh Alī Muttaqī says that Shaytān should be fought against by zikr-ullāh [The remembrance of Allāh].

These four main enemies are constantly attacking man in order for him to be deprived of faith and eventually enter the eternal hellfire. It is necessary that we have these four characteristics. And for these four characteristics to be developed, it is very necessary for each and every individual to be in one way or another associated with a Shaykh. It is he who will guide that person through the maze of the world. And in today's world, as business people will tell you, it is referred to as a 'Dog-eat-Dog' world. This maze that we live in, is known as 'The Modern World'.

May Allāh ﷻ gift us with a Shaykh who is able to guide us through this maze. It is our personal duty to find such a Shaykh. Alḥamdulillāh, we are gifted with one, [i.e. Hadhrat Maulānā Yūsuf Motālā Sāhib Dāmat Barakātuhum].

Verse 54

وَقَالَ الْمَلِكُ ائْتُوْنِيْ بِهِ اَسْتَخْلِصْهُ لِنَفْسِيْ ج

فَلَمَّا كَلَّمَهُ قَالَ اِنَّكَ الْيَوْمَ لَدَيْنَا مَكِيْنٌ اَمِيْنٌ ﴿٥٤﴾

And the King said, "Bring him to me. I shall single him out for myself."
Then when he spoke to him, he said, "Be assured this day, Thou art of a high standing with us, Invested with all trust."

It seems that Yūsuf ﷺ had not yet appeared before the king. The king's order in the terms mentioned in verse fifty led to a message from Yūsuf ﷺ and the subsequent public proceedings with the ladies. Now that Yūsuf's ﷺ innocence, wisdom, truthfulness and trustworthiness had been proved and confirmed by the splendid tribute of the wife of Azīz, the king was very much impressed and decided to appoint him to serve as his own person as his trustworthy and confidential wazīr [Prime Minister].

According to ancient traditions, the king who made Yūsuf ﷺ his Prime Minister and committed into his hands the entire administration of Egypt, was 'Apepia'. He was one of the Hyksos King. [161]

---

[161] Tafsīr Mājidī 378:2.

"Then when he spoke to him..." He became even more impressed and addressed him with some of the most noble praises.

Some narrations say that Yūsuf ﷺ upon being released, washed himself, put on the special clothes provided to him, and entered the king's courtyard. He said, 'As-salāmu Alaykum'. The king was unaware of this type of greeting and enquired about its reality. Yūsuf ﷺ replied that this has been the preferred way of my forefathers; Ibrāhīm ﷺ, Is'hāq ﷺ, and Yā'qūb ﷺ. They were all men of Allāh and submitted themselves to the order of Allāh.

It has also been narrated that when Yūsuf ﷺ was leaving the prison, those prisoners whom he left behind were very grieved. The prison officer had acted with great kindness to all the prisoners due to Yūsuf ﷺ. In fact, he had made Yūsuf ﷺ their leader. Therefore, it was inevitable that some of the prisoners even started to cry upon the departure of Yūsuf ﷺ. Yūsuf ﷺ consoled them and promised to do for them whatever was in his capacity. [162]

Verse 55

قَالَ اجْعَلْنِيْ عَلٰى خَزَآئِنِ الْأَرْضِ ۚ اِنِّيْ حَفِيْظٌ عَلِيْمٌ ﴿٥٥﴾

Yusuf said, "Set me over the store house of the land [i.e. treasures of the country]. I am a good keeper, possessing good knowledge."

During the conversation, they probably discussed the dream of the king and its interpretation. The king said, 'How is it possible to tackle this huge famine? Indeed, it is a great task which requires wisdom, ability and honesty.' Yūsuf ﷺ put forward a detailed plan and the king began to wonder, who but Yūsuf ﷺ can put this into practice. He must have said something, which indicated his inclination towards Yūsuf ﷺ. And so Yūsuf ﷺ offered his services. He asked to be put in charge of the granaries and storehouses. He was prepared to take the burden of guarding the reserve stock in the time of plenty so that it may be utilised in the lean years to come.

The king gladly agreed to the suggestion. He embraced Islām upon Yūsuf's ﷺ hands and appointed him as the *Wazīr*, the Prime Minister and the superintendent of the royal granaries. The previous Azīz was relieved of his

---

[162] Ma'limul Irfān, Pg. 714.

duties and now Yūsuf 🕮 was the Azīz of Egypt. Some suggest that he was given a much higher rank and more powers than the previous Azīz. He was especially selected to carry out a great emergency policy to meet the very difficult times of austerity that were foretold. He was given plenary powers and the fullest confidence that a king could give to his most trusted *Wazīr*.

The books of *tafsīr* have mentioned that the previous Azīz died, and Yūsuf 🕮 was wedded to his wife Zuleikhā. He was thirty [30] years of age at the time. They had two sons Ifrayim and Meesha. Ifrayim had a son named '*Noon*' who was the father of '*Yusha*', the successor of Mūsā 🕮. He also had a daughter named '*Rahmat*' who became the wife of Ayyūb 🕮.

It is also said that after their marriage, Yūsuf 🕮 said to Zuleikhā, 'Is this not better than that to which you were calling me?' She felt deeply regretful and replied, 'O Prophet of Allāh! My husband was very weak [impotent], he had no desire for me, whereas I was young, and could not help myself in falling for your outstanding beauties.'

Some also narrate that when Yūsuf 🕮 was honoured by the king when he passed by Zuleikhā, she observed his shining splendour and said, 'All praise is due for Allāh who turned the slaves into kings because of their obedience to Him, and turned the kings into slaves because of their disobedience to Him.'

Note: The *Sūfīs* point to the fact that Yūsuf 🕮 had endured many hardships from the jealousy of his brothers to slavery and then imprisonment for a good few years. Yet, Allāh 🕮 saw his patience and rewarded him with the highest status. The same is the case of every *sālik*; every hardship is a foundation for bounties. [163]

Note: Allāma Uthmānī 🕮 writes, 'Hadhrat Yūsuf 🕮 himself made the request for the guardianship of the treasures. This was in order to benefit the creation of Allāh 🕮 generally and especially in the forthcoming famine period. It shows that the Prophets possessed perfect wisdom in worldly affairs too, and they did not think that to hold financial responsibilities for public welfare is against prophethood or holiness. Moreover, if a good

---

[163] Rumooz Pg. 50.

practicing Muslim thinks honestly that he is capable of carrying out a certain task and others will not be able to do it properly or will oppress innocent people, he can request for that in order to benefit his fellow Muslims brothers or human beings in general. If he has to describe some of his qualifications in order to gain that post he will not be considered proud and arrogant or a self-admirer [which is of course not allowed, as the Prophet ﷺ said, *'He will not enter paradise who has pride in his heart though it may be as little as the weight of a mustard seed].'* [164]

There is a *Hadīth* of Abdur Rahmān Ibn Samurah ؓ which says, *'Never ask for leadership, because if you are given leadership without request, [i.e. you are forced to accept it] you will be assisted, [by Allāh and His Angels] whereas if you are given leadership through insistence [and applications] you will be left to yourself.'* [165]

Also, another *Hadīth* of Abū Mūsā Ash'arī ؓ states, 'I came with two other friends to the company of the Prophet of Allāh ﷺ. The two requested to be appointed upon a certain post. The Prophet ﷺ disliked their attitude.' Abū Mūsā said, 'Forgive me, O Prophet of Allāh ﷺ! I had no knowledge of what they had in their minds.' He said, *'We do not appoint upon these posts who request for them. But you, O Abū Mūsā, you may go to accomplish so and so task.'*

The two *Hadīth* refer to people who are greedy and want to gain high posts in order to achieve worldly benefits, who are not sincere in their intentions. When a person lacks sincerity from the beginning, then what is there to expect from him in a later period?

Note: A notable point here is that Yūsuf ﷺ agreed to work for a *kāfir*. Although some *Mufassirūn* say that King Rayyān Ibn Walīd embraced Islām and thus Yūsuf ﷺ was working for a Muslim, nevertheless there is no concrete evidence for this. Whatever the case, it is permissible to work for a *kāfir*.

The Sahāba ؓ used to do labour work for the wealthy Jews. Hadhrat Alī ؓ and his family were once struck by hunger. He worked for a Jew and earned

---

[164] Ṣaḥīḥ Muslim #172.
[165] Bukhārī 6227, Muslim 3120.

some barley. He brought it home and Fātima, his wife, grinded one third of it and made some food. Suddenly, a poor beggar approached them and asked for something to eat. They gave it to him. Then she prepared another third portion and when that was ready, an orphan came to ask for something to eat.

They gave the food to him. Then she prepared the last portion. When it was ready, one *mushrik* [polytheist] prisoner suddenly appeared and asked for something to eat. They gave it to him and spent the night in hunger. Allāh ﷻ was so pleased with their gesture that He revealed a verse in the Qur'ān, '*And they feed, for the love of Allāh, the indigent, the orphan, and the captive.*' [166]

However, if that particular job involves something which is contrary to the laws of Allāh ﷻ, then it will not be permissible, e.g. bank managing, insurance brokering, serving wine, working in breweries, even though you may only be transporting alcohol from one place to another. If you have to hurt or kill innocent people for your job, then this is also not allowed. Before you apply for a job, one should consult a *Muftī*.

Note: The first half of Yūsuf's ﷺ story has come to a close at this point. The tests and hardships conclude here. The latter part, which involves bounties, favours and dignity will now commence.

Among the lessons learnt so far are as follows:

1. *Zinā* is a major sin. One must try to refrain from it until his last possible limits. If one indulges in it, he is viewed as having oppressed the whole community.

One *Hadīth* says, 'When *Zinā* spreads among a community, they will be struck with the punishment of Allāh.' [167] Moreover, in another *Hadīth*, the Messenger of Allāh ﷺ said, 'When vulgarity becomes prominent in a community to the extent that they practice their wrongdoing openly, such illnesses and plague will befall them that had not afflicted their

---

[166] Qur'ān 76:8.
[167] Mustadrak #2308.

predecessors.' [168] AIDS, and Cancer are just two examples which come to mind.

2. The person who turns towards the One and only, Almighty God, will surely be assisted and protected from evil by Him.

Verse 56

وَكَذَلِكَ مَكَّنَّا لِيُوْسُفَ فِي الْأَرْضِ ج يَتَبَوَّأُ مِنْهَا حَيْثُ يَشَآءُ ط

نُصِيْبُ بِرَحْمَتِنَا مَنْ نَّشَآءُ وَلَا نُضِيْعُ أَجْرَ الْمُحْسِنِيْنَ ﴿٥٦﴾

And thus did We establish Yūsuf in the Land so that he might settle therein wherever he pleased, We bestow of Our Mercy on whomsoever We will, and We waste not the reward of those who do good.

'*And thus We established Yūsuf...*' The boy, whom his jealous brothers got rid of by throwing him into the well, who was sold in the Egyptian Market for a meagre price, and who was thrown into prison for a good few years, now becomes the most trusted dignitary in a foreign land, chief minister in one of the greatest empires of the world.

It seems that the dark passages that came within the space of a few years were leading to the shining daylight, which lay ahead of him. Had he stayed in the company of his father and not been thrown in the well, would he have been picked up by the caravan? If the caravan had not sold him in the Egyptian Market, would he have ever reached the courtyard of the Azīz? And if the woman had not shown her desire and then her anger, would he have gone to prison? If he hadn't gone to prison, would his eminence and his high character ever have shone before the king? And when the king would not realise his status, how would he have chosen him for such a high post? So this is all a chain in the elevation of Yūsuf ﷺ. This world is a place of means. And Allāh ﷺ conducts His affairs through various means. This is why Allāh ﷺ gradually took Yūsuf ﷺ through these stages. It is said that he was barely thirty years old when he became ruler of Egypt.

---

[168] al-Bayhaqī #3401.

Khāzin mentions that when Yūsuf ﷺ gained full control over Egypt, he made preparations for the collection and safekeeping of the crops. He constructed special storage houses and gathered the food in them. He distributed wealth wisely. He upheld justice and the men and women of Egypt loved Yūsuf ﷺ.

The first seven years passed away with the bounties and favours of Allāh ﷻ at their highest level. Then came the years of test and tribulation. Yūsuf ﷺ was well prepared. The first person to be struck with hunger was the king. He tolerated it until one half of the day had passed then he shouted, 'Oh Yūsuf! The hunger is killing me.' Yūsuf ﷺ said, 'This is just the beginning of the drought.'

Then within the first year, the people of Misr consumed whatever they had saved for themselves, and then they started to purchase from Yūsuf ﷺ what he had saved for these years of famine. At first, they bought food with their wealth. When they had no dirham and no dīnār left, they bought with them their slaves, and then their properties. There came a certain time when they were even prepared to give their children for food.

Then a time came in Egypt when not a single person, male or female, free or slave, remained without being indebted to Yūsuf ﷺ. They were all almost slaves of Prophet Yūsuf ﷺ. The people of Egypt said, 'We have never seen a ruler as mighty and powerful as Yūsuf ﷺ.' Then Yūsuf ﷺ asked the king, 'How do you see towards that which Allāh has given me? What do you think I shall be doing with the people of Egypt?' The king replied, 'The decision is yours. We are your followers.' Yūsuf ﷺ said, 'I take Allāh as witness and also make you a witness that I have freed the whole of Egypt and that I return to them whatever assets they offered.'

It is also said that Yūsuf ﷺ never ate to his fill during the testing times. Someone asked him, 'Why do you stay hungry when the treasures of the Earth are in your command?' He replied, 'I fear that if I eat to my fill I might forget those who are hungry.' [169]

One similar story is narrated regarding Hadhrat Umar ibn Khattāb ﷺ. Ibn Abd il-Barr narrates from Zirr ibn Hubaish who says, 'I saw Umar, bold and reddish. I mentioned this to one of his sons who said, 'Our father was white

---

[169] Khāzin pg. 425.

in complexion, but during *Ām Al-Ramādah* [the year of the ash] [170], he ceased the consumption of meat and butter. He would only eat bread with olive oil. For this reason, the colour of his skin changed.' Allāhū Akbar! Our forefathers were so courteous of others, that they forsook their luxuries due to the poor.

Bishr Hāfī [a pious saint who resided in Baghdād] was once seen shivering in cold weather, even though he had warm clothes by his side. Upon enquiring, he replied, 'There are many poor people out there who are shivering. I do not have any clothes to comfort them, so the least I can do is emulate them so that I can realise how they are feeling.' One of the wisdoms behind fasting is that the person fasting may realise the pangs of hunger, which strike the poor day in, day out.

'*We bestow Our Mercy...*' Maybe the justice of Yūsuf ﷺ is meant here by the word mercy, or the Prophethood, or the kingdom, wealth and similar favours. [171]

'*We do not waste the reward...*' Ibn Abbās ؓ says: *Muhsinīn* here means '*Sābirīn* [the patient ones]'. The indication is towards the patience of Yūsuf ﷺ as well as towards his honesty and piety.

Verse 57

وَلَأَجْرُ الْاٰخِرَةِ خَيْرٌ لِّلَّذِينَ اٰمَنُوْا وَكَانُوْا يَتَّقُوْنَ ﴿٥٧﴾

And verily, the reward of the hereafter is better for those who believed and used to be obedient to Allāh [by abstaining from all kinds of sins and evil deeds, and by performing all kinds of righteous good deed].

'*And the reward of the hereafter...*' The reward of the hereafter is specially for the believers and those who fear Allāh ﷻ, even if they are kings of the Earth. Their portion of the hereafter will be better for them than the worldly

---

[170] In the eighteenth year after the *Hijra*, during the caliphate of Umar ibn al-Khattāb ؓ, the skies dried, crops died and animals perished. The famine was in and around the city of the Messenger ﷺ, and lasted for nine months. It was given the name *Ām al-Ramādah*, because the earth had turned black, resembling ashes.

[171] Khāzin, Nasafi.

favours which were bestowed upon them. In fact, a just ruler will be among those who are closest to Allāh ﷻ on the Day of Judgement, taking rest in the shade of the throne of Allāh ﷻ when there will be no alternative shade.

Imām's Bukhārī and Muslim narrate from Abū Hurairah ؓ that the poor among the *Muhājirīn* [migrants, from Makkah to Madīnah] complained to the Prophet ﷺ that, 'The wealthy have gone forth with the high ranks and eternal bliss. They pray like us, they fast like us, yet they donate with their remaining/excessive wealth whereas we cannot do this.' The Prophet ﷺsaid, '*Shall I not tell you something with which you can catch those who have overtaken you and you can go ahead of those who are behind you and no one can do better than what you can do?*' They replied in the affirmative. The Prophet ﷺ instructed them to recite *Subhān-Allāh, Alhamdulillāh* and *Allāhū Akbar* thirty-three times [33] after each *salāh*. They practiced this for some time then they came again only to say that the wealthy have come to know of our act and they also perform it. The Prophet ﷺ said, 'That is the grace of Allāh ﷻ, He bestows upon whom He wishes.' [172]

Verse 58

﴾ وَجَآءَ اِخْوَةُ يُوْسُفَ فَدَخَلُوْا عَلَيْهِ فَعَرَفَهُمْ وَهُمْ لَهُ مُنْكِرُوْنَ ٥٨ ﴿

And the brethren of Yūsuf came and entered his presence. He recognised them while they did not recognise him.

Mājidī narrates, 'And the sons of Israel came to buy corn among those that came: for the famine was also in the land of Canaan. And Joseph was the governor over the land, and it was he who sold to all the people of the land.' [173]

Allāma Uthmānī ؒ comments: Hadhrat Shāh Sahib says, 'When Hadhrat Yūsuf ؑ became the ruler of Egypt, he cultivated the earth for seven years in accordance with the dream of the King, and the nation's stock increased. Then during the seven years of the famine, he rationed the food at a value; it was the same for the countrymen and the foreigners, but more than a camel-

---

[172] Bukhārī 798, Muslim 936 - Al Maraghi 8:5.
[173] Genesis 'The First Book of Moses' 42:5,6 – Tafsīr Mājidī Pg. 379.

load was not given to the latter. Thus, people were delivered from the miseries of famine and the royal treasure multiplied. News had travelled that grain was cheaply available in Egypt spread far and wide, and so Yusuf's brothers came to purchase it.' [174]

When they came to Yūsuf ﷺ, they did not recognise him because he was a boy when they threw him in the well, but Yūsuf ﷺ recognised them at once because no spectacular change in their physique had taken place. Moreover, the list of the foreigners might have been prepared for the sake of administration and submitted to Yūsuf ﷺ daily, as is the general custom among all countries, and Yūsuf ﷺ according to the revelation in his early age might have been waiting for them. It is said that they had described their lineage. But a common man cannot dare to ask the name and lineage of the kings, so the brethren could not have asked Yūsuf ﷺ his name. In short, they could not know Yūsuf ﷺ. It was the wisdom [hikmah] of Allāh ﷻ, the Great, who had determined to fulfil the period of examination of Hadhrat Yā'qūb ﷺ. [175]

Verse 59

وَلَمَّا جَهَّزَهُمْ بِجَهَازِهِمْ قَالَ ائْتُوْنِيْ بِاَخٍ لَّكُمْ مِّنْ اَبِيكُمْ ۚ

اَلَا تَرَوْنَ اَنِّيْ اُوْفِى الْكَيْلَ وَاَنَا خَيْرُ الْمُنْزِلِيْنَ ﴿٥٩﴾

And when he had furnished them with provision [suitable] for them, he said, 'Bring unto me a brother ye have, of the same father as yourselves, [but a different mother]. Do you not see that I give out full measure and that I do provide the best hospitality.'

Allāma Uthmānī ﷺ says: 'Hadhrat Yūsuf ﷺ had hosted them with great hospitality and gave them one camel load each. When the brothers saw his generosity and conduct with them, they requested him to give one more camel for their half-brother [Binyāmīn]. He was unable to leave his elderly father who was aggrieved at the loss of his [Binyāmīn's] full brother [Yūsuf], who was incredibly beloved to him; he was [allegedly] killed in the jungle

---

[174] Mūzihul Qur'ān 1077:2.
[175] Tafsīr Uthmānī 1077:2.

long ago. The brothers said it would be very kind on the part of the king, Azīz-e-Misr, if he gave the share of Binyāmīn as well. Hadhrat Yūsuf ﷺ said it was against legislation to entrust the share of one who was absent. If they returned with him, they would be given his share. Yūsuf ﷺ further said that they had seen his hospitality and behaviour with them, so there was no question of Binyāmīn being harmed if they were to return.' [176]

Verse 60

فَاِنْ لَّمْ تَأْتُوْنِيْ بِهِ فَلَا كَيْلَ لَكُمْ عِنْدِيْ وَلَا تَقْرَبُوْنِ ﴿٦٠﴾

"But if you do not bring him to me, you shall have no measuring [of corn] from me nor shall you even come near me."

Hadhrat Yūsuf ﷺ continued that if they would not bring him, they would be deemed as liars who wanted to take one extra camel load by deception. The punishment then would be that their own shares would be forfeited, and they would be denied entry into Egypt.

Verse 61

قَالُوْا سَنُرَاوِدُ عَنْهُ اَبَاهُ وَاِنَّا لَفٰعِلُوْنَ ﴿٦١﴾

They said, "We shall try to win him from his father: indeed, we shall do it."

In other words, they said, 'Though it is very difficult to seperate him from his father, yet we shall try to win over our father. We hope that by some way or the other, we will succeed in convincing our father and bringing Binyāmīn to your presence.'

Verse 62

وَقَالَ لِفِتْيٰنِهِ اجْعَلُوْا بِضَاعَتَهُمْ فِيْ رِحَالِهِمْ لَعَلَّهُمْ
يَعْرِفُوْنَهَآ اِذَا انْقَلَبُوْٓا اِلٰٓى اَهْلِهِمْ لَعَلَّهُمْ يَرْجِعُوْنَ ﴿٦٢﴾

And he [Yūsuf] said to his servants, "Put their merchandise into their saddle bags, so that they will find it when they reach back to their household, perchance they may return."

Mājidī writes: 'Then Joseph commenced to fill their sacks with corn, and to restore every man's money into his sack and to give them permission for the way.' [177]

Imām Rāzī writes: There is wisdom behind returning their money in their sacks secretly:

1. Yūsuf ﷺ felt uneasy taking money from his parents and his brothers. It was against his hospitality as well as his honour.

2. He thought that it is possible they might not have any more money at home, and they might not return.

3. He wanted to do them a favour in a manner that they would not feel embarrassed. If he were to openly return the money, they might have refused to take it.

4. When they reached their destination and found their money in their sacks, their truthfulness would urge them to return and enquire about the return of the money. Was it a mistake? Then this money is not ours. It should be returned to the king. If it was given back deliberately, why?

5. When their father would see that the king of Egypt is so kind, he would feel at ease in sending Binyāmīn with them.

In short, Yūsuf ﷺ exceeded the limits in hospitality, good treatment, and kindness, as much as his brothers had exceeded the limits when they were jealous of him, ill treated him and tortured him. [178]

A question may arise in the mind of the reader of the Qur'ān, that Yūsuf ﷺ had gained a very high status and was living a luxurious life. He spent

---

[177] Genesis 'The First Book Of Moses' 42:25 – Tafsīr Mājidī.

[178] Ma'āriful Qur'ān [Kāndhlawī] 46:4.

seven years in such a state. Why is it that he never felt the need to inform his bereaved old father? He could even have told his brothers about himself. Instead, he opted to call upon his real brother Binyāmīn, which further aggravated the grief of his father.

It is important to keep in mind that whatever Yūsuf ﷺ did, was done by the order of Allāh ﷻ. It was Allāh's ﷻ will that Ya'qūb ﷺ should endure patience for some more time so that his rank may be raised among other Prophets, and he may be raised up to the ranks of Ibrāhīm and his sons ﷺ.

Verse 63

$$ فَلَمَّا رَجَعُوٓا اِلٰٓى اَبِيْهِمْ قَالُوْا يٰٓاَبَانَا مُنِعَ مِنَّا الْكَيْلُ $$

$$ فَاَرْسِلْ مَعَنَآ اَخَانَا نَكْتَلْ وَاِنَّا لَهٗ لَحٰفِظُوْنَ ﴿٦٣﴾ $$

So when they returned to their father they said, "Dear father! No more measure of grain shall we get [unless we take our brother] so send our brother [Binyāmīn] with us so that we may get our measure and we will indeed take care of him."

Khāzin writes, 'When they returned to their father, they praised the hospitality of the Egyptian ruler. They said that he was very kind and generous, even our family members would not be as kind to treat us in this manner. Ya'qūb ﷺ said to them, 'When you go back to him, give him my thanks, and say to him that our father sends salāms to you and prays for you, because of your favours to us.'

Now, since the most urgent matter for them was to take back their brother with them, they begged their father to let him go with them and made a firm promise to look after him, just like they had done with Yūsuf ﷺ.

Verse 64

$$ قَالَ هَلْ اٰمَنُكُمْ عَلَيْهِ اِلَّا كَمَآ اَمِنْتُكُمْ عَلٰٓى اَخِيْهِ مِنْ $$

$$ قَبْلُ ۭ فَاللّٰهُ خَيْرٌ حٰفِظًا ۤ وَهُوَ اَرْحَمُ الرّٰحِمِيْنَ ﴿٦٤﴾ $$

He [Yā'qūb] said, "Shall I trust you with him with any result other than that when I trusted you with his brother aforetime? But Allāh is the best to take care and He is the Most Merciful of those who show mercy!"

Yā'qūb 🙵 said, 'You said the same words when you took Yūsuf with you [we shall take every care of him]. So how should I believe in your promise? Since there is grave necessity, which cannot be ignored, I shall let him go with you. But I keep my faith in Allāh 🙵 to take care of him.'

Khāzin says, 'These words indicate to the fact that in the end, Yā'qūb 🙵 let Binyāmīn go with them. He knew that they ill-treated Yūsuf, but the reason for letting Binyāmīn go with them is that they had not shown jealousy and malice towards Binyāmīn, which they had shown towards Yūsuf 🙵. Also, time had passed, they had grown up and learnt their lessons, the famine was also heavy and they desperately needed the extra grain for Binyāmīn, so he permitted Binyāmīn to go with them.'

Note: These days some people who claim to be the followers of *Hadīth* say that it is not permitted to say '*Khudā Hāfiz*' [A phrase in Persian, meaning 'May The Lord protect you']. They say it is *Bid'ah*. If they had read the Qur'ān, they would have known that it is in the Qur'ān. The reader will surely understand what Yā'qūb 🙵 said here: 'But Allāh 🙵 is the best to take care of him.' When we say '*Khudā Hāfiz*', we pray to Allāh 🙵 to take care of the person who is leaving. When the Prophet 🙵 would say farewell to someone, he would say, 'I entrust Allāh 🙵 your deen, your faithfulness and your final deeds.'

When a layman cannot memorise this *duā*, as with many other *duā's*, he could say in short '*Khudā Hāfiz*'. However, one should not forget the *masnūn* [Prophetic] greeting which is '*Assalāmū Alaykum*'. One should try to say them both. [i.e *Salām* and '*Khudā Hāfiz*].

Verse 65

$$وَلَمَّا فَتَحُوْا مَتَاعَهُمْ وَجَدُوْا بِضَاعَتَهُمْ رُدَّتْ اِلَيْهِمْ ۚ قَالُوْا يَاۤ اَبَانَا مَا$$

$$نَبْغِيْ ؕ هٰذِهٖ بِضَاعَتُنَا رُدَّتْ اِلَيْنَا ۚ وَنَمِيْرُ اَهْلَنَا وَنَحْفَظُ اَخَانَا وَنَزْدَادُ$$

$$كَيْلَ بَعِيْرٍ ؕ ذٰلِكَ كَيْلٌ يَّسِيْرٌ ﴿٦٥﴾$$

Then when they opened their baggage, they found their goods returned to
them. They said, "O our father! What more can we desire? This is our goods
returned to us. So we shall get [more] supply [of food] for our family and we
shall [also] take care of our brother and add [at the same time] a full camel's
load [of grain to our provisions]. This is an easy measure."

The brothers narrated the generosity of the Egyptian King and requested
their father to send Binyāmīn with them. Thereafter, they opened their
baggage. And to their amazement, they found their money [stock-in-trade]
returned to them. This further supported their request to take Binyāmīn.
Thus, they said, 'What else do we desire? The king has returned our goods;
he himself wants us to return to him for more goods. So when we are making
a firm promise to take care of Binyāmīn, you should let him come with us.
There are two benefits in this:

1. We will get an extra load of grain.

2. The king will be pleased with us, and we are hoping to get some extra out
of him.'

The brothers mention three reasons why their father should choose to trust
them; firstly, because their intentions are not to fill their own stomachs, but
to feed their family, thus making this request a selfless one. If fulfilled, it
would benefit their father greatly. Secondly, they mention that they will
protect Binyāmīn to remove the fear in Yā'qūb's ﷺ heart; and thirdly, the
obvious fact that they will be able to bring back more provisions in this
difficult time. It was an opportunity not to be missed.

Verse 66

$$ قَالَ لَنْ أُرْسِلَهُ مَعَكُمْ حَتَّىٰ تُؤْتُوْنِ مَوْثِقًا مِّنَ اللهِ لَتَأْتُنَّنِيْ بِهِ اِلَّا اَنْ يُّحَاطَ بِكُمْ ۚ فَلَمَّا اٰتَوْهُ مَوْثِقَهُمْ قَالَ اللهُ عَلٰى مَا نَقُوْلُ وَكِيْلٌ ﴿٦٦﴾ $$

He [Yā'qūb] said, "I will by no means send him with you unless you give me a solemn pledge with Allāh that you will bring him back to me, unless it so happens that you yourselves are surrounded [and made powerless]." Then when they gave him their assurance, he said, "Allāh is the witness and guardian over what we say."

Allāma Uthmānī ﷺ writes, 'Hadhrat Yā'qūb ﷺ said to the brothers of Yūsuf ﷺ, that if unfortunately, a divine decree was to take place, wherein they were surrounded from all sides and without any escape - he would say nothing about such a misfortune [i.e. he would recgonise it to be from Allāh]. Indeed, it was necessary for them to look after Binyāmīn as much as realistically possible. After taking this solemn promise and pledge he said, 'Allāh ﷺ is the witness and guardian over what we say,' for greater emphasis and to stress caution. It meant that they had passed responsibility to Allāh regarding the pledge that they had undertaken and if someone betrayed the pledge or violated it, then Allāh ﷺ would punish him. It may also mean that though they were making the pledge according to their desired satisfaction, the main purpose behind the covenant could only be accomplished by the protection and security of Allāh ﷺ. If Allāh ﷺ does not will, then all measures and planning are doomed to failure.'

Hadhrat Shāh Sahib ﷺ said, 'The external measures [i.e. planning] were managed strongly and trust was put in Allāh ﷺ - this is a rule for everyone [i.e. utilise one's means before seeking trust in Allāh]'. [179]

Khāzin writes, 'It has been narrated from Kā'b Al-Ahbār ﷺ that when Yā'qūb ﷺ said, 'Allāh ﷺ is the best to protect them...' Allāh ﷺ said, 'By My Honour and My Majesty, I shall return both to you [Yūsuf and Binyāmīn] because you have put your faith in me, and you have handed your affairs to me.'

---

[179] Tafsīr Uthmānī 1080:2.

Verse 67

$$وَقَالَ يٰبَنِيَّ لَا تَدْخُلُوْا مِنْ بَابٍ وَّاحِدٍ وَّادْخُلُوْا مِنْ اَبْوَابٍ مُّتَفَرِّقَةٍ ط$$

$$وَمَآ اُغْنِيْ عَنْكُمْ مِّنَ اللهِ مِنْ شَيْءٍ ط اِنِ الْحُكْمُ اِلَّا لِلّٰهِ ط عَلَيْهِ تَوَكَّلْتُ ج$$

$$وَعَلَيْهِ فَلْيَتَوَكَّلِ الْمُتَوَكِّلُوْنَ ﴿٦٧﴾$$

And he said, "My Sons! Do not enter by one gate but enter by different gates,
and I cannot avail you against Allāh at all; Judgement is for none but Allāh. On
Him I rely, and on Him should the relying put their trust."

'Do not enter from one gate but go from different gates...' Due to the famine, Yā'qūb
﷽ was compelled to send Binyāmīn with his brothers, and so he did, placing
his trust in Allāh ﷻ. However, he instructed them to take special care when
entering the Egyptian city. Since his sons excelled others in beauty, he feared
that some evil gaze might fall upon them, and be a cause of grief to them.

The brothers of Yūsuf ﷽ had formerly entered the city like common
travellers without distinction, but the people must have raised their eyes
upon them when they saw the special treatment they received from Yūsuf
﷽. The second journey was characterised with new spirits and new visions,
because they were invited by Yūsuf ﷽ himself, together with Binyāmīn. So,
Hadhrat Yā'qūb ﷽ thought that the collective entering of eleven youthful
and handsome brothers, with glory and grandeur, would definitely attract
the attention of the Egyptians, especially after having observed the scene of
their exclusive treatment in the previous journey.

The influence of the evil eye is true - modern mesmerism is proof of the
influence of the eye - hence Hadhrat Yā'qūb ﷽ tried to save them from the
influence of the evil eye and its bad effects. In the whole universe, the
command of Allāh ﷻ prevails, and all mortal arrangements and efforts are
futile against divine command. Allāh ﷻ has not prohibited us to plan and use
different means for further success, or to bring about measures in order to
save us against impending disasters, so Yā'qūb ﷽ directed them to enter
through different gates. We are taught to put trust in Allāh ﷻ alone, whilst
also using the worldy means available to us, knowing that Allāh ﷻ is the one
who gives cause to good and bad.

The Prophet ﷺ has said, 'The influence of the evil eye is true.' [180]

Another *Hadīth* says, 'If there was something which could compete with the Decree [of Allāh ﷻ], it would surely be the evil eye.' [181]

In the Muwattā of Imām Mālik, we read that one Sahābī, Hadhrat Sahl Ibn Hūnaif ؓ had taken off his upper garment and was having a bath. Another person, Āmir Ibn Rabī'a ؓ, happened to pass by and his eyes fell upon the chest of Sahl and his beautiful soft skin. He remarked, 'What a handsome person! I have not even seen a beautiful woman who could be that handsome!' As soon as he had said this, Sahl fell to the ground [he suffered something similar to a fit]. Someone ran to the Prophet ﷺ and informed him. He enquired, 'Do you blame someone to be the cause of this?' They mentioned Āmir. The Prophet ﷺ called on him and admonished him, 'Why do you have to kill your brother? Why did you not say, '*Bārak-Allāh fika* [May Allāh bless you]?' Thereafter, he ordered Āmir to wash himself. The water that was saved was splashed upon Sahl. As soon as this was done, Sahl recovered as though nothing had happened. [182]

Today, we see many people complaining of the effects of Jinn and black magic. Very few of these cases are true. In fact, the majority of such cases are mainly due to underlying psychological issues.

I myself have experienced this. Once I went to a friend's house who said that he was checked by a *bāpū* [a person who treats the effects of jinn and black magic], and was told that someone had done black magic on him. He felt really ill and heavy, and was unable to work. He had a job in a council department. Fortunately for him, a Maulānā from Makkah was with me at the time, who was also a Khalīfah of Hadhrat Shaykh al-Hadīth Maulānā Muhammad Zakariyā ؒ. He was very experienced in this field. I requested the Maulānā to check the young man. He checked and said that there was nothing to worry about. My friend asked, 'Then why do I get such bad feelings.' The Maulānā said, 'It is the evil eye. You are a handsome young man with a nice job and a nice family. People envy you and look at you with the

---

[180] Bukhārī 5299, Muslim 4057.

[181] Muslim 4058.

[182] Muwatta Mālik 1472, Musnad Ahmed 15143, Ibn Mājah 3500.

evil eye, which is causing this.' He then prescribed some *wazīfa* [prayers] for safeguarding oneself from the evil gaze.

Many people have fun in lying and blaming jinn or black magic for their failure. Maulānā Adam Loonat Sahib of Leicester had to deal with many such cases. Once a family came to him and complained that a Jinn had possessed their daughter, and that she had started doing funny things. Maulānā checked and said that she has not been possessed and that she is fine. She is just acting. Upon their insistence for *tā'wīz* [amulet], the Maulānā gave them a pen and paper, and told them to scribble something on it. He then wrapped the paper and stood in the hallway while the girl was in the other room. He then said loudly, 'Give this *tā'wīz* in her hand and as soon as she holds it, she will be possessed by the jinn.' Her guardian then told her to hold the *tā'wīz*. When she did this, she suddenly fell on the floor and started screaming. Her guardian realised the truth and took her away.

The best way in casting away the effects of the evil gaze is what is mentioned in the *Hadīth*. We read in Mishkāt Shareef that the Prophet ﷺ would read the following prayers upon his grandsons, Hasan and Hussain, and he would say that Hadhrat Ibrāhīm ﷺ would read the same upon Ismā'īl and Is'hāq ﷺ.

$$\text{أُعِيْذُكُمَا بِكَلِمَاتِ الله التَّامَّاتِ مِنْ شَرِّ}$$

$$\text{كُلِّ شَيْطَانٍ وَهَامَّةٍ وَمِنْ كُلِّ عَيْنٍ لَامَّةٍ ـ}$$

'I give you both refuge in the words of Allāh which are most complete, from the evil of every Satan, and whatever treads on the earth, as well as from every eye that strikes its gaze upon you.' [183]

The affected person may also read the *Muawwazatain* [Sūrahs Falaq and Nās], Sūrah Ikhlaas, Sūrah Fātiha, Ayatul Kursī, each of them three times, and then blow on one's palms, and wipe them over the whole body. Do this after every fardh salāh for forty [40] days. Don't forget to also read Durūd Sharīf three times before and after. Inshā-Allāh Allāh will provide a cure.

---

[183] Bukhārī 3120, Tirmidhī 1986.

Verse 68

وَلَمَّا دَخَلُوا مِنْ حَيْثُ اَمَرَهُمْ اَبُوْهُمْ ۗ مَا كَانَ يُغْنِىْ عَنْهُمْ مِّنَ اللهِ مِنْ
شَيْءٍ اِلَّا حَاجَةً فِىْ نَفْسِ يَعْقُوْبَ قَضٰهَا ۗ وَاِنَّهٗ لَذُوْ عِلْمٍ لِّمَا عَلَّمْنٰهُ
وَلٰكِنَّ اَكْثَرَ النَّاسِ لَا يَعْلَمُوْنَ ﴿٦٨﴾

And when they entered in the manner their father had enjoined, it did not
profit them in the least against [the plan of] Allāh. It served only to satisfy
Yā'qūb's heartfelt desire. Verily, he was endued with knowledge for We had
taught him; but most people know not.

Allāma Uthmānī 🙿 comments that Yūsuf's 🙿 brothers entered the city
through different gates as their father had directed them, and thus they were
not affected by any evil stare, but the divine decree [i.e. of tribulation] came
from another side. [Binyāmīn was detained under the charge of theft, as we
will read in the next chapter]. What is destined cannot be avoided.

Those who have knowledge put faith in divine decree and also utilise
[worldly] means. Those without knowledge remain between the two; if they
adopt one, they leave the other. Either they deny destiny and totally rely on
[worldy] means, or they are lazy and rely on fate and forgo planning.
However, the 'Ārif [a person who recognises Allāh] maintains both the
qualities accordingly: taqdīr [divine decree] and the tadbīr [human planning].

Verse 69

وَلَمَّا دَخَلُوْا عَلٰى يُوْسُفَ اٰوٰى اِلَيْهِ اَخَاهُ قَالَ
اِنِّىْ اَنَا اَخُوْكَ فَلَا تَبْتَئِسْ بِمَا كَانُوْا يَعْمَلُوْنَ ﴿٦٩﴾

And when they entered in to Yūsuf's presence, He received his [full]
brother [Binyāmīn] to stay with him and said [to him], Indeed I am thy own
brother; so do not grieve over what they have been doing.

The brothers arrived in Egypt and Yūsuf ﷺ again received them with hospitality, as they had complied with his request in bringing Binyāmīn.

When Yūsuf ﷺ was given some privacy with Binyāmīn, he informed him quietly that I am your real brother Yūsuf. He must have enquired about the status of his parents, and then he advised Binyāmīn to forgive and forget what their [half] brothers had done to them. Yūsuf ﷺ might have deduced the fact that the brothers had ill-treated Binyāmīn on their way to Egypt, for it was the first time they were able to separate him from their father. So following the custom of the beloved of Allāh ﷻ, Yūsuf ﷺ taught Binyāmīn to forgive his brothers.

Imām Shāf'ī ﷺ says, 'I have forgiven anyone who has caused me any harm whatsoever, be it with regards to health, wealth or gossip etc. How can I distress Muhammad ﷺ on the Day of Judgement regarding his *ummah*?'

Verses 70-75

فَلَمَّا جَهَّزَهُمْ بِجَهَازِهِمْ جَعَلَ السِّقَايَةَ فِيْ رَحْلِ اَخِيْهِ ثُمَّ اَذَّنَ مُؤَذِّنٌ اَيَّتُهَا الْعِيْرُ اِنَّكُمْ لَسٰرِقُوْنَ ﴿٧٠﴾ قَالُوْا وَاَقْبَلُوْا عَلَيْهِمْ مَّاذَا تَفْقِدُوْنَ ﴿٧١﴾ قَالُوْا نَفْقِدُ صُوَاعَ الْمَلِكِ وَلِمَنْ جَاءَ بِهٖ حِمْلُ بَعِيْرٍ وَّاَنَا بِهٖ زَعِيْمٌ ﴿٧٢﴾ قَالُوْا تَاللّٰهِ لَقَدْ عَلِمْتُمْ مَّا جِئْنَا لِنُفْسِدَ فِي الْاَرْضِ وَمَا كُنَّا سٰرِقِيْنَ ﴿٧٣﴾ قَالُوْا فَمَا جَزَآؤُهٗ اِنْ كُنْتُمْ كٰذِبِيْنَ ﴿٧٤﴾ قَالُوْا جَزَآؤُهٗ مَنْ وُّجِدَ فِيْ رَحْلِهٖ فَهُوَ جَزَآؤُهٗ ۚ كَذٰلِكَ نَجْزِى الظّٰلِمِيْنَ ﴿٧٥﴾

And when he provided them with their furnishing, he put the drinking cup in his brother's saddle bag. And then, a crier cried, 'O Camel Riders! Ye are surely thieves. They said as they turned unto them, 'What is it that ye have lost?' They said, 'We have lost the king's cup. And he who bringeth it shall have a camel load, and I am answerable for it.' They said, 'By Allāh! Ye know very well that we have not come to cause any uproar in this land, nor are we thieves.' They said, 'Then what shall be the penalty for this, if ye are proved liars?' They said,

'It's penalty is that he in whose bag [the cup] is found shall himself be the recompense thereof. Thus we punish wrong-doers.'

Hadhrat Maulānā Idrīs Kāndhlawī ﷺ writes, 'When Yūsuf ﷺ got some privacy with his brother, he asked, 'What is your name?' He replied, 'Binyāmīn.' Yūsuf ﷺ asked, 'And your mother's name?' 'Rahīl' was the reply. Yūsuf ﷺ asked, 'Do you have a real brother?' Binyāmīn said, 'I had one, but he died.' Yūsuf ﷺ asked, 'If I became your brother as a replacement to your lost brother, will you be happy?' Binyāmīn said, 'Where would I find a brother better than you, but you were not born to Yā'qūb and Rahīl.' Yūsuf ﷺ said, 'Do not be grieved, I am your real brother Yūsuf.' The joy of Binyāmīn upon hearing this cannot be estimated. Then, Yūsuf ﷺ said, 'I want to keep you in my company and I may have to execute a plan in which your good name may be [temporarily] tarnished.' Binyāmīn exclaimed, 'This doesn't bother me, as long as I get to spend some time in your company.' [184]

Yūsuf ﷺ ordered that his valuable silver cup should be hidden in the saddle bag of Binyāmīn or, as Qurtubī states, Yūsuf ﷺ himself carried out this act. When the caravan left the city, they had not gone far, when all of a sudden, someone called out that a theft had been committed against Yūsuf ﷺ.

The caravan had been kept in the special guesthouse of Yūsuf ﷺ. When they left, the place was due to be cleaned and checked that everything was alright. The caretaker realised that an expensive beaker was missing. The first doubt was upon those who had stayed in that guesthouse, so he proclaimed, 'You are thieves!'

Looking back at the story, one may object, that how did Yūsuf ﷺ call them thieves or allow them to be called thieves, when he himself had put the cup in one of their saddlebags?

Answers to this objection have been given by the *Mufassirūn*. Some have written that this cry was not from Yūsuf ﷺ, rather it was the caretaker of the guesthouse who called out to them. And he was oblivious of what had taken place beforehand.

Imām Fakhruddīn Rāzī ﷺ states, 'If, for instance, this call was made by Yūsuf ﷺ, then this is due to 'tawriyah' (precautionary dissimulation). The

[184] Ma'āriful Qur'ān.

reality is that when a person steals something, he hides it, and then derives benefit from it. The brethren had hidden Yūsuf 🌿 in the well, and then they had sold him to the caravan for a meagre price, so in fact, within the context of the whole story, they were the thieves.'

Some commentators say that it is possible that the letter *hamza* which is used for *istifhām* [which indicates to an interrogative sentence] has been omitted from the sentence. Thus, the statement of Yūsuf is a question, and not an informative sentence i.e. 'Are you thieves?'

Some say that all this had taken place through the order of Allāh 🌿 and, *'He cannot be questioned for what he does, whereas they [his bondsmen] will be questioned.'* The wisdom behind this, could be that by separating Binyāmīn after the separation of Yūsuf 🌿, Allāh 🌿 was completing the *Ibtilā* [test] of Yā'qūb 🌿.

Note: The *heela* [trick] carried out by Yūsuf 🌿 indicates that it is permissible to do such a thing in order to obtain your lawful rights. However, where the intention of such *heela* would be to avoid the rightful duties, or to obtain something in an unjust way, then it will not be permissible.

The *Hanafī Fuqahā* [jurists] say that carrying out such *heela* to protect oneself or to get out of a sticky situation has been narrated from the prophets, and are therefore permissible. When Ibrāhīm 🌿 feared for his wife Sarah, he said to the tyrant, 'She is my sister.' He meant sister in deen, because all Muslims are brothers and sisters.

In Sahīh Bukhārī, we read from Ka'b Ibn Mālik that when the Holy Prophet 🌿 intended to go for a battle, he would carry out *tawriyah*, i.e. he would take the name of a place which is in the direction of the route he is intending to take, and he would keep secret the actual destination. [185] If one travels from Manchester to London, Birmingham comes along the way, so upon being questioned about his destination, he replies, 'I am going towards Birmingham,' he will not be lying.

Also in Sahīh Bukhārī, we read in the story of the execution of Ka'b Ibn Ashraf [the accursed Jewish leader], that when the Sahābī, Muhammad Ibn Maslama sought permission from the Prophet 🌿 to say something which

---

[185] Bukhārī 2728.

would appear to be an insult, whereas he meant something else, the Prophet ﷺ granted him that permission. [186]

We have many more examples to prove this. For an understanding person, even one would be enough, whereas, for someone who has no intellect, then volumes are insufficient.

The *Hanafī Fuqahā* [May Allāh ﷻ grant them great rewards for their efforts] have explained this with minute details in specific chapters within the books of Fiqh. They have tried their best to make practicing Islām as easy as possible. They have put forward solutions to the trickiest situations.

An example of solving a tricky situation can be taken from the following incident. Once an Abbāsid king was sitting with his wife at night under the light of the full moon. During the conversation he said, 'If you are not more beautiful than the full moon, I will give you three talāqs.' The queen immediately rushed behind the curtain, assuming she was definitely divorced. The King realised his stupidity, and spent the whole night restlessly.

The following day, he gathered the *ulamā* and put his dilemma before them. They unanimously said that she has absolutely been divorced. One *Ālim* was sitting quietly. The King asked him to speak. He said, 'In my humble opinion, the Queen is not divorced, because Allāh says in the Holy Qur'ān: '*Indeed we have created the humankind in the best of forms.*' [187] Therefore, a human being is the most beautiful of the creation and he/she has a better form than the full moon. Therefore, the divorce cannot be taken into account. [188]

Note: In the *Sharī'ah* of Ibrāhīm ﷺ, the punishment for a thief was that he would be handed over to the person whose goods he stole. He would have to serve him for a full year. This is what is meant by verse seventy-five [75]. Yūsuf ﷺ wanted them to speak out this sentence, so that it would be easy for him to keep his brother in his company.

---

[186] Bukhārī 2807.
[187] Qur'ān 95:4.
[188] Tarāshe pg.16.

Verse 76

$$\text{فَبَدَاَ بِاَوْعِيَتِهِمْ قَبْلَ وِعَآءِ اَخِيْهِ ثُمَّ اسْتَخْرَجَهَا مِنْ وِّعَآءِ اَخِيْهِ ط كَذٰلِكَ}$$

$$\text{كِدْنَا لِيُوْسُفَ ط مَا كَانَ لِيَاْخُذَ اَخَاهُ فِيْ دِيْنِ الْمَلِكِ اِلَّاۤ اَنْ يَّشَآءَ اللّٰهُ ط}$$

$$\text{نَرْفَعُ دَرَجٰتٍ مَّنْ نَّشَآءُ ط وَفَوْقَ كُلِّ ذِيْ عِلْمٍ عَلِيْمٌ ﴿٧٦﴾}$$

So he began [the search] with their baggage before the baggage of his brother,
then he bought it [the King's cup] out of his brother's sack. Thus did We plan for
Yūsuf. He could not have taken his brother by the law of the king, except if
Allāh willed. We exalt in degrees whomsoever We will, and above every
knowing one is a Knower.

When the brothers themselves mentioned the punishment for stealing,
Yūsuf ﷺ ordered a search. He began with the eldest brother's belongings and
gradually came to the youngest brother, Binyāmīn. [189]

'Thus we planned for Yūsuf...' Maulānā Idrīs Kāndhlawī ﷺ and Khāzin write,
'We made Yūsuf's brethren proclaim the sentence of a thief and they were
caught by their own admission. The reason for this plan was that under
Egyptian law, if someone stole something, he would be beaten up, and he
would have to return the price of the stolen goods in twofold. The brethren
would not have been in a position to return twice the price of the golden
cup.'

'Except if Allāh willed...' i.e. Allāh's ﷻ will is always superior and whatever He
wills is bound to take place. None can escape the will of Allāh ﷻ. There is a
saying among the Egyptian people:

$$\text{أنا أريد وأنت تريد ـ والله يفعل ما يريد ـ}$$

'I will, you will, but Allāh fulfils whatever He wills.'

---

[189] Genesis 'The First Book of Moses' 44:11-12 – Tafsīr Mājidī.

'We exalt...' Khāzin writes, 'This exalting is due to knowledge. Yūsuf ﷺ was a man of knowledge, therefore Allāh ﷻ raised his rank. The verse indicates that knowledge is the most precious thing, and of the highest rank in the eyes of Allāh ﷻ.'

'And above every...' Ibn Abbās ؓ says, 'Above every learned person, there is someone who knows more than him, until the knowledge reaches Allāh ﷻ who is above all knowledgeable persons. This is because He is the Independent, who is not in need of teaching.'

Ibn al-Anbāri ؓ says, 'An *Ālim* should taunt himself [if he does not know something]. He should feel humbleness and humility within himself, and should think of the bounties and favours of Allāh ﷻ. He should never attempt to show his power because there is no such *Ālim* above whom there is none.

Verse 77

قَالُوْٓا اِنْ يَّسْرِقْ فَقَدْ سَرَقَ اَخٌ لَّهُ مِنْ قَبْلُ ۚ فَاَسَرَّهَا يُوْسُفُ فِيْ نَفْسِهٖ
وَلَمْ يُبْدِهَا لَهُمْ ۚ قَالَ اَنْتُمْ شَرٌّ مَّكَانًا ۚ وَاللّٰهُ اَعْلَمُ بِمَا تَصِفُوْنَ ﴿٧٧﴾

They said, "If he steals, then there was a brother of his who stole before [him]. But Yūsuf concealed this in his heart and did not disclose it to them. He said, "You are in more evil plight, and Allāh is the best knower of what he ascribe."

Many readers might have forgotten the sequence of events that are taking place in Yūsuf's ﷺ story. I will mention a brief account of what is going on. Yūsuf ﷺ informed his brother Binyāmīn that he was the long lost brother who was once thrown in the well, and that he had worked out a plan to keep him in Egypt for some time. Thereafter, a golden cup [or silver cup] was placed in Binyāmīn's baggage, and later it was announced that the King's cup was missing. The brothers' belongings were searched and the cup was revealed from Binyāmīn's bags, who as 'punishment', was to stay in the service of the king for one year.

When the cup was found in Binyāmīn's belongings, the brothers accused him of theft, and without defending Binyāmīn, or trying to enquire about the incident, they in fact confirmed the event and went further by recalling another incident which had taken place many years beforehand. They said that among the children of Yā'qūb ﷺ, these two, who are of a different mother than us, are both thieves. They boasted of their piety and innocence, and attempted to validate the alledged crimes of Binyāmīn and Yūsuf ﷺ. Little did they realise that they were playing into the hands of Yūsuf ﷺ.

Yūsuf ﷺ did not lose his self-control upon hearing this remark. He kept quiet and thought in his heart, 'Allāh knows the reality of your accusations.'

The *Mufassirūn* have narrated here different stories regarding the accusation made upon Yūsuf ﷺ. Khāzin writes:

1. Sa'īd Ibn Jubair ﷺ and Qatādā ﷺ say that Yūsuf's ﷺ maternal grandfather had an idol which he worshipped. Yūsuf ﷺ took it secretly and broke it into pieces and threw it along the footpath so that he would not be able to worship it.

2. Mujāhid ﷺ says that once a beggar came and asked for something. Yūsuf ﷺ took an egg and gave it to him.

3. Sufyān ibn Uyaynah ﷺ says, 'He once gave a chicken to a beggar.'

4. Wahb bin Munabbih ﷺ says that he used to hide food for the poor people.

5. Muhammad ibn Is'hāq ﷺ says that there was an elder sister of Hadhrat Yā'qūb ﷺ who possessed the belt of Hadhrat Ibrāhīm ﷺ. It was their custom that the belt was kept by the eldest person in the family. She, being the eldest, inherited it from her father Is'hāq ﷺ. When Yūsuf ﷺ was born, he was given into her care. Naturally she loved her nephew very much. When he grew up, Hadhrat Yā'qūb ﷺ desired to take him back. She refused to return him saying that she could not bear his separation. But Hadhrat Yā'qūb ﷺ made repeated requests for his return. One day, she tied the belt around the waist under the clothes of Hadhrat Yūsuf ﷺ and returned him, then she searched for the belt hither and thither. At last it was found with Yūsuf ﷺ, and according to their *Sharī'ah*, Yūsuf ﷺ was handed to her and stayed with her until she passed away.

Hadhrat Yūsuf ﷺ was a mere child when this incident took place. He had nothing to do with his aunt's actions. Nevertheless, the brothers took this to be theft and made false accusations upon Yūsuf ﷺ.

Similar is the case of many *Ahl-ullāh* [friends of Allāh] of our time. People accuse them of things which they never did or had nothing to do with.

Yūsuf's ﷺ patience and forbearance comes to light in his concealment of the truth. The divine *hikmat* [wisdom] did not demand the disclosing of the secret. It would also have been premature to express any feelings at this moment in time.

Verse 78

قَالُوْا يٰٓاَيُّهَا الْعَزِيْزُ اِنَّ لَهٗٓ اَبًا شَيْخًا كَبِيْرًا فَخُذْ اَحَدَنَا مَكَانَهٗ ۚ اِنَّا نَرٰىكَ مِنَ الْمُحْسِنِيْنَ ﴿٧٨﴾

They said, "O Azīz [the exalted one] he has a father who is an old man, very aged, so take one of us in his stead. For we see thou art [gracious] in doing good.

Maulānā Idrīs Kāndhlawī ﷺ writes: 'When the guards were ordered to take Binyāmīn away, the brothers' pride started to fade, and they realised that they had no choice but to appear infront of the the *Azīz* [i.e. Yusuf] . Thus, they said, 'Take one of us in his place.'"

Verse 79

قَالَ مَعَاذَ اللهِ اَنْ نَّأْخُذَ اِلَّا مَنْ وَّجَدْنَا مَتَاعَنَا عِنْدَهٗٓ ۙ اِنَّآ اِذًا لَّظٰلِمُوْنَ ﴿٧٩﴾

He said, "Allāh forbid that we take anyone other than Him with whom we found our property. Indeed [If we did so] we would be unjust."

Here, Yūsuf ﷺ used the words, 'him with whom we found our property', rather than, 'the thief' even though this would have been much shorter. The reason is that Yūsuf ﷺ knew that Binyāmīn had not committed any theft.

This is the second time in the sūrah that Yūsuf ﷺ uses the words 'Allāh forbid'. The first was when Zuleikhā attempted to seduce him, fearing the violation of the right of Allāh. On this occasion, he feared the violation of the right of his brother, so again he says 'Allāh forbid', in order to remind him that Allāh is the Being in Whom we can take refuge from committing acts of oppression.

Verse 80

فَلَمَّا اسْتَيْئَسُوْا مِنْهُ خَلَصُوْا نَجِيًّا ۚ قَالَ كَبِيْرُهُمْ اَلَمْ تَعْلَمُوْٓا اَنَّ اَبَاكُمْ قَدْ اَخَذَ عَلَيْكُمْ مَّوْثِقًا مِّنَ اللهِ وَمِنْ قَبْلُ مَا فَرَّطْتُّمْ فِيْ يُوْسُفَ ۚ فَلَنْ اَبْرَحَ الْاَرْضَ حَتّٰى يَأْذَنَ لِيْٓ اَبِيْٓ اَوْ يَحْكُمَ اللهُ لِيْ ۚ وَهُوَ خَيْرُ الْحٰكِمِيْنَ ﴿٨٠﴾

Then when they despaired of him, they counselled together privately. The eldest of them said, "Do you know that your father has taken assurance from you in the name of Allāh, and how before this, you had failed in your duty towards Yūsuf. Therefore, I will by no means go forth from this land until my father gives me leave or Allāh commands me. Indeed, he is the best to command."

Allāma Shabbīr Aḥmad Uthmānī ﷺ writes, 'When they became despondent of a positive reply from Hadhrat Yūsuf ﷺ, they conferred privately, away from the gathering. The majority of them opined that they should return home. The eldest of them in age and wisdom, said, 'How will you go before your father? What answer will you give to him about the pledge he had taken from us? We have already committed one mistake regarding Yūsuf ﷺ, the after effects of which we are still bearing. Returning without Binyāmīn shall be utter shamelessness and inhumanity. So for me, I will never return and I will not move from here unless father gives me an order to move from here, or some heavenly decision should finish the matter', meaning either I die or I arrange for the release of Binyāmīn.

'*The eldest of them said...*' Khāzin states, 'There are three opinions regarding who is taken into account as being the eldest:

1. Ibn Abbās ﷺ says, 'The eldest in wisdom and in knowledge, and this was *Yahūda*.'

2. Mujāhid ﷺ says, 'The leader of them all and this was *Sham'ūn*.'

3. Dhahhāk ﷺ says, 'The eldest in age and this was *Rubīl*.' [190]

Abdullāh Yūsuf Alī ﷺ writes, 'His name is not given in the Qur'ān. The eldest brother was *Reuben*. But according to the biblical story, the brother who had taken the most active part in this transaction was *Judah*, one of the eldest brothers, being the fourth son after Reuben, Simeon and Levi and of the same mother as these. It was Judah who stood surety to Jacob for Binyāmīn.' Therefore, it is natural that Judah should, as here, offer to stay behind. [191]

Verse 81

اِرْجِعُوٓا اِلٰۤى اَبِيْكُمْ فَقُوْلُوْا يٰٓاَبَانَآ اِنَّ ابْنَكَ سَرَقَ ۚ وَمَا
شَهِدْنَآ اِلَّا بِمَا عَلِمْنَا وَمَا كُنَّا لِلْغَيْبِ حٰفِظِيْنَ ﴿٨١﴾

Return to your father and say: "O our father! Verily thy son committed a theft.
We bear witness only to what we know and we have no idea of the unseen
thing."

Allāma Uthmānī ﷺ writes, "The eldest son continued: 'Leave me here and all of you go to our father, and say that such an event has taken place beyond expectation.'

Hadhrat Shāh Sahib ﷺ mentions that the son said, 'We had given our word based on our own knowledge. How could we know that Binyāmīn would be

---

[190] Khāzin 35:3.
[191] Genesis xliii.9 – Abdullāh Yūsuf Alī 580.

arrested for theft?' or 'We described the punishment for theft according to our own *Sharī'ah*, but we did not know that our brother was a thief.'

Verse 82

وَاسْأَلِ الْقَرْيَةَ الَّتِىْ كُنَّا فِيْهَا وَالْعِيْرَ
الَّتِىْ اَقْبَلْنَا فِيْهَا ۚ وَاِنَّا لَصٰدِقُوْنَ ﴿٨٢﴾

And ask the town where we have been and the caravan in which we have been, indeed we are telling the truth.

They said to their father, 'If you do not believe us, then investigate the matter by sending some reliable persons to that city where the event took place, or ask the caravan with which we have come. It will prove that we are truthful in our statement.

Verse 83

قَالَ بَلْ سَوَّلَتْ لَكُمْ اَنْفُسُكُمْ اَمْرًا ۚ فَصَبْرٌ جَمِيْلٌ ۚ عَسَى
اللّٰهُ اَنْ يَّأْتِيَنِىْ بِهِمْ جَمِيْعًا ۚ اِنَّهٗ هُوَ الْعَلِيْمُ الْحَكِيْمُ ﴿٨٣﴾

He [Yā'qūb] said, "Nay but have yourselves contrived a story [good enough] for you. So, patience is the most fitting [for me] maybe Allāh will bring them all back to me. For He, and only He is indeed full of knowledge and wisdom."

Allāma Uthmānī ﷺ writes, 'Some commentators have interepreted this verse to mean that Hadhrat Yā'qūb ﷺ rebuked his sons as if to say, 'How could you even promise to protect him when you did not even question the possibility that someone else might have placed the cup in his goods deliberately? The mere finding of the cup in Binyāmīn's baggage does not prove he is guilty.' They did not defend Binyāmīn; rather they corroborated his crime by saying that his brother had also committed theft previously. If they weren't corrupt, they would not have acted in such a manner. Now, they had come to fabricate lies. Nevertheless, Hadhrat Yā'qūb ﷺ would remain patient and would not complain at all. It was not beyond Allāh's ﷺ mercy and power that He might gather Yūsuf and Binyāmīn 🕮, and the brother who was left there on account of Binyāmīn, all together with their father. Allāh 🕮 knows the circumstances of everyone and deals with everyone according to his *hikmat*.'

It shows that the hearts of the Messengers do not get despondent even in the most severe and disappointing circumstances, and even after a great lapse of time, they always believe in the mercy of Allāh 🕮 and always cherish the hope of Divine kindness.

Yā'qūb 🕮 had lost trust in his sons. They had made the same lame excuse regarding Yūsuf 🕮, that a wolf had eaten him and this is his shirt. At that point, Yā'qūb's 🕮 remarks were exactly the same. He could not bring himself to believe them, yet he could not reprimand them. Thus he said, '*Fa-Sabrun Jamīl*.'

Among the Prophets 🕮, there are some who are famous for their patience. Regarding Ayyūb 🕮, Allāh 🕮 says in the Qur'ān: '*Truly we found him full of patience. How excellent is the servant! Indeed, he was penitent [one who would turn to God frequently].*' [192]

And He says: '*And [remember] Ismā'īl, Idrīs and Zul Kifl [men] of constancy and patience. We admitted to them Our mercy, for they were of the religious ones.*' [193]

Allāh 🕮 commands us, '*O ye who believe! Observe patience and constancy; outside all others in endurance; strengthen each other; and fear Allāh so that you may prosper.*' [194]

He also says: '*And obey Allāh and his Messenger; and do not fall into disputes, lest ye lose heart; and be patient: for Allāh is with those who Patiently persevere.*' [195]

Allāh 🕮 gives us glad tidings: '*And give glad tidings to those who are tolerant who say, when afflicted with calamity: 'To Allāh we belong, and to Him we return: they are those on whom [descend] blessings from their Lord and mercy. And they are the ones that receive guidance.*' [196]

---

[192] Qur'ān 38:44.
[193] Qur'ān 21:85.
[194] Qur'ān 3:200.
[195] Qur'ān 8:46.
[196] Qur'ān 2:155-157.

Allāh ﷻ praises his patient servants in another verse, He says: *'Those who show patience [firmness and self control] who are true [in word and deed] who worship devotedly, in the early hours of the morning.'* [197]

May Allāh ﷻ grant us the ability to exercise beautiful patience in any turbulence and afflictions that we may face, and may He rank us among the sābirīn. Āmīn

Verse 84

$$ وَتَوَلَّىٰ عَنْهُمْ وَقَالَ يَاأَسَفَىٰ عَلَىٰ يُوسُفَ $$

$$ وَابْيَضَّتْ عَيْنَاهُ مِنَ الْحُزْنِ فَهُوَ كَظِيمٌ ﴿٨٤﴾ $$

And he turned away from them and said: "Alas, my grief for Yūsuf!"
And his eyes were whitened due to the (tears of sorrow), thus he was a
suppressor (of his grief).

Hadhrat Yā'qūb ﷺ was absolutely stunned by the story that Binyāmīn had committed theft. He could not bring himself into believing that his darling little Binyāmīn, whose innocence he knew very well, would commit such a grave crime. Thus he exclaimed, 'All I can do is be patient and seek help from Allāh.' Yet one sorrow brings up the memory of another and a greater one. Binyāmīn has gone! Oh but Yūsuf! His pretty dream of boyhood! His greatness foretold! And now how dark was the world! If only he could weep! Tears might give him relief, and his red and swollen eyes might yet regain their light! But his grief was too deep for tears. His eyes lost their colour, and became dull white. [198]

Readers may wonder as to why Allāh ﷻ put Yā'qūb ﷺ through so many hardships. The answer is provided by The Messenger ﷺ, who said: 'We, the party of messengers, are put through the hardest tests, then [after the prophets, the ones to be tested the most] are those who bear the most resemblance with the Prophets.'

Allāh ﷻ puts the Prophets to tests according to their wisdom and according to their capacities, as He wills. So in Yā'qūb's ﷺ case, the love of Yūsuf ﷺ was

---

[197] Qur'ān 3:17.
[198] Abdullāh Yūsuf Alī 582.

cast into his heart and then he was separated so terribly. The shock was severe but he did not give in, nor did he complain. Despite years of tearful crying and his burning heart, he did not fail to perform divine obligations. The more his heart wept, the closer he got to Allāh ﷻ and gained more insight.

Hadhrat Shāh Sahib ؓ writes, 'Such great pain was controlled for such a long period. Only a Prophet could bear this.' [199]

Ibn Kathīr ؓ relates from Sa'īd ibn Jubair ؓ, who said, 'No nation apart from the nation of Mohammed ﷺ was gifted with the words *Innā Lillāhi wa Innā Ilaihi Rāji'ūn* [a duā made at the time of a loss, meaning 'Indeed, we belong to Allāh and to Him is our return']. This is highlighted by the statement of Yā'qūb ؑ when he said, '*Alas! My grief for Yūsuf...*' He remained silent and inwardly puts his case before Allāh ﷻ alone [i.e. He did not say 'Innā Lillāh...'].

The *Mufassirūn* have two opinions regarding the whiteness of the eyes of Yā'qūb ؑ:

1. Muqātil ibn Hayyān ؓ says, 'He turned blind and remained in this state for a period of six years.'

2. Some say that due to excessive crying, his eyes had whitened, and his eyesight was severely weakened. [200]

Maulānā Idrīs Kāndhlawī ؓ writes, 'As his eyesight continued to weaken, his foresight continued to strengthen.'

Abul Barkat Al-Nasafī writes ؓ in '*Madārik al-Tanzīl*', 'At the time there was none more virtuous than Yā'qūb ؑ upon the face of this earth. Yet he cried and cried. This shows that there is no harm in crying due to grief.'

We see that our Holy Prophet ﷺ cried when his son Ibrāhīm died. Upon being questioned, he replied: '*Indeed the heart feels sorrow, the eyes shed tears, yet we only say such words that please our Lord. O Ibrāhīm! We are indeed grief stricken due to your separation.*' [201]

---

[199] Mūzihul Qur'ān.
[200] Khāzin 37:3.
[201] Bukhārī 1220, Muslim 4279.

Although crying is permitted, the *Sharī'ah* has drawn a line, and has deemed certain practices to be prohibited; shouting, slapping the cheeks, beating the chest and tearing the clothes. Also prohibited is proclaiming such phrases which call upon the displeasure of Allāh ﷻ, e.g. 'Why did Allāh ﷻ afflict me with this grief? Could he not find someone else? I have lost faith in Him, I have no hope of recovering', and statements of the ilk. We can also understand from here that the *mātam* [lamenting] of Shi'ās which takes place in the blessed month of *Muharram* has nothing to do with Islām. In fact, it is not allowed in Islām, and is against the teachings of Islām.

Verse 85

$$ قَالُوْا تَاللهِ تَفْتَؤُا تَذْكُرُ يُوْسُفَ حَتّٰى تَكُوْنَ $$

$$ حَرَضًا اَوْ تَكُوْنَ مِنَ الْهٰلِكِيْنَ ﴿٨٥﴾ $$

They said: "By Allāh thou will never cease remembering Yūsuf
until thy health is ruined or thou art of those who perish."

The sons tried to comfort their father saying it seems that you are never going to get over the grief of Yūsuf ﷺ. You are so deeply engrossed in his love that you will keep on remembering him, even after so many years, until you reach the last extreme of illness, or until you die.

Mujāhid ﷺ says: '*Haradan*' literally means 'close to death.'

Ibn Is'hāq ﷺ says: 'It means one whose body has rotten and whose intellect has faded away.' In our present time, we could interpret it as 'severe depression'.

Khāzin writes: 'It is strange that one cannot benefit even from himself due to severe grief, sorrow, pain and worries.'

Verse 86

$$ قَالَ اِنَّمَآ اَشْكُوْ بَثِّيْ وَحُزْنِيْ اِلَى اللهِ $$

$$ وَاَعْلَمُ مِنَ اللهِ مَا لَا تَعْلَمُوْنَ ﴿٨٦﴾ $$

He said, "I expose my distress and anguish only
unto Allāh, and I know that which ye know not."

Yā'qūb ﷺ replied, 'How can you teach me patience? The impatient is he who
complains before the creation against the pain sent from Allāh ﷻ. I express
my pain only before He who gave it to me, and I know from Allāh ﷻ that
Yūsuf ﷺ and his brother are alive and they will certainly be returned to me.'

Ya'qūb ﷺ uses two words to describe his grief: *bathth* and *huzn*. Both are
similar in meaning, but are deliberately used in different contexts, and add
to the literary flavour of the Qur'ān. *Bathth* literally means the sorrow and
grief which has been caused over a long period of time, and *huzn* means the
sorrow and grief which has been caused by something recent. In the context
of the story of Hadhrat Yā'qūb ﷺ, he suffered both long term grief (the
disappearance of Yūsuf) and was afflicted by a very recent grief [the
accusation levelled against Binyāmīn]. How beautiful is the language of the
Qur'ān, that in two words, it has captured two entire stories!

Verse 87

يَٰبَنِيَّ اذْهَبُوا فَتَحَسَّسُوا مِنْ يُّوسُفَ وَاَخِيهِ وَلَا تَيْئَسُوا مِنْ رَّوْحِ

اللهِ ۚ اِنَّهُ لَا يَايْئَسُ مِنْ رَّوْحِ اللهِ اِلَّا الْقَوْمُ الْكٰفِرُوْنَ ﴿٨٧﴾

"Go, O my sons! And search for Yūsuf and his brother, and never give up hope
of Allāh's mercy; truly no one despairs Allāh's mercy except those who have no
faith.'

Yā'qūb ﷺ taught his sons patience and to be hopeful of Allāh's ﷻ mercy. He
had this feeling that the three of them might be together in Egypt, also their
stock of grain might have been running low. Thus, he advised his sons to go
and search for their brothers.

Khāzin has narrated here a detailed letter written by Yā'qūb ﷺ to the king
of Egypt, Yūsuf. He mentions the high status of his forefathers Is'hāq and
Ibrāhīm ﷺ. Thereafter, he requested him to return Binyāmīn safely;
otherwise, he would be compelled to supplicate to Allāh ﷻ against the
Egyptian ruler. When Yūsuf read this letter, he shrieked and cried profusely.

Then he revealed himself to his brothers as is mentioned in the following verses. [202]

Verse 88

فَلَمَّا دَخَلُوْا عَلَيْهِ قَالُوْا يٰٓاَيُّهَا الْعَزِيْزُ مَسَّنَا وَاَهْلَنَا الضُّرُّ وَجِئْنَا بِبِضَاعَةٍ مُّزْجٰةٍ فَاَوْفِ لَنَا الْكَيْلَ وَتَصَدَّقْ عَلَيْنَا ۗ اِنَّ اللهَ يَجْزِى الْمُتَصَدِّقِيْنَ

﴾٨٨﴿

Then when they came before him, they said: 'O Azīz! [The exalted one] distress has seized us as well as our family and we have brought poor merchandise, so give us full measure and be charitable to us. Verily Allāh does reward the charitable.'

"And when they came..." When they left their father and undertook the journey to Egypt, they arrived in the courtyard of Yūsuf ﷺ. They were in desperate need for sustenance as the famine had a severe impact upon their physical health.

They started off their plea in a different manner to that of the previous two journeys. They sounded very humble and admitted their weakness. They said to Yūsuf ﷺ, 'What merchandise we have brought with us is very minimal. It is not even suitable to be put before you, therefore we beseech your favours and request you to be charitable towards us and give us a full measure of grains, like you had done on the previous two occasions.'

Ibn Abbās ﷺ says: 'The dirhams they had were counterfeit.'

Some commentators say: 'They had empty sacks and ropes.' Some say, 'They had some materials which the Bedouins would use, and were made from wool.' Some say, 'They had animal skins and slippers.'

Khāzin writes, *'Muzjāt'* literally means to push slowly and whatever price they had brought to pay for goods was something to be refused and deemed

---

[202] Khāzin 39:3.

unacceptable. This is why the wording of the *Mufassirūn* differ in describing the nature of their possessions.' [203]

"And be charitable to us..." The *Mufassirūn* have two opinions regarding the interpretation of 'charity' in the above verse:

1. Sufyān Ibn Uyaynah ﷺ says that charity here means alms giving. The *sadaqah* money was *halāl* for the previous Prophets ﷺ and their families. As for our Prophet Muhammad ﷺ, accepting *Sadaqah* is not allowed. His personality is very high. Thus we should offer him gifts and presents, not the *Zakāh* and *Sadaqah* money for which we hope for reward from Allāh ﷺ, and which is a means of cleaning up our wealth. The same is the case with the family of our Holy Prophet ﷺ. To this date, the majority of *Ulamā* are of the opinion that it is NOT permitted to give *Sadaqah* to the progeny of the Messenger ﷺ.

2. The majority of *Ulamā*, when interpreting the above verse, say that charity is not taken into account here. They mention that charitable money was not suitable for any of the Prophets ﷺ, and not accepting charity is in fact, the distinguishing feature of a Prophet. Thus, being charitable means to be generous, hospitable, and to give them full measurement as before, and not lessening it due to the meagre amount they have put forward.

The implication of the word charity is the same as it is in the *Hadīth*, 'It is a *Sadaqah* which Allāh ﷺ bestowed you with, so accept His *Sadaqah*.' [204]

The Prophet ﷺ said this when he was questioned regarding the reduction of 4 *rak'āts salāh* to 2 *rak'āts* during a journey. He described the reduction of 2 *rak'āts* as charity.

Note: Hasan Basrī ﷺ and Mujāhid ﷺ disliked the following supplication of a person, 'O Allāh, be charitable to me.' The reason being that charity is given

[203] Khāzin 39:3.
[204] Tirmidhi #3034.

by someone who is hoping for reward. Hasan Basrī said to the person, 'Say: O Allāh give me, have mercy on me, and bestow on me.'

"Verily Allāh does reward the charitable..." Ibn Juraij ﷺ and Dhahhāk ﷺ say that the brothers did not say, 'Allāh will reward you', because they did not know that the Azīz was a believer.

Verse 89

قَالَ هَلْ عَلِمْتُمْ مَّا فَعَلْتُمْ بِيُوسُفَ وَاَخِيْهِ اِذْ اَنْتُمْ جٰهِلُوْنَ ﴿٨٩﴾

He said, "Remember what you did to Yūsuf and his brother while you were ignorant?"

'He said, Remember...' Muhammad Ibn Is'hāq ﷺ says, 'When the brothers pleaded to Yūsuf ﷺ, in a very humble manner and described their poverty, Yūsuf ﷺ could not control himself. He cried and disclosed the secret. It seems that he had sensed that the testing times were over. Maybe he had received some revelation in this regard.'

'While you were ignorant...' Look at the great characteristics of a great Prophet. He did not taunt them, rebuke them nor did he mention a fraction of the distress they had caused him when they mercilessly threw him in the well. Rather he himself, makes an excuse for their wrongdoing: that you were ignorant of the facts, which made you do what you did. The Holy Prophet ﷺ once described a prophet who was tortured by his people to the extent that his face was covered in blood. Still he was supplicating, 'O Allāh, forgive my nation, because they know not.' It seems that he was referring to himself. When the pagans of Makkah attacked him in the battle of *Uhud*, wounded his cheeks, broke his front teeth, his face was heavily bleeding. Fātima ﷺ, his daughter, tried to stop the bleeding with cold water but it would only increase. So she burnt some palm leaves and put the ashes on the wound, which brought a halt to the bleeding. In this state, he once said, *'How can a nation which covered its Prophet's face with blood be successful.'* Thereafter, he prayed, *'O Allāh! Forgive my nation because they do not know.'*

Verse 90

قَالُوٓا أَءِنَّكَ لَأَنْتَ يُوْسُفُ ، قَالَ اَنَا يُوْسُفُ وَهٰذَآ اَخِيْ ، قَدْ مَنَّ اللهُ

عَلَيْنَا ، اِنَّهُ مَنْ يَّتَّقِ وَيَصْبِرْ فَاِنَّ اللهَ لَا يُضِيْعُ اَجْرَ الْمُحْسِنِيْنَ ﴿٩٠﴾

They said, "Art thou indeed Yūsuf." He replied, "I am Yūsuf and this is my
brother; Allāh has surely been gracious to us. Verily, he who fears and endures
affliction, then Allāh does not spoil the reward of those who do good."

The brothers were totally taken aback by Yūsuf's words. They said in utter
surprise, 'Are you really Yūsuf?'

Perhaps their father's words, the shaping of events, Yūsuf's open fondness
of Binyāmīn despite him being a prisoner, and perhaps a recollection of
Yūsuf's dream - all these things suddenly 'clicked' and had mentally prepared
them to ask, 'Are you really Yūsuf?' Yūsuf ﷺ also gave them a direct reply,
'Yes, I am Yūsuf, and if you still have doubt of my identity then here is
Binyāmīn, ask him. We have suffered much, but Allāh ﷻ at last rewards
patience and right conduct. He has changed separation into union, disgrace
into respect, pain into comfort, poverty into prosperity. He who was sold for
a petty price as a slave is now made the king of Egypt.'

Ibn Kathīr ﷺ says, 'The reason for their amazement is that they had been
coming to Yūsuf for over a period of two years or more, and yet they could
not recognise him. And he in turn knew them, yet was able to conceal
himself.'

Khāzin says the reality of taqwā is constant awareness of the commands of
Allāh. And sabr means to halt oneself from whatever is forbidden by Allāh ﷻ
and to make oneself punctual of his duties towards his master.

Mujāhid ﷺ says, 'Whoever refrains from forbidden acts and is patient in the
prison.'

Ibn Abbās ﷺ says, 'Whoever refrains from Zinā and is patient when being
single [a bachelor].'

Muhsinīn means those who do good deeds. These words have been
mentioned in many other verses. Allāh ﷻ says in Sūrah Āl-e-Imrān, '...those
who spend [freely] whether in prosperity or in adversity; who restrain anger and
pardon [all] men; for Allāh loves the Al-Muhsinīn'

In Sūrah Al-Mā'idah: '*And those who believe and do deeds of righteousness, there is no blame for what they ate [in the past], when they guard themselves from evil and believe and do deeds of righteousness, then again guard themselves from evil and believe, then guard themselves from evil and do good. For Allāh loves those who do good.*' [205]

In Sūrah Yūnus, we read, '*For those who have done good is the best reward and even more.*' [i.e. having the honour of glancing at the countenance of Allāh, as mentioned in a *Hadīth* in Sahīh Bukhārī].

The *Hadīth Jibra'īl* explains the meaning of *Ihsān* – '*What is Ihsān?*' '*That you worship Allāh as though you are looking at him. Because if you don't see him, he is watching you.*' [206]

Allāma Tībī ◈ says, '*Ihsān* literally means to do good. When you worship in the correct manner, you are doing good to yourself by gaining maximum reward.' If one worships whilst one's mind is occupied with worldly thoughts, and with no *Khushu'* [devotion/ concentration], then your *thawāb* [reward] will be reduced.'

The Prophet ◈ is teaching us that the best form of fulfilling any duty towards our Lord Almighty, and that is whether we are performing *salāh*, engaged in *dhikrullāh*; daily *tasbeeh* or in reciting the Qur'ān, giving alms, fasting or performing *Hajj*. We should always be conscious that our Lord is always watching us.

Hāfiz Ibn Rajab ◈ says, 'It is a very suitable reward for those who do good, that Allāh will let them glance at Himself. In this world they worshipped Him as though they are looking at Him, so in the next world, He will be fulfilling this desire by actually letting them see Him.'

Verse 91

قَالُوْا تَاللهِ لَقَدْ اٰثَرَكَ اللهُ عَلَيْنَا وَاِنْ كُنَّا لَخَاطِئِيْنَ ﴿٩١﴾

They said, "By Allāh! Indeed Allāh has preferred you over us,
and we certainly have been guilty of wrong doing."

---

[205] Qur'ān 5:93.
[206] Muslim #8.

When they realised that the king who was conversing with them was their own brother, they confessed to their guilt and admitted that Allāh ﷻ has selected Yūsuf ؑ and has given him preference over them.

Jealousy cannot bring about any good, and no matter how hard the jealous person tries, he is unable to cause harm except that which Allāh ﷻ wills. Piety and patience have brought their fruits and jealousy has become void.

'*Allāh has preferred you...*' Ibn Abbās ؓ says, 'By giving you kingdom.' Abū Sālih ؒ narrates: 'By patience.' Some say: 'By gentleness and forgiveness.' Khāzin says: 'By knowledge and understanding.' [207]

'*We have been guilty...*' The word '*Khāti'īn*' is derived from '*Khata'a*', which means to commit a sin with will and intention. It is not from the word '*Akhta'a*', which means 'to make a mistake'. Thus it means that we confess to our sins, we did not fear Allāh ﷻ nor did we have any patience. Please forgive us from your part and ask Allāh ﷻ to forgive our ill treatment to such a wonderful brother.

Verse 92

قَالَ لَا تَثْرِيْبَ عَلَيْكُمُ الْيَوْمَ ط يَغْفِرُ

اللهُ لَكُمْ ز وَهُوَ اَرْحَمُ الرّٰحِمِيْنَ ﴿٩٢﴾

He replied: "Let no reproach be [cast] on you on this day. May Allāh forgive you and He is the Most Merciful among those who show mercy."

Allāma Uthmānī ؒ writes: 'Hadhrat Yūsuf ؑ did not like to hear even these words from his brothers. He said: 'Do not talk like that. Today I do not accuse you, [nor will I ever do so in the future], I have pardoned all your faults. The words which I said were only to expresse [my] gratitude unto Allāh and the result of patience and piety. I shall never repeat your faults and I pray to Allāh that He may also forgive you. He is the Kindest of the Kind and Most Merciful among those who show mercy. My kindness too is the reflection of His Kindness.'

---

[207] Khāzin 40/3.

Note: Nasafī 🙪 narrates here that the day when our Holy Prophet Muhammad 🙪 conquered Makkah, he stood at the door of the Kā'bā. The *Quraish* had gathered around him. He asked them: *'How do you expect me to deal with you?'* They replied: 'You are an honourable brother and the son of an honourable brother, our fate is in your hands.' He said: *'I will say what my brother Yūsuf said, 'Let no reproach be upon you.'* [208]

Hadhrat Maulānā Abul-Hasan Alī Nadwī 🙪 has mentioned this in some detail. I narrate here his blessed words from his book, 'Muhammad: *Rasūl-ullāh*' He writes: 'The Apostle 🙪 stood at the door of the Kā'bā, holding its frame, while the *Quraish* arranged themselves in front of him in the courtyard. The Apostle 🙪 then addressed them, saying: *'There is no God but Allāh alone; He has no associate. He has made good His promise and helped His servant. He has alone overthrown all the confederates. Lo! All the privileges and claims to retaliation and blood are beneath my feet except the custody of the Kā'bā and watering of the pilgrims. O' ye people of Quraish, God has abolished the haughtiness of paganism and the pride of lineage. Man springs from Ādam and Ādam sprang from dust.'*

Thereafter the Apostle 🙪 recited the Qur'ānic verses: *'O Mankind! Lo! We have created you from a male and female, and have made you nations and tribes that ye may know one another. Lo! The noblest of you, in the sight of Allāh, is the best in conduct. Lo! Allāh is Knower, Aware.'*

He also writes: 'A cousin of the Apostle 🙪 whose name was Abū Sufyān ibn al-Hārith happened to meet the Prophet 🙪 on the road. He tried to get to the Apostle 🙪 but was given the cold shoulder by him. Abū Sufyān had insulted, as well as persecuted the Apostle 🙪 in Mecca. Feeling distressed and disconsolate at the indifference of the Prophet 🙪, he approached Ali 🙪 to put forth his lamentation. Alī 🙪 advised him to go again to the apostle 🙪 and say what the brothers of Yūsuf 🙪 had said to him: 'By Allāh, verily Allāh hath preferred thee above us, and we are indeed sinful.' The Apostle 🙪 never likes anybody to exceed him in words, kindness and comforting. Abū Sufyaan did as advised by Alī 🙪 and got the reply from the Apostle 🙪, 'Have no fear this

---

[208] Khāzin and Nasafī 41:3.

day! May Allāh forgive you, and He is the Most Merciful of those who show mercy.' Abū Sufyaan accepted Islām and was thereafter known for his piety and strength of faith, but he was forever ashamed of his past misdeeds. He always talked to the Prophet with downcast eyes and never dared to look into his face.' [209]

Verse 93

اِذْهَبُوْا بِقَمِيْصِيْ هٰذَا فَاَلْقُوْهُ عَلٰى وَجْهِ اَبِىْ

يَاْتِ بَصِيْرًا ۚ وَاْتُوْنِيْ بِاَهْلِكُمْ اَجْمَعِيْنَ ﴿٩٣﴾

"Go with this shirt of mine, and cast it over the face of my father,
he will become clear sighted and bring me all your family."

It seems that Yūsuf asked about the condition of his father and was told of the loss of his sight. He said: 'I am not in a position to go to our native land [Can'ān] and bring the family to Egypt. So you go and bring my parents and all the family to me. In order to make the journey easy, put this cloak on my father's face, he will regain sight and will be able to undertake the journey to Egypt.'

Shāh Sahib says: 'Allāh has the remedy to every disease. Yā'qūb's eyes had lost sight due to the sorrow of separation. It was recovered by the rubbing of a cloth of the separated one. This was a miracle of the Prophet Yūsuf .'

Allāma Uthmānī says: 'Today, it has been established through observations and experiences, that sometimes the blind recover their eyesight by the effect of some serious shock or extraordinary joy.' [210]

Hadhrat Maulānā Idrīs Kāndhlawī writes: 'This is similar to the incident of Muhammad , who put his blessed hand over the eye of a Sahābī and applied his saliva, whereby the sahābī regained his sight.' [211]

[209] Reference from Ml Ali Miya book.
[210] Uthmānī 1094:2.
[211] Ma'āriful Qur'ān 62:4.

Dhahhāk ؏ says: 'The shirt was made from the cloth of Jannah.' Mujāhid also says: 'Hadhrat Jibra'īl ؏ had told Yūsuf ؏ to send his shirt to his father's aid.'

When Ibrāhīm ؏ was made naked and thrown in the fire, Jibra'īl ؏ brought this shirt from Paradise and clothed him. When he died, he passed it onto his son Ishāq ؏ who passed it onto Yā'qūb ؏. When Yā'qūb ؏ feared for Yūsuf ؏, he put this shirt in a *ta'wīz* and made Yūsuf ؏ wear it. Thereafter, when Yūsuf ؏ was thrown into the well, Jibra'īl ؏ came and opened the *ta'wīz*, took the shirt out and put it on Yūsuf ؏. It was this same shirt which was sent to Yā'qūb ؏. It had the fragrance of Paradise and when it would be put on an ill person, he would be cured. [212]

'*...Bring your whole family...*' Kalbī ؏ says, 'They were approximately seventy people. Masrūq ؏ says, 'They were seventy-three [73] men and women.'

Verse 94

وَلَمَّا فَصَلَتِ الْعِيرُ قَالَ اَبُوْهُمْ اِنِّىْ لَاَجِدُ

رِيْحَ يُوْسُفَ لَوْلَاۤ اَنْ تُفَنِّدُوْنِ ﴿٩٤﴾

And when the caravan had departed, their father
said, "Surely, I feel the fragrance of Yūsuf, though ye may call me dotard."

'*When the caravan had departed...*' Khāzin narrates here that Yūsuf ؏ sent - along with his brothers - a protocol of two-hundred [200] personnel and made a lot of other necessary arrangements in order that his parents could have a peaceful journey. [213]

'*Surely, I feel the fragrance of Yūsuf...*' Sūfī Abdul Hamīd Suwatī ؏ writes in his commentary of the Qur'ān, '*Ma'ālimul Irfān*', 'When Yūsuf ؏ was less than ten miles from Can'ān [When Yūsuf was thrown into the well], Yā'qūb ؏ had no idea of his whereabouts, but when the caravan set off from Egypt, which is approximately two-hundred and fifty [250] miles away, he felt that Yūsuf ﷺ was alive and the time for reunion was nigh.

If one ponders over the reason for this difference, one comes to the conclusion that the Prophets do not possess the knowledge of the unseen. Rather, they only know what they are told by Allāh ﷻ. Allāh ﷻ did not want to inform Yā'qūb ﷺ when Yūsuf ﷺ was in the well because he had willed to test Yā'qūb ﷺ. When, after about forty years of separation, Yā'qūb ﷺ had passed his test with full marks, Allāh ﷻ informed him about Yūsuf ﷺ just as the caravan left from Egypt.

Similar is the case of our Holy Prophet Muhammad ﷺ. There are numerous incidents in which he did not know matters of the unseen. For example, when the hypocrites accused our mother Ā'ishā ﷺ, the Prophet ﷺ stayed in the state of confusion for over a month. When revelation finally cleared up the matter, he proclaimed the innocence of Ā'ishā ﷺ. If he had known her innocence from the beginning, he would have declared earlier, that this is only an accusation, and that Ā'ishā ﷺ was innocent.

Similarly, when Jibra'īl ﷺ came down in the form of a human being and asked the Prophet ﷺ, 'What is *Īmān*?' He gave a full reply. Then Jibra'īl ﷺ asked, 'What is Islām?' He gave a clear description. 'What is *Ihsān*?' He explained. But when he asked, 'What is the exact time of the final hour?' The Prophet ﷺ replied, '*The person who is questioned does not know more than the questioner.*' [214]

However, there are plenty of incidents when the Prophet ﷺ told something of the unseen. He said to Alī ﷺ and a few other Sahāba ﷺ, 'Go to the garden of *Khākh*. There you will find a lady who is travelling alone and who has a letter from Hātib Ibn Abī Balta'a to the Pagans of Makkah.' [215] [Hātib had informed them regarding some private matters of the Prophet ﷺ].

Likewise, he was on his deathbed when he revealed the news that Firōz Daylamī ﷺ had killed the tyrant, the impostor, Aswad Anasī. His words were, 'The pious man, Firoz Daylami has killed him.'' [216]

---

[214] Bukhārī 48.
[215] Bukhārī 2785.
[216] Tahdib al-Asma 1/567.

He was in Madīnah when he informed the people that Zaid, Jā'far and Abdullāh Ibn Rawāha ﷺ had all been martyred in the battle field of Mūta. Tears were flowing from his eyes while he was saying these words. [217]

He was in Madīnah when he said, '*A friend of yours, As'hama has died in Habasha [Ethiopia]. Let us perform his janazah prayer.*' [218] Thereafter, he made the Sahabah ﷺ stand in a row and performed the *janāza* as though it was in front of them. This list can go on and on.

In short, the Prophets knew a lot of the unseen, but only if the will of Allāh ﷺ prevailed with it. Otherwise they were human beings. We also believe that our Prophet ﷺ had been given the knowledge of previous people as well as those who are yet to come, and he is the most knowledgeable person who has set foot on the face of this earth.

However, he cannot be called '*Aalim of ghayb*'. This is because *Ilm* of *ghayb* is to know each and every little detail of everything in the universe. This is a *sifat* [attribute] of Allāh ﷺ. We should avoid using such attributes for anyone else. The incidents mentioned above could be classed as '*Ittilaa alal ghayb*' having been informed of some *ghayb*. This is upto Allāh ﷺ. He informs whoever He wills, with whatever He wills.

'*If ye do not call me a dotard...*' A dotard is a person who has a weakness in memory due to old age, who keeps engaged in useless talk. Yā'qūb ﷺ feared that they might call him a dotard, so he advised them from the beginning so that they control their tongue.

Our Prophet ﷺ has used this word in a *Hadīth*, where he describes the laxity of a person towards his preparation for *Ākhirah*. He says:

مَا يَنْتَظِرُ اَحَدُكُمْ اِلَّا غِنًى مُطْغِياً اَوْ فَقْرًا مُنْسِيًا اَوْ مَرْضًا مُفْسِدًا اَوْ هَرَمًا مُفْنِدًا اَوْ مَوْتًا مُجْهِزًا اَوِ الدَّجَّالَ فَالدَّجَّالُ شَرُّ غَاءِبٍ يُنْتَظَرُ اَوِ السَّاعَةَ فَالسَّاعَةُ اَدْهى وَاَمَرُّ ـ

'[It seems as though] You are only waiting for wealth which makes you a transgressor, or poverty which would result in forgetfulness, or illness which

---

[217] Bukhārī 3474.
[218] Bukhārī 1242, Nasāi 1954.

ruins your body, or old age which would make you a dotard, or death which would come all of a sudden, or the Dajjal in which case the Dajjal is the most evil person who could be waited for, or the hour in which case the hour is the most shocking and the most bitter thing.' [219]

Verse 95

$$ قَالُوْا تَاللهِ اِنَّكَ لَفِيْ ضَلٰلِكَ الْقَدِيْمِ ﴿٩٥﴾ $$

They said, "By Allāh! Thou art in thy old-time illusion."

'*They said....*' The People surrounding Hadhrat Yā'qūb ﷺ said to Hadhrat Yā'qūb ﷺ that the old ideas about Yūsuf ﷺ, his hope for meeting Yūsuf ﷺ again, and his extreme love for him, were seated in his heart and these emotions were [mistakenly, in their eyes] being transformed in the fragrance of Yūsuf ﷺ.

Khāzin says: 'It was the grandsons of Yā'qūb ﷺ and his other family members who had uttered these words. His sons were in Egypt and they were bringing the good news.'

The word '*Dhalāl*' means to be diverted off the right track. Here it means that the right thing to do is to completely forget Yūsuf ﷺ, because, it was assumed that he was dead. His relatives were in disbelief that even now, Yā'qūb ﷺ could not get thoughts of a reunion with Yūsuf ﷺ out of his mind. This, seemingly, was his error and a delusion.

In Sūrah Duhā, Allāh ﷻ says to the Holy Prophet ﷺ: "*Did he not find thee an orphan and give thee shelter. And he found thee wandering and he gave thee guidance. And he found thee in need and he made thee independent.*" [220]

In the middle of the verse, the word '*Dhalāl*' is used, which has been translated here using the word '*wandering*'. Before he was blessed with Prophethood, our Prophet Muhammad ﷺ was putting a huge effort in his quest for the truth. Sometimes he would go to a cave and sit there for hours on end, pondering over the creation and its Creator, worshipping in the way he had learnt, with what was left from the religion of his forefather Ibrāhīm

---

Tirmidhī 2306.
Qur'ān 93:6-8.

🕮. He had never, for once, bowed down to an idol, nor had he ever believed that the idols could take a person closer to God, or that the angels were the daughters of God. He never committed fornication, never consumed wine, and never lied, nor was he dishonest, he never talked bad about other people, to the point that historians have written that he had never opened his *awra* [*satar* - the bare parts of the body which should be covered. For men, the navel to the knees] in front of anyone even though those practices were widespread and common at the time.

Verse 96

فَلَمَّآ اَنْ جَآءَ الْبَشِيْرُ اَلْقٰهُ عَلٰى وَجْهِهٖ فَارْتَدَّ بَصِيْرًا ج

قَالَ اَلَمْ اَقُلْ لَّكُمْ ج اِنِّىْ اَعْلَمُ مِنَ الله مَا لَا تَعْلَمُوْنَ ﴿٩٦﴾

Then when the bearer of glad tidings arrived, he cast it [the shirt] upon his face and he became clear sighted. He said, "Did I not tell you that I knew from Allāh what you do not know."

'Then when the bearer of....' Khāzin narrates from Suddī who said that this was Yahūzā. He was the one who had brought Yūsuf's 🕮 shirt, clogged in blood and said that a wolf had devoured Yūsuf 🕮. He wanted to make amends for that. He wanted to make his father happy just as he had caused him so much grief earlier.

'He regained his sight...' As mentioned before, this was a miracle of Yūsuf 🕮. Allāh 🕮 had bestowed his Prophets with such miracles.

Here, Abdullāh Yūsuf Alī has written words which grieved me. He writes: 'Both his physical and mental visions now became clear and bright as before.'

How can a Prophet's mental vision not be clear and bright? Is he trying to say that a Prophet of Allāh 🕮 had become insane? *Astaghfirullāh!* It is an established fact that Allāh 🕮 had chosen for Prophethood only those who were the best of creation at that particular time. Among the requirements of Prophethood is to be complete physically and mentally.

Abdullāh Yūsuf Alī does not realise that when the mental vision does not stay right, then one no longer has the capability of receiving revelation.

Allāh ﷻ says to our Prophet ﷺ: 'Thou art not, by the grace of thy lord, mad or possessed, nay for thee, is a reward entailing. And surely thou hast sublime morals.' [221]

Khazin narrates here that when he regained his sight, the first thing he asked was, 'How is Yūsuf ﷺ?' Yahūzā replied, 'He is the king of Egypt.' Yā'qūb ﷺ asked, 'What have I to do with being a king? How is his *deen*?' Yahūzā replied: 'He is on the *deen* of Islām.'

There is a great lesson for us in these questions. How worried are we about the *deen* and *imān* of our offspring? Are we guiding them straight or are we neglecting our duty towards their upbringing?

Verse 97

قَالُوْا يٰٓاَبَانَا اسْتَغْفِرْ لَنَا ذُنُوْبَنَآ اِنَّا كُنَّا خٰطِئِيْنَ ﴿٩٧﴾

They said, "Father! Ask for forgiveness of our sins. For we were truly at fault."

They requested Yā'qūb ﷺ to ask Allāh ﷻ to forgive their sins. They had committed heavy blunders. They meant to say, that first Yā'qūb ﷺ should forgive them and then ask Allāh ﷻ with a clean heart for their forgiveness. [A person who himself does not forgive, cannot be expected to beseech Allāh ﷻ for forgiveness]. [222]

Verse 98

قَالَ سَوْفَ اَسْتَغْفِرُ لَكُمْ رَبِّىْ ۙ اِنَّهٗ هُوَ الْغَفُوْرُ الرَّحِيْمُ ﴿٩٨﴾

He said, "Soon I will ask my Lord for forgiveness for you:
for He, only He, is the Oft Forgiving, Most Merciful."

'Soon I shall ask...' Yā'qūb ﷺ replied by saying, 'let the moment of acceptance come and I shall definitely ask forgiveness for you.' There are two opinions with regards to this moment:

---

[221] Qur'ān 68:2-4.
[222] Tafsīr Uthmānī 1095:2.

1. The time of *Tahajjud*, just before the break of dawn. Ibn Kathīr ﷫ narrates: Umar ﷜ would come to the Masjid at the time of *sahr* [pre-dawn]. He would hear a person supplicating, 'O Allāh, You called upon me and I am here. You ordered me and I obeyed, this is the time of *sahr*, so forgive me.' He listened carefully and noticed that the voice was from the house of Abdullāh Ibn Mas'ūd ﷜. He asked Ibn Mas'ūd ﷜ about this. Ibn Mas'ūd ﷜ replied, 'Ya'qūb ﷫ delayed his son's request up to the time of *sahr*, when he said, *'Soon I will ask for forgiveness for you from my Lord.'* This is an indication from Ibn Mas'ūd ﷜ of the time of the acceptance of *dua* on the basis that it was during this time that Ya'qūb ﷫ had asked for forgiveness for his children.

One *Hadīth* says that when the last portion of the night is left, Allāh ﷻ calls out from the sky, *'Who is there to call Me, so that I may answer his call, who is there to ask Me for forgiveness, so that I may forgive him...'* [223]

In another *Hadīth*, the Prophet ﷺ was asked, 'Which *dua* is most accepted?' He replied, *'Any dua made in the middle of the last portion of the night and after fardh salāh.'* [i.e If you divide the night into six parts for example, then the middle of the last part which is the best time for *Tahajjud*, this is also the best time for *dua*]. [224]

Khāzin writes, 'When the time of *sahr* arrived, Ya'qūb ﷫ performed his *salāh*, then he raised his hands and supplicated to Allāh ﷻ, 'O' Allāh ﷻ, forgive me, my yearning for and crying over Yūsuf ﷫, and my impatience over him, and forgive my children for what they did to Yūsuf ﷫.' Allāh ﷻ revealed upon Ya'qūb ﷫, 'I have forgiven you and them all.'

2. The second opinion is narrated from Ibn Abbās ﷜, who says, 'He delayed his supplication to the night of Jumu'ah.'

Verse 99

فَلَمَّا دَخَلُوْا عَلٰى يُوْسُفَ اٰوٰى اِلَيْهِ اَبَوَيْهِ وَقَالَ

[223] Bukhārī 5846, Muslim 1261.
[224] Tirmidhī 3421.

$$ \text{﴿٩٩﴾ ادْخُلُوْا مِصْرَ اِنْ شَاءَ اللهُ اٰمِنِيْنَ} $$

Then when they entered unto Yūsuf, he took his parents unto himself and said,
'Enter Misr [Egypt] in safety and security Inshā-Allāh.'

'*Then when they entered unto Yūsuf...*' The ulamā say that due to the request of
Yūsuf 灘, his whole family migrated from Can'ān and moved to Misr [Egypt].
When the news came that they are now approaching the city, Yūsuf 灘 came
out of the city to welcome them. It is said that the great king of Egypt also
came out to greet them. An army of four thousand [4000] soldiers
accompanied him. Many Egyptians also came with them. When Yā'qūb 灘
saw the huge crowds and the horsemen, he asked, 'Is this the Pharaoh of
Egypt?' His son Yahūzā replied, 'No, this is your son, Yūsuf.'

When they came closer, they dismounted and hugged each other. They
greeted each other in a way a father would greet his long lost son, and a
loving son would greet his respectful father. Tears streamed down their
cheeks. Yūsuf 灘 said to his father, 'Father! I heard that you cried so much
over my separation that your sight was lost. Were we not to gather on the
Day of Judgement?' Yā'qūb 灘 replied, 'Yes, but I was afraid that your dream
might be snatched from you, in which case there would never be any reunion
in the hereafter.' [225]

'*He provided you a place...*' He gave his parents a respectable place near him.

Suddī 灘 says, 'His mother had died. His father then married his maternal
aunt.' Since an aunt is like a second mother, as the *Hadīth* says, '*The maternal
aunt is like a mother.*' [226] The Qur'ān used the phrase, 'His parents.'

However, Hasan Basrī 灘 is of the opinion, that this was his real mother and
she was still alive. Hāfiz Ibn Kathīr 灘 also says that there is no evidence to
prove that his mother had died. The clear verse of the Qur'ān says that she
was still alive and that seems to be the case.

---

[225] Khāzin.
[226] Abū Dāwūd 2278.

'Enter Misr with peace Inshā-Allāh...' Some commentators say that the condition 'Inshā-Allāh' is related to peace. That is to say that they had no fear of famine or any other issues in this city.

Some say that people would be afraid of the rulers when they entered Egypt. They had this custom of seeking refuge from the King before entering the city. So Yūsuf ﷺ said to his family that there is no need for this. You will be staying here with peace and tranquillity.

Some say that 'Inshā-Allāh' is for tabarruk [attain Baraka - blessings]. It is the same as when our Prophet ﷺ would enter a graveyard he would say, 'Peace be upon you, O dwellers of the house of believers! Inshā-Allāh we will soon be joining you.' So Inshā-Allāh here is for barakah because death is inevitable.

Verse 100

وَرَفَعَ اَبَوَيْهِ عَلَى الْعَرْشِ وَخَرُّوْا لَهُ سُجَّدًا ۚ وَقَالَ يَاَبَتِ هٰذَا تَأْوِيْلُ رُءْيَايَ مِنْ قَبْلُ ۫ قَدْ جَعَلَهَا رَبِّيْ حَقًّا ؕ وَقَدْ اَحْسَنَ بِيْ اِذْ اَخْرَجَنِيْ مِنَ السِّجْنِ وَجَآءَ بِكُمْ مِّنَ الْبَدْوِ مِنْ ؕ بَعْدِ اَنْ نَّزَغَ الشَّيْطٰنُ بَيْنِيْ وَبَيْنَ اِخْوَتِيْ ؕ اِنَّ رَبِّيْ لَطِيْفٌ لِّمَا يَشَآءُ ؕ اِنَّهُ هُوَ الْعَلِيْمُ الْحَكِيْمُ ﴿١٠٠﴾

And he raised his parents high on the throne. And they all fell down into prostration before him and said, "Father! This is the interpretation of the dream which I saw long ago: My Lord has now made it come true; He was indeed good to me when He took me out of prison and brought you [all here] out of the desert, after Satan had stirred strife between me and my brethren. Verily my Lord plans deep what He wills, no doubt He is All-Knowing, All Wise."

Allāma Uthmānī ﷺ writes: 'Yūsuf ﷺ paid homage to his parents and seated them high with grace and esteem. However, Yūsuf ﷺ could not avoid the homage which was given to him by Allāh ﷻ. According to the customs of that time, the parents of Yūsuf ﷺ and all his brothers fell down into prostration before him. This sajdah was that of reverence which had been lawful up to the era of Hadhrat Īsā ﷺ since the days of Ādam ﷺ, according to the well-known commentator, Ibn Kathīr ﷺ. It has been made unlawful by the *Sharī'ah* of Islām as highlighted by many traditions. Hadhrat Shāh Abdul Qādir Sahib ﷺ has expounded on the unlawfulness of the *sajdah* of reverence.

Note: Reverence and worship are two different things. Reverence of another is permissible, but worship is never permissible for anything beside Allāh ﷻ. Worshipping other than Allāh ﷻ is clear polytheism. The *sajdah* of worship has never been allowed in any heavenly constitution. Of course the *sajdah* of reverence was permissible in the previous constitutions only for the show of respect within certain limits. The *Sharī'ah* of Muhammad ﷺ has cut the root of this *sajdah* because the degree of *tawhīd* in Islām is the most supreme.

Shāh Walīullāh Sahib ﷺ has dealt with many kinds of *shirk* in his famous book *'Hujjat-ullāh al-Bāligah'* in a succinct manner.

Shāh Sahib has explained that if a person prostrates in front of an idol, he will instantly be classed as a *mushrik*, because the *Sharī'ah* has classed some acts to be clear *kufr* [disbelief], for example: wearing a cross, swearing at Allāh ﷻ, or any of his Prophets ﷺ, throwing the Qur'ān in a tip, or prostrating before an idol, amongst other actions.

However, if somebody prostrates in front of another human being, or in front of a grave, we cannot instantly rule them out of Islām, or label them a *mushrik*, committing *shirk*. They will be questioned about the very reason for their prostration. If they say that their intention was to worship that particular person, then they will be classed as *mushrik*.

However, if the reason for their prostration was to pay respect to the person, then they will have committed a *harām* act; therefore, the person would be considered a *fāsiq* [open sinner], and not a *mushrik*.

Many ignorant people do not know the difference, and then go on to label people with *shirk*. This is a very abhorrent thing to do.

Imām Abū Hanīfā ﷺ used to say that if there were ninety-nine [99] interpretations of a person's ambiguous statement which would deem him a *kāfir*, and only one interpretation which would keep him a Muslim, then we would call him a Muslim due to that one interpretation.[227] This is why we see

---

[227] Minah ul-Rawdh al-Azhar Fi Sharh al-Fiqh al-Akbar, p.445

many sects came into being in the time of the *salaf* [members of the first 3 generations after The Messenger ﷺ], especially the *Mu'tazila*, *Khawārij*, *Rawāfidh* and the *Qadariyyah*. They had misguided beliefs, yet the *salaf* called them 'The Misguided Sects'. Never did any of the *salaf* label them as *kāfirs*.

The conclusion is that one should be very cautious in the *mas'ala* [ruling] of *imān* and *kufr*, and one should not keep a narrow mind by driving people out of the fold of Islām. Rather, one should be broadminded, and try keeping Islām as broad as possible. May Allāh ﷻ give us the correct understanding of *Dīn. Āmīn.*

Sūfī Abdul Hamīd Sahib ﷺ says, 'The trials of separation were over. Reunion had taken place. Two years had passed in the famine. Five years were left. Due to the excellent organisation of Yūsuf's ﷺ ration, the stock was distributed equally and fairly. A whole country had been saved from death by starvation. That is why Yūsuf ﷺ said, 'Enter in peace and security.' This is why everyone bowed down in prostration to Yūsuf ﷺ.

'*And brought you out of the desert...*' This indicates that living in a town or a city is better than living in a village. The Prophet ﷺ says, '*Whosoever lives in the desert shall become hard hearted* [due to a lack of exposure to civilisation].' [228]

'*And Satan had stirred...*' See how humble and understanding Hadhrat Yūsuf ﷺ was. He does not utter a single word which would embarrass his brothers. On the contrary, he curses Shaytān for stirring between them. His words take off a great amount of weight from the shoulders of his brothers.

'*Verily my Lord plans deep...*' It was His plan to take me out of the well and into the courtyard of the Azīz of Misr, and then to the throne. Indeed, He is All-Wise, All-Knowing.

---

[228] Mishkāt.

Verse 101

رَبِّ قَدْ اٰتَيْتَنِيْ مِنَ الْمُلْكِ وَعَلَّمْتَنِيْ مِنْ تَاْوِيْلِ الْاَحَادِيْثِ ۚ فَاطِرَ
السَّمٰوٰتِ وَالْاَرْضِ ۖ اَنْتَ وَلِيِّ فِي الدُّنْيَا وَالْاٰخِرَةِ ۚ تَوَفَّنِيْ مُسْلِمًا
وَّاَلْحِقْنِيْ بِالصّٰلِحِيْنَ ﴿۱۰۱﴾

My Lord! Thou has bestowed on me some power and has taught me of the
interpretation of discourses. Creator of the heavens and the earth! Thou art my
patron in this world, and in the hereafter, cause me to die as a Muslim, and join
me with the righteous.

Hāfiz ibn Kathīr ﷺ writes: 'When Allāh ﷻ completed his favours upon Yūsuf
ﷺ, by uniting him with his parents and his brothers, and by giving him a
kingdom as well as Prophethood, he pleaded to his Lord to give him death
while he was a Muslim, and to join him with his pious predecessors, the
prophets and messengers who were sent before him.'

We note here two essentials:

Firstly, to die as a Muslim. One *Hadīth* says, '*Actions are according to their
endings.*'[229] i.e. No matter what a person does in his entire life, when the later
part of his life is in accordance to the requirement of *Sharī'ah*, then Allāh ﷻ
will judge him by that. Many a time, a person lives a sinful life, but before
death, he turns towards Allāh ﷻ, repents from all sins, and becomes one of
His accepted servants.

Hadhrat Shaykh al-Hadīth, Maulānā Muhammad Zakarīyā ﷺ narrates a
heart-rending story in '*Fadhā'il-e-Sadaqāt*'. He writes:

Shaykh Abdul Wāhid bin Zaid ﷺ [a well-known spiritual leader of the Chistī
order of Sūfīs], has narrated the following story: 'Once we were travelling on
a ship, when a storm blew our ship to an island, where we landed and saw a
man engaged in idol worship. We said to him, 'Whom do you worship?' He
pointed towards the idol. We said, 'You have moulded your God with your
own hands! Our Lord whom we worship has created all this and is the Creator
of all things. Handmade idols are not worthy of worship.' The man asked,

---

229 Bukhārī 6117.

'Whom do you worship?' We replied, 'We worship Allāh; the Sacred Being Whose Throne is above the heavens, Who controls the affairs of the world, Whose Majesty and Glory transcends everything.' The man said, 'How did you come to know of Him?' We said, 'Our Lord sent us His apostle who was noble of birth and most excellent of character. This prophet taught us all these things.' He said, 'Where is that prophet now?' We said, 'After conveying the message of his Lord, his obligation was fulfilled, so our Lord called him back to Him, in order to grant him good recompense and reward him for conveying His message completely and properly.' The man said, 'Did this Prophet leave behind any signs of his Apostleship [any source of guidance] for you?' We said. 'He left for us the Word of Allāh, the Holy Qur'ān'.

The man asked to be shown the Qur'ān, and we placed the Holy Qur'ān before him. He said that he did not know how to read, and then requested us to recite from the Qur'ān. We recited a sūrah from the Qur'ān, to which he listened, with tears flowing from his eyes. After we had recited it up to the last verse, he said, 'We owe it to Him Who revealed this Book, that we never disobey His commandments.' After this, he accepted Islam, and we taught him the fundamentals of Islam, and some of the commandments of Allāh. We also taught him a few sūrahs of the Holy Qur'ān. At nightfall, after observing the Ishā *salāh*, as we were preparing to go to bed, the man said, 'Does your Lord also sleep?' We said, 'He is the Living, the Eternal, neither slumber nor sleep overtakes Him.' [230] He then said, 'How impudent of you to sleep while your Lord is Awake!' We were amazed at his words. When we were going to leave the island, the man asked us to take him with us, saying that he wished to learn more of the new faith. We took him on board, and our boat sailed back to the city of Abadhaan. On reaching there, I said to my friends, 'Let us make contribution for our newly converted brother, for he must be needing money for his provision.' We collected some dirhams and presented the money to him. He asked, 'What is this?' We told him that it was something to help him for his needs. He recited, '*Lā Ilāhā Illallāh*.' He then said, 'You have shown me a path, which you are not following yourselves. I lived in an island and worshipped an idol instead of worshipping Allāh and still He did not destroy me, nor let me die of hunger, though I did not know Him. How can

---

[230] Qur'ān 2:255.

He destroy me now, when I know Him [and worship Him!?]' Three days later, we were told that he was on his deathbed, and his last hour had drawn near. We visited him and asked him if he had any wish. He replied, 'He who sent you to the island for my 'Hidāyah' has fulfilled all my wishes.'

As we sat here, I [Abdul Wāhid] dozed off and dreamt that I saw a green and pleasant garden, in which there stood a magnificent domed building. A throne was placed in a room of the building, on which there sat a most beautiful damsel, the like of whom, in beauty, I had never seen before. She was saying, 'O, send him to me quickly, I beseech you in the name of Allāh; I am so fond of him that I cannot bear to be separated from him anymore.' I woke up and saw that his soul had departed from the body. We washed him, shrouded him and laid him to rest in the grave, after offering his funeral prayers.

That night I saw the same garden and the same dome in a dream, with the same beautiful maid reclining on her throne, while I saw a man reciting this verse, 'The angels enter unto them from every gate, saying: Peace be upon you [glad tidings of being protected against all manner of affliction], because you persevered [held fast to deen]. Ah! Sweet passing will be the sequel of [heavenly] home. [231]

These are the miraculous manifestations of Allāh's ﷻ Infinite Bounty and His Forgiveness! The man spent his life in worshipping an idol, but when his hour of death drew near, Allāh ﷻ raised a storm to blow a boat to the island, and thus the man was granted eternal heavenly bliss through the guidance of the people on board.

'O Sovereign Lord of the Universe! No one can withhold what You give, nor can anyone give what You have witheld.'

In one Hadīth, the Prophet ﷺ says, 'O Allāh, make the best portion of my life the last one, and my best deeds the final ones, and my best the day I meet you.'

The second supplication Yūsuf ﷺ made, was 'to be joined with the pious ones.' Not only did Yūsuf ﷺ supplicate in this manner, but Sulaimān ﷺ also supplicated with the same words:

$$ \text{وَاَدْخِلْنِيْ بِرَحْمَتِكَ فِيْ عِبَادِكَ الصّٰلِحِيْنَ} \bigcirc $$

"And admit me by thy grace to the ranks of thy righteous servants." [232]

---

[231] Qur'ān 13:23-24.
[232] Qur'ān 27:19.

Our Prophet ﷺ also supplicated with the words:

$$ اَللّٰهُمَّ اِنِّى اَسْأَلُكَ الْفَوْزَ عِنْدَ الْقَضَاءِ وَنُزُلَ الشُّهَدَاءِ $$

$$ وَعَيْشَ السُّعَدَاءِ وَمُرَافَقَةَ الْاَنْبِيَاءِ وَالنَّصْرَ عَلَى الْاَعْدَاءِ^{233} $$

'O Allāh, I beseech you for success in whatever you destine for me, for the hospitality of the martyrs and for living like the fortunate ones, and for the company of the Prophets, and for assistance against the enemies.' [234]

This shows how important and effective good company is, especially when a person has some dominion over people, his contact will mostly be with the worldly people, therefore he should constantly supplicate in these words. The love for these pious people should be kept in mind.

A poet says:

$$ أُحِبُّ الصَّالِحِيْنَ وَلَسْتُ مِنْهُمْ $$

$$ لَعَلَّ اللهَ يَرْزُقُنِيْ صَلَاحًا ـ $$

'I love the pious even though I am not from them,
Maybe Allāh will gift me with a little piety.'

Allāma Uthmānī ﷺ writes that Hadhrat Yūsuf ﷺ led the administration of the country during the lifetime of Hadhrat Yā'qūb ﷺ. After his death, he left the administration by his own will. The commentators have written that Hadhrat Yā'qūb ﷺ in his last will had decided that he should be buried in his native land, Shām. So Hadhrat Yūsuf ﷺ brought the coffin to Shām according to his father's will. Hadhrat Yūsuf ﷺ had said that a time would come when the Banū Isrā'īl would get out of Egypt, so they should also take his coffin with him. When Hadhrat Mūsā ﷺ left Egypt with the Banū Isrā'īl, he also took the coffin of Hadhrat Yūsuf ﷺ with him.

Note: Here one may ask, 'Why did a Prophet of Allāh ask for death?' We have been instructed not to desire for our death. A *Hadīth* in Musnad Ahmed states:

---

[233] Tirmidhī 3419
[234] Sunan Tirmidhī and Ibn Khuzaima.

'*None of you should desire for death due to any hardship which befalls him.*' One should not supplicate for death to come before its destined time, except if one has complete reliance on his deeds [which is impossible]. When a person dies, his deeds are terminated. A true believer can only increase his good deeds.

Therefore, to supplicate or call upon death is very much disliked. Several answers could be put forward in reply to this question:

1. This was permissible in the *Sharī'ah* of Yūsuf 🙾 and it has been prohibited from our *Sharī'ah*. Qatādā says: 'No Prophet besides Yūsuf 🙾 asked for death. [235]

2. He supplicated when his time of departure drew near and he was about to leave this world. It is the same as when our Prophet said in his last words: 'O Allāh! I request for the loftiest companion.' i.e. Yourself.

3. He did not ask for death to arrive instantly. The words of his *duā* indicate that he meant to say that whenever the time comes, sooner or later, he wishes to die as a Muslim, and to be joined with his forefathers. It is the same when we pray, 'O Allāh! Let us live as Muslims, and let us die as Muslims, and join us with the pious ones.'

Ibn Kathīr 🙾 mentioned the above answers and he goes on to say that the prohibition is related to desiring for death due to some hardships of the *dunyā*, i.e. worldly affairs such as poverty, ill health etc.

However, if the *fitna* is in one's *dīn*, then he may ask for death. The proof of this is in the story of the magicians of Firoun. When Firoun warned them with grave punishment, and they feared that the tyrant might force them into disbelief, they supplicated:

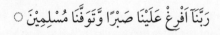

رَبَّنَآ أَفۡرِغۡ عَلَيۡنَا صَبۡرًا وَّتَوَفَّنَا مُسۡلِمِيۡنَ ۞

---

[235] Khāzin.

"O our Lord, pour out on us patience and consistency, and let us die as Muslims." [236]

When Hadhrat Maryam ﷺ feared her tribe, she said:

$$يٰلَيْتَنِيْ مِتُّ قَبْلَ هٰذَا وَكُنْتُ نَسْيًا مَّنسِيًّا ۝$$

"How I wish that I had died before this and become a forgotten thing." [237]

The duā in the *Hadīth* of Mū'āz ﷺ in Musnad Ahmed and Tirmidhī:

$$وَاِذَا اَرَدْتَّ بِقَوْمٍ فِتْنَةً فَتَوَفَّنِيْ غَيْرَ مَفْتُوْنٍ ـ$$

'When you [O Allāh] intend to send some fitna upon a nation, then call me to you without getting indulged in the *fitna*.'

Hāfiz Ibn Kathīr ﷺ mentions in his tafsīr, that when Hadhrat Alī ibn Abī Tālib ﷺ realised during his last days that the affairs are getting out of hand and matters can only get worse, he prayed:

$$اَللّٰهُمَّ خُذْنِيْ اِلَيْكَ فَقَدْ سَئِمْتُهُمْ وَسَئِمُوْنِيْ ـ$$

'O Allāh! Take me to thyself, indeed I have become sick of them and they are also tired of me.'

When Hadhrat Imām Bukhārī ﷺ was involved in the *fitna*, with the *Amīr* of Khurāsān, he supplicated:

$$اَللّٰهُمَّ قَدْ ضَاقَتْ عَلَيَّ الْاَرْضُ بِمَا رَحُبَتْ فَاقْبِضْنِيْ اِلَيْكَ ـ$$

'O Allāh! The earth, although being so broad and wide has become cramped for me, therefore take me to yourself.'

---

[236] Qur'ān 7:126.
[237] Qur'ān 19:23.

Verse 102

$$\text{ذٰلِكَ مِنْ اَنْبَآءِ الْغَيْبِ نُوْحِيْهِ اِلَيْكَ ۚ وَمَا كُنْتَ}$$

$$\text{لَدَيْهِمْ اِذْ اَجْمَعُوْٓا اَمْرَهُمْ وَهُمْ يَمْكُرُوْنَ ﴿١٠٢﴾}$$

"This is from the news of the unseen, which we reveal upon you. And you were not with them when they agreed upon their plan and began to devise."

The story of Hadhrat Yūsuf ﷺ has ended.

In the forthcoming verses Allāh ﷻ declares proof for the Prophethood of Muhammad ﷺ. He says: 'O Muhammad, you have never been to a college nor any school. Nor have you read a book of history. The majority of the people in your vicinity are illiterate. You have also not had the opportunity to benefit from a human teacher. You were not present when the brothers of Yūsuf made a plot against him and threw him into the well. In spite of all this, you narrate in great detail an event which took place several hundred years ago. History can make mistakes, however, your description is so accurate that even the people of the book hasten towards you, so that they can correct their gospels. This cannot be possible except through divine revelation. And divine revelation can only be sent down upon a Prophet. Therefore, you are a Prophet.'

Maulānā Idrīs Kāndhlawī ﷺ writes that Allāh ﷻ declared this proof because the pagans of Makkah had enquired about the story of Yūsuf ﷺ in order to test Prophet Muhammad ﷺ. So Allāh ﷻ says, 'You have seen the proof; is it not time to accept the truth?'

Verse 103

$$\text{وَمَآ اَكْثَرُ النَّاسِ وَلَوْ حَرَصْتَ بِمُؤْمِنِيْنَ ﴿١٠٣﴾}$$

And most men will not believe even though you maybe ever so eager.

In this verse, Allāh ﷻ says that even though the clear proofs are there, you, O prophet, are also very eager to bring the people closer to God Almighty. Most people will not believe. Most people are arrogant, stubborn, in pursuit of their whims and desires, and always aiming to follow the false traditions of their forefathers. Therefore, they don't accept the clear message of Almighty Allāh ﷻ.

History shows most people have strayed and have refused to follow the truth. Even today, four-fifths of the world's population are deprived of believing in the true message.

Verse 104

$$وَمَا تَسْأَلُهُمْ عَلَيْهِ مِنْ اَجْرٍ ط$$

$$اِنْ هُوَ اِلَّا ذِكْرٌ لِّلْعٰلَمِيْنَ ﴿١٠٤﴾$$

And you do not demand from them any reward for this:
it is nothing but an admonishment for the whole world.

'O Prophet! Why do people do this when the advice you are giving them is for free? You have never asked them for any remuneration. All the prophets before you have been doing the same. Surely there is enough admonishment and advice in this Qur'ān for people who want to understand!'

It is notable here that people often like following leaders who demand money; they accept them and put their faith in them. People who follow different cults and shower their money on bāpūs, fake pīrs and bogus liars, whereas the Godly people are mostly ignored. No attention is paid towards them. It seems that people fail to realise the value of the Ahl-ullāh [people of Allāh], and are unable to differentiate between falsehood and truth. It seems this has been the custom from the ancient times.

Verse 105

$$وَكَاَيِّنْ مِّنْ اٰيَةٍ فِى السَّمٰوٰتِ وَالْاَرْضِ$$

$$يَمُرُّوْنَ عَلَيْهَا وَهُمْ عَنْهَا مُعْرِضُوْنَ ﴿١٠٥﴾$$

And there are so many signs in the heavens and the earth that
they do pass by, yet they turn [their faces] away from them.

In the aforementioned verses, Allāh ﷻ had mentioned that although Muhammad ﷺ is unschooled, he has narrated the story of Yūsuf ﷺ in great detail. This is a sign of his Prophethood. In the following verses, Allāh ﷻ says: 'Leave aside this one sign, there are so many other signs in the heavens and the earth that people pass by and yet they never ponder over them.'

The whole universe is a reflection of its Creator. The sun, moon, stars and sky itself testify to their Creator. The cycle of the sun and moon has been going on for thousands of years, yet there is not one single setback in their routine. The skies have no pillar holding them, even though the roof of a small house cannot be held up without support. It is Allāh ﷻ who holds the skies with his great power. In the earth there is a sign of God in everything that surrounds us. Billions of human beings, birds, animals, flowers, mountains, events taking place around us; someone is born, someone is dying. People with different colour, language, attitudes, qualities, and anything that happens; good or ill health, good or bad fortune. Hence, in a nutshell, the whole universe and its events bear testimony to the existence of God, His power, His majesty, His control, His qualities and to His infinite mercy.

An Arabic poet says:

$$\text{فَيَا عَجَبًا كَيْفَ يُعْصَى الْإِلهُ} \quad \text{اَمْ كَيْفَ يَجْحَدُهُ الْجَاحِدُ}$$

$$\text{وَفِيْ كُلِّ شَيْءٍ لَهُ ايَةٌ} \quad \text{تَدُلُّ عَلَى اَنَّهُ وَاحِد}$$

'How strange! How can one disobey the Lord
or how can a refuser refuse His existence?
When there is a sign of Him in each and everything
which proves that He Himself is the One and Only?'

Hadhrat Alī ﷺ would say:

$$\text{عَرَفْتُ رَبِّيْ بِفَسْخِ الْعَزَائِمِ ـ}$$

'I recognise my Lord through the cancellations of my firm intentions.'

i.e. many a time, I had organised and prepared, but suddenly something came up and I had to cancel my plans. This made me think that there is a power which has full control over me and sometimes shows itself.

Allāma Uthmānī ﷺ writes: 'As they do not believe in you hearing the Qur'ānic verses, similarly, they do not receive lessons of Divine Oneness whilst observing the signs of the universe. The fact is that their hearing and seeing is only cursory. Had they pondered over the signs and the verses of God, they would have obtained some benefit. But when there is no pondering, how can they obtain *imān*?'

Sir Isaac Newton once said, 'The link, attachment, and connection between the particles of the universe, even though thousands of years have passed over them is such that it is impossible for them to be balanced except by the One Being who is before everything, and who has the knowledge of and control over everything.' [238]

Professor Lenny says, 'God, full of knowledge and power, opens Himself before me in His mysterious and amazing ways and leaves me wondering. In each and everything, no matter how small it may be, His wisdom is manifest and the power of creation is evident.' [239]

Verse 106

وَمَا يُؤْمِنُ اَكْثَرُهُمْ بِاللهِ اِلَّا وَهُمْ مُّشْرِكُوْنَ ﴿١٠٦﴾

And most of them do not believe in Allāh except by associating others [as partners] with Him.

Allāma Uthmānī ﷺ writes: 'Most people believe in God by their tongue that their creator and Lord is Allāh. But despite this declaration, they are generally indulged in various types of associations.'

There are some who are indulged in associating idols as the Divine's partners. In Sahīh Muslim, it is narrated that the *mushrikīn*, while performing *tawāf* of Ka'bā, would say in their *talbiya*: 'I am here O Lord, I am at your service, You have no partners, except for that partner, who himself, and

---

[238] Translated from Makhzan-e-Akhlāk, Pg. 116.
[239] Translated from Makhzan -e-Akhlāk, Pg. 117.

whatever he possesses, is under your command.' When they would say, 'You have no partners...' the Prophet ﷺ would quietly say, 'Stop! Stop!' i.e. don't add any more words.

The Jews, Christians, and Hindus, while believing in God and His attributes, give power and control to others and worship them. Some say that God has a son whom He sacrificed for the sins of others, and therefore we should worship His son. Some believe that idols have the power to cure, give daily bread, give life, and take life, amongst other beliefs.

Among Muslims are those who pay respect beyond limits to some, other than Allāh ﷻ. This includes prostrating in front of graves, circumambulating them, asking them for daily needs, asking a pious saint to cure an illness, to give a child or ease the suffering of an individual or even to forgive one's sins.

Hasan Basrī ؓ would interpret the above verse with shirk e khafī [The lesser shirk]. Shirk is of two types: Jalī [major] and Khafī [lesser]. The first is to declare openly that God has taken others as partners to Him. The second is to believe in His oneness, but to worship Him without sincerity, with the intention of showing off. This is the habit of hypocrites.

Allāh ﷻ says: 'When they [the hypocrites] stand up to prayer, they stand without earnestness. They want to be seen by people, and little do they hold Allāh in remembrance.' [240]

Hāfiz Ibn Kathīr ؓ narrates that the Prophet ﷺ says, 'Allāh declared, 'I am absolutely free from the assossiation of partners. Whosoever performs a deed while assossiating someone else with me within that action, I will abandon him and his shirk.' [241]

In another narration, he says, 'Such a person [who does good actions to please others] should seek his reward from the one who he wanted to show.' [242]

The Prophet ﷺ says, 'The thing I fear most over you is the lesser shirk.' [243]

Imāms Ahmed, Abū Dāwūd, and Tirmidhī ؓ narrate that Abū Bakr Siddīq ؓ said, 'O Prophet of Allāh ﷺ, teach me something that I can say in the morning, evening and when I retire to bed.' He replied, 'Say: 'O Allāh! Creator

[240] Qur'ān 4:142.
[241] Muslim 530.
[242] Musnad Ahmed 9246.
[243] Musnad Ahmed 22528.

of the heavens and the earth, knower of all that is hidden and open, Lord of everything and the owner of it! I bear witness that there is none worthy of worship besides thee. I seek refuge in You from the evil of my ego [nafs] and from the evil of Satan and his associating [shirk].' [244]

May Allāh ﷻ protect us from all forms of *shirk*, and may He grant us the pure and clear *tawhīd*. *Āmīn*.

Here, I would like to narrate some words of wisdom from a great *sūfī* of his time, Shaykh Walī Raslān Ad-Dimashqī ﴾ (he is better known as Arsalān Ad-Dimashqī). Indeed, only the *sūfī* can write such wonderful and beautiful words. I have read them over and over again, and each time I get a new feeling. May Allāh ﷻ give us the ability to appreciate what these pious devotees put before us and to practice on what they teach us. *Āmīn*

Shaykh Walī Raslān [d. 540 AH] says in his book '*Risala fit-Tawhīd*' [His book is called risāla al-tawhīd]: 'Know, that the whole of you, is hidden polytheism [*Shirkun Khafiyyun*] and your realisation and affirmation of oneness [*tawhīd*] will not become evident to you, until you exit from yourself.'

Shaykh Alī Ibn Atiyya Al Hamawī [d. 926] explains the meaning of this. He writes, 'Now then, the most meritorious of all good works and the most excellent of all forms of worshipful obedience, is self-abasement, contrite humility, and casting oneself down at the gate of the Lord in the utmost state of destitution. You must therefore cast yourself down, O tender-hearted brother, at the gate of your Master. You must purify your clothes by ridding them of the filthy stain of polytheism so that you may experience the real meaning of your ritual prayer and attain true nobility.

You must also know that if you adopt an attitude of strict impartiality and view your situation with a discerning eye, and if the gifts of grace assist you in the process, you will come to understand what he [Walī Raslan] means when he says, speaking as one who knows from direct experience, 'The whole of you is covert polytheism.'

What he is saying, in effect, is that every aspect and facet of your being, your dealings and your attitudes, your appetites and your behaviour, all amount to a form of polytheism that is manifestly evident from the perspective of those with developed faculties of insight, although it is covert

---

[244] Tirmidhī 3314, Abū Dāwūd 4405, Musnad Ahmed 7620, Darimī 2573.

from the standpoint of someone who has not reached that stage of development, and whose conscience is not yet clear.

When someone attaches little importance to worshipful servitude, he takes a pretentious view of his own deeds and a distorted view of his own words, and it is only to someone who is seriously committed to worshipful servitude that the significance of this concept can be fully apparent.

As an example of such dedicated commitment, let us consider the case of our Master, the Caliph, Umar Ibn al-Khattāb ﷺ, and how he once surprised Hudhaifa ﷺ by asking him the question, 'Am I one of the hypocrites?' 'No', replied Hudhaifa, 'You are not one of them, and no one after you will ever be as innocent of hypocrisy as you are!' If a man like Umar ﷺ could harbour such a grave suspicion about his own lower self, and could subject it to this kind of scrutiny, what does this tell us about everybody else?

That [kind of dedicated commitment] develops out of a lack of satisfaction with the lower self, that it is the very root of all forms of worshipful obedience. The root of every act of worshipful obedience, of every moment of vigilant awareness, and of every virtue, is the lack of satisfaction with the lower self, just as positive satisfaction with it, is the root of every sinful act of disobedience, every moment of heedless negligence and every lustful indulgence.

Shaykh Abul Hasan ash-Shādhilī ﷺ was making a very similar point when he said: 'If someone dies without having penetrated deeply into this science of ours, he may die while still persisting in the commission of major sins.'

He was stating the simple truth when he uttered these words, and he was stating it without exaggeration. As a matter of fact, he was elucidating and clarifying one of the sayings of the chief of the masters of perfection, Sayyid Arbāb al-Kamāl ﷺ, namely:

'There are three things that lead to salvation, and there are three things that lead to perdition. As for the things that lead to salvation, they are:

1. Dutiful devotion to Allāh, ﷻ both in private and in public.
2. Speaking the truth, whether one is in a state of contentment or a state of exasperation.
3. Frugality in affluence and poverty alike.

As for the three things that lead to perdition, they are:

1. A whimsical passion pursued.
2. A mean-spirited impulse obeyed.
3. A man's conceited satisfaction with his own lower self, this being by far the most serious of them all.'

Pay close attention to his words: 'This being by far the most serious of them all.' Having stated that the causes of perdition are three in number, namely, ostentation, envy and vanity, he declares that vanity is by far the most serious of the three. So tell me, O my brother, do we know of any person who performs the ritual prayer without taking conceited pride in his performance of that prayer? Do we know of any person who keeps the fast without taking conceited pride in his observance of the fast?

Of course, we know of no such person, unless it is someone who Allāh ﷻ has enabled to succeed by virtue of His providential care, and whom He has enfolded in the blessed grace of His saints and His special friends, for they are the physicians who are qualified to treat the diseases of our hearts. They can fairly be described as the tried and tested antidote to the poison that are sins. I urge you therefore, O my brother, to spend time in their company, in order that you may reap the blessed benefits of associating with them and gather their ripe fruit. As a result of this, your habitual pattern of faults and failings will become apparent to you, and, through the blessed grace of their instruction, you will be cleansed of every form of polytheism that screens you from the One who knows all mysteries through and through.

Once you have progressed to this level of purification, you will come to be detached from your ordinary human characteristics. You will come to be far removed from any characteristic that is incompatible with worshipful servitude. The realisation and affirmation of Oneness will come to be evident and plainly manifest. Your lower self will fade into non-existence and you will make your exit from it. And that is the greatest bliss!

As he [Walī Raslān] ؓ has said, 'And your realisation and affirmation of Oneness will not become evident to you until you exit from yourself.' In other words, the spiritual station of the affirmation of Oneness will not become a reality for you, the pure wine of its true meaning will not be imbibed by you, nor one of its distinctive features will be glimpsed by you, and nearness to its inner courtyard and sanctuary will not be permitted to you, not until you exit from your own self, that is, from your lower self, through your detachment from your ordinary human characteristics, the abandonment of your own personal preferences and considerations, and confirmation of the fact that you have, indeed, arrived at the station of worshipful servitude.

'Then, and only then, the lights of the affirmation of Oneness will shine upon you, and the rays of direct knowledge and singular devotion will stream forth from your heart. As far as your outwardly visible form is concerned, you will be in the company of your fellow creatures, but your inner being will be in the company of the Divine Truth. Your outwardly visible form will be dedicated to the practice of the Sacred Law, while your inner being will be dedicated to the experience of reality.

You will demonstrate the distinction between truth and falsehood, not only your tongue, but all the other members of your body will bear witness thereto. The lights of integration will radiate upon you, so that your innermost being, your spirit and your heart's core will come to be imbued therewith.

'You will eat from the fruit of the tree of 'Laa Ilāhā ilallāh' with your Lords permission at any time and on any occasion. You will parade in the splendid clothes of Muhammad *Rasūlullāh* ﷺ, so every spectator will look upon you with honour and every eye will view you with favour.'

'You will advance from the station of faith to the station of active goodness, at which point reality will be disclosed to you, and the true state of affairs will become manifestly obvious to your sight. You must therefore seek forgiveness for all the patterns of behaviour by which your character has previously been defined. You must also confess your sins, for the gifts of grace encompass one who confesses to having sinned.'

Shaykh Walī Raslān goes on to say, 'When your passion has faded away, the door of *haqīqa* [reality] will be unveiled for your benefit, so that your own will is annihilated and *wahdāniyya* [oneness] is unveiled to you and then you will realise that it is He, not you.'

'If you surrender to Him, He will draw you close, but if you argue with Him, He will keep you at a distance.'

'If you draw near through Him, He will bring you close, but if you draw near through yourself, He will keep you at a distance.'

'If you seek Him for your own sake, He will burden you, but if you seek Him for His sake, He will pamper you.'

'Your nearness to Him is your separation from yourself, while your distance from Him is your attachment to yourself.'

'If you come without you, He will accept you, but if you are ignorant of Him, you will be restless. Therefore, the point is that He should be and you should not be.'

'As for the common folk, their works are suspect and as for the elite, their works are good deeds, and as for the elite of the elites, their works are degrees of spiritual progress.'

'Whenever you shun your passion, your faith is reinforced, and whenever you shun your own essence, your realisation and affirmation of oneness is reinforced.'

Creatures are a screen and you are a screen, but the Lord of Truth is not one to be secluded, and he is concealed from you because of yourself, and you are concealed from yourself because of you. So separate from yourself, and you shall witness Him. [245]

The meaning of the last sentence is that all creatures are a *hijab* [veil]. Your *nafs* is also a veil. The Lord is not behind any veil, He is open and He is with you wherever you maybe. You cannot see Him because you are engrossed in your *nafsānī khwāhīshāt* [Lowly Desires]. You do not realise who you are and what your status is because of your *nafs*. So abandon all attachment to your personal characteristics and you shall witness Him. That means you are about to enter *maqām ul-ihsān* [the stage of worshipping Allāh as if you can see Him], therefore you must refrain from indulging in personal inclinations. A *Hadith* says: *'Pay careful attention to Allāh and He will take good care of you. Pay careful attention to Allāh and you will find Him face to face with you. If you have a request to make, you must put your request to Allāh, and if you need to ask for help, you must ask for help from Allāh.'* [246]

---

[245] Al-Risala, P.g 9.
[246] Tirmidhī 2400, Musnad Ahmed 2537.

The *Hadīth* of Jibra'īl defines *Ihsān* as, 'You worship Allāh as though you are seeing Him, because if you don't see Him, He is definitely watching you.' [247]

Verse 107

اَفَاَمِنُوۤا اَنْ تَاْتِيَهُمْ غَاشِيَةٌ مِّنْ عَذَابِ اللهِ اَوْ

تَاْتِيَهُمُ السَّاعَةُ بَغْتَةً وَّهُمْ لَا يَشْعُرُوْنَ ﴿١٠٧﴾

"So do they then feel secure against this, that there may come upon them an all-encompassing cover from the torment of Allāh, or that there may come upon them the Final Hour all of a sudden while they are unaware."

The above verses could be explained through some other verses from Sūrah Al-Nahl. Allāh ﷻ says: *'Do those who devise evil [plots] feel secure that Allāh ﷻ will not cause the earth to swallow them up, or that the punishment will not seize them from directions they little perceive? Or that He will not seize them in the midst of their strutting about, without a chance of their frustrating Him? Or that He may not call them to account by a process of slow wastage? For thy Lord is indeed full of kindness and mercy.'* [248]

In Sūrah Al-A'rāf, Allāh ﷻ says: *'Do the people of the towns feel secure against the coming of Our wrath by night while they sleep? Or did they feel secure against its coming in broad daylight while they played about [care-free]? Did they then feel secure against Allāh's devising? But no one can feel secure from the plan of Allāh, except those [doomed] to ruin.'* [249]

The earthquake in Turkey in the recent past proves that Allāh's ﷻ wrath can strike by night and take thousands of lives. The earthquake in Bhuj [Gujrāt, India] bears testimony that it can strike in broad daylight when people are busy in their day to day engagements. It is a pity that we hear these things on the news, but pay little attention to them. When Allāh ﷻ can send down such a huge punishment on a whole community, why then can He not send down His wrath on any individual? Indeed, He is full of kindness

---

[247] Bukhārī.
[248] Qur'ān 16:45-47.
[249] Qur'ān 7:97-99.

and mercy that He keeps on forgiving and does not punish us for every single evil deed we commit. He says in one place: *'If Allāh were to punish men for their wrongdoing, He would not leave on earth a single living creature; but he gives them respite for a stated term. When their term expires, they would not be able to delay [the punishment] for a single hour, just as they would not be able to bring it forth [for a single hour].'* [250]

The Holy Prophet ﷺ would often supplicate:

$$\text{اَللّٰهُمَّ لَا تُؤْمِنَّا مَكْرَكَ وَلَا تُنْسِنَا ذِكْرَكَ وَلَا}$$

$$\text{تُهْتِكَ عَنَّا سِتْرَكَ وَلَا تَجْعَلْنَا مِنَ الْغَافِلِيْنَ ـ}$$

O Allah! Do not make us senseless towards your hidden devising, and do not let your remembrance die out from our hearts, and do not remove your covering over our faults [which is concealing our sins], and do not make us from among the neglectful.'

Verse 108

$$\text{قُلْ هٰذِهٖ سَبِيْلِيْ اَدْعُوْا اِلَى الله ۗ عَلٰى بَصِيْرَةٍ اَنَا}$$

$$\text{وَمَنِ اتَّبَعَنِيْ ۖ وَسُبْحٰنَ الله وَمَا اَنَا مِنَ الْمُشْرِكِيْنَ ﴿١٠٨﴾}$$

Say thou [O Prophet], 'This is my way. I do invite unto Allāh, resting upon an insight – I and those who follow me. Glorified is Allāh! And I am not of the associators [Those who join partners with Allāh]."

'This is my way....' i.e. my way is one of pure *tawhīd*. I myself say *'Laa Ilāhā Illallāh.'* I call people towards Allāh ﷻ and not towards myself. I do not want people to worship me. I want them to worship the One and Only Allāh ﷻ. I am free from all of the forms of *shirk* and I want to free others as well. I do this with clear insight.

---

[250] Qur'ān 16:61.

'Basīrah' means the knowledge and recognition with which one can differentiate between *Haq* [truth] and *Bātil* [falsehood]. [251]

In Sūrah An'ām we read, *'Now there has come upon you from your Lord the 'Basā'ir' [the clear proofs] to open your eyes. If any will see, it will be for [the good of] his own soul. If any will be blind, it will be to his own [harm].'* [252]

In Arabic, 'Basārah' means to see with the physical eyes, whereas, 'Basīrah' means to see with the eyes of the heart – the insight. So, here Allāh ﷻ orders the Prophet ﷺ to say that this invitation towards *tawhīd* is not based upon any blind following. Rather, it is through clear insight, careful thought and complete understanding - and first establishing *tawhīd* myself - that I have begun to call people towards Faith in one Allāh and the religion of Islam.

In Sūrah Al-An'ām we read, *'Say verily, my Lord hath guided me to a way that is straight – a religion of right – the path trod by Abraham, the true in faith and He certainly did not join Gods with Allāh. Say: 'Truly, my prayer and my service of sacrifice, my life and my death are all for Allāh – the Cherisher of the worlds. He hath no partners. This is what I have been commanded, and I am the first who submits to His will.'* [253]

Allāma Uthmānī ﷺ writes: 'My way is the one of pure *tawhīd*. I invite the whole world to come unto one God, denouncing all whims and fancies, and to obtain the right knowledge of divine oneness, divine attributes, divine perfections and divine commands, through the right way. My companions and I are treading this path in light of reason and argument, discernment and insight. God has given me a light, which has enlightened the hearts of my companions. There is no blind following here. The follower of pure *tawhīd*, perceiving the light of recognition and discernment in his interior at every step and realising the exquisite deliciousness of God's absolute servitude in all movements of absorption, calls out spontaneously:

$$\text{وَسُبْحٰنَ اللهِ وَمَا اَنَا مِنَ الْمُشْرِكِيَنَ ۝}$$

"Allāh be glorified and I am not of the associators [those who join partners with Allāh]."

---

[251] Khāzin.

[252] Qur'ān 6:104.

[253] Qur'ān 6:161-163.

'*And those who follow me...*' Tafsīr Nasafī states here that according to Arabic grammar, these words could be connected to one or two things:

1. 'I invite you towards Allāh', In this case, the verse means, 'I myself, as well as my companions, call people towards Allāh.'

2. 'Resting upon an insight.' i.e. my companions and I myself are resting upon an insight.

Khāzin narrates here from Ibn Abbās ♦ who says: 'Indeed Muhammad ﷺ and his companions were upon the most beautiful path and upon the best guidance. And they are the mines of knowledge and the treasures of faith, and the army of the merciful.'

Abdullāh Ibn Mas'ūd ♦ says: 'Whoever wants to follow, then he should follow those who have died. [In another narration he adds: 'Because those who are alive, can never be safe from *Fitnah* which could deviate them from religion. In that case, those who follow them will also be deviated]. They are the companions of Muhammad ﷺ. They were the best of this nation, with the most virtuous hearts, with the deepest of knowledge and with the least of pretending. They were such that Allāh ﷻ chose them for the company of His Prophet Muhammad ﷺ and for transmitting His religion, Islam. So, emulate their characters [not the characters of the *Kuffār*] and follow their path. They were indeed upon the straight path.' [254]

In *Mazāhir-e-Haq*, the author explains that in the last portion of Ibn Mas'ūd's ♦ life [d. 33AH], some sects had begun to take birth. Ibn Mas'ūd ♦ warned his students not to be deceived by those so-called religious sects. He commanded them to hold firmly to the path of the *Sahāba*. He did not mean that they should only follow those *Sahāba* who had died, and not those who are alive. We consider every single person from amongst the *Sahāba* to be stars of guidance.

Similarly, today we see some sects who say we should only follow the Qur'ān, because a large number of *Hadīth* are forged, so we cannot differentiate between the right and wrong. Some say we should only follow

---

[254] Khāzin, Razeen, Mishkāt, Mazahire Haq, P.g 226. Vol 1.

the *Hadīth* and should not look anywhere else. Both these sects are misguided.

In order to fully understand the commandments of *Sharī'ah*, we have to look at all the sources of *Fiqh*. We have to keep in mind whatever the *Salaf-e-Sālihīn* have transmitted to us. We have to trust the scholars of our time. It is they who can explain the *Sharī'ah* to us. This matter needs a lot of careful writing. I am not in the position to go down that line at the moment. Maybe, if Allāh ﷻ grants me the *tawfīq*, I will concentrate on it in future.

However, we just need to understand that *Muftiyaane Kirām* and *Ulamā-e-Izaam* do not make jurisdical rulings from their own pockets, they simply derive them from the ocean of knowledge at their disposal, and then explain it to us. They are more fearful than us in their duty and in their accountability on the Day of Judgement.

Verse 109

وَمَآ اَرْسَلْنَا مِنْ قَبْلِكَ اِلَّا رِجَالًا نُّوْحِیْ اِلَیْهِمْ مِّنْ اَهْلِ الْقُرٰی ط اَفَلَمْ یَسِیْرُوْا فِی الْاَرْضِ فَیَنْظُرُوْا كَیْفَ كَانَ عَاقِبَةُ الَّذِیْنَ مِنْ قَبْلِهِمْ ط وَلَدَارُ الْاٰخِرَةِ خَیْرٌ لِّلَّذِیْنَ اتَّقَوْا ط اَفَلَا تَعْقِلُوْنَ ﴿۱۰۹﴾

And We did not send before you [as messengers] anyone but men unto whom We revealed [our message]. Men from among the people of the towns. Have they then not travelled throughout the earth so that they may observe the end of those before them? And surely the abode of the hereafter is best for the God-fearing. Do you then not reflect?"

'*And we did not send...*' i.e. It was men whom Allāh ﷻ chose to reveal His message to, so that they may explain that message to the people. He did not choose angels, Jinns or even women to be messengers.

The verse indicates that Prophets were raised among the men-folk only, no woman has ever attained Prophethood. There is a slight difference of opinion here among the *ulamā*:

1. Ibn Hazm ☙ says that some women did reach the rank of Prophethood. Among them are: Maryam, mother of Īsā ☙; Sārah, wife of Ibrāhīm ☙, and the mother of Mūsā ☙.

Some *ulamā* do take this view into account. Their proof is that Angels spoke to these three ladies, as we read in Sūrah Āle Imrān:

1. *'Behold! The angels said: 'O Mary! Allāh Hath chosen thee and purified thee. He has chosen thee above the women of all nations.'* [255]

2. *'And we gave her [Sarah] glad tidings of Ishāq and after him of Yā'qūb.'* [256] It was the angels through whom this good news was given to her.

3. *'And We sent this inspiration to the mother of Moses, Suckle [thy child], but when thou hast fears about him, cat him in to the river.'* [257]

Hāfiz Imādud-dīn Ibn Kathīr ☙ after narrating this view of the said scholars, comments that, 'Although these women had the privilege of speaking to, or receiving the message from the angels, this does not necessarily mean that they have become prophets.' Talking to angels is not sufficient to attain Prophethood.

2. Ibn Kathīr ☙ narrates from Imām Abul-Hasan Al-Ash'ari ☙ who said, 'There is no Prophet among the women. Nevertheless, there have been amongst them the *Siddīqāt* [the truthful ones, those who were exceptionally pious].'

When Allāh ☙ mentions the ranks of those whom he has favoured, He begins with the Prophets, then the *Siddīqīn* [among whom is Abū Bakr Siddīq ☙], then the *Shuhadā*, [The martyrs, among whom is Umar, Uthmān and Alī ☙), then the *Sālihīn.* [258]

---

[255] Qur'ān 3:42.
[256] Qur'ān 11:71.
[257] Qur'ān 28:7.
[258] Qur'ān 4:69.

When Allāh ﷻ mentions the high rank of Maryam ؏, He says, 'Christ, the son of Mary was no more than a messenger; many were messengers that passed away before him. His mother was Siddīqāh.' [259]

In another verse, He says: 'And she testified to the truth of the words of her Lord and of His revelations, she was one of the devout servants.' [260]

If she was a prophet, this would surely have been mentioned when he was praising her for her devotion and servitude.

The majority of the ulamā hold this view, which is also supported by the verse in discussion, i.e. that Allāh ﷻ sent the messengers only among the men-folk. When Allāh ﷻ mentions the Prophets, He often clarifies their Prophethood, e.g. regarding Ismā'īl ؏, He says, 'And Ismā'īl was a messenger and a prophet.'

Sūfī Abdul Hamīd Suwāti ؏ says: 'Allāh ﷻ has created men and women with different qualities. Therefore, neither responsibilities are same nor are their rights. The woman is not compelled to go out for Jihād, Jumu'ah salāh or salāh in a Masjid, amongst other acts of worship. For her own safety, Allāh ﷻ has instructed her to stay in the house and not roam around town like the women of Jāhiliyyah used to do so. Our respected ladies can train and teach girls in their personal matters, however, to go out and work for a living is a responsibility that has been put upon the shoulders of the men-folk.'

A Prophet is a person upon whom Allāh ﷻ sends his revelations so that he may convey the message of Allāh ﷻ to Allāh's people and call them towards the path of Allāh ﷻ. For this purpose, he will have to go out, call people, sit with them, answer their questions and he will have to be patient if faced with abuse or torture. A woman is, by nature, physically weaker than a man. She may not have the strong character to face the difficulties that lie with this mission.

It is imperative for us to understand that women and men *are* different, which doesn't necessarily mean one is inferior to the other, or that we are unequal. Allāh ﷻ has made both genders so than we can complement one another, not compete with one another. Consider the example of a football team and the players within the team. Each player has a different role; the striker's job is to score goals, although at times he is asked to defend. The

---

[259] Qur'ān 5:75.
[260] Qur'ān 66:12.

defender's job is to defend his goal from the opposition, although at times we find them capable of scoring goals! Men and women are part of the same team, not to rival one another, but to help one another. We have our own roles within our families, homes and societies, because we have different skill sets. At times, we are – temporarily - better placed to overtake responsibilities, but generally, we stick to what is within our capabilities.

Women have been modelled and made to carry out certain roles, like bearing children, breastfeeding them, and nurturing them, amongst many other responsibilities. Men have been made physically stronger, which makes them more suitable for working in places like factories, especially those which deal with heavy goods. Of course, there are exceptions to the rule, but some aspects of nature can never be changed. This is why we see men and women separated when participating in most sports, due to the physical advantage of males. No person would be ignorant enough to suggest men and women playing rugby together would define equality, and no person would conclude from the fact that they played separately, that women were automatically inferior to men. Different, yes, inferior, no.

Note: After the departure of our beloved Prophet, Hadhrat Muhammad Mustafā ﷺ from this world, certain people claimed to be prophets in their localities. Among them was a woman named Sijāh al-Aslamiyyah [according to Hāfiz ibn Kathīr, in al Bidāya wan-Nihāya, her name was Sijāh bint al-Hārith, the wife of Musaylama Kadhdhāb] from the tribe of Aslam. She would say, 'The Prophet Muhammad ﷺ has said:

لا نبيّ بعدى ـ

'No male prophet will come after me'.

He did not say:

لا نبيّة بعدى ـ

'No female Prophet will come after me.'

Therefore, it is possible that Prophethood among the men folk is finished, but women could come as prophets. It is clear that this poor lady was disillusioned and misguided by the instigation of Shaytān. Otherwise, the Qur'ān has declared the Prophet ﷺ as 'The Seal of the Prophets', and then there could be no question of a new prophet or new *Sharī'ah* coming after him. Maybe this is why when the Caliph, Abū Bakr Siddīq ﷺ fought these imposters and brought them back to the straight path, this lady, Sijāh, also denounced her own claims and became a proper muslimah. There was another imposter named Tulaiha Ibn Khuwailid, who has also repented from his false claims of Prophethood. And amazingly the two of them, although from a different background, wedded each other and then lived happily ever after.

Another narration is that Sajāh later married Musaylama, accepted him as prophet, then after he was killed in battle of Yamāma, she accepted true Islam

The verse in connection also indicates that none of the angels were made prophets.

Dhahhāk ﷺ narrates from Ibn Abbās ﷺ, 'They were not from the people of the sky, as the *mushrikīn* had repeatedly requested.' The infidels would argue that why did Allāh not send down an angel? How can a human be made prophet? The Qur'ān, in one place replied that if there were angels living on the earth, he would surely have sent an angel. Since the inhabitants of the earth are humans, we have to send down a human being.

'*Men from among the people of towns...*' This indicates that the prophets were raised from people who lived in towns and cities, and not from those who lived in villages or in the jungles or deserts. The wisdom behind this is that the people of towns have a better understanding of the circumstances of people, their culture, their lifestyle, how to communicate politely and how to explain critical matters, provide solutions for problems etc. On the other hand, most Bedouins are void of this quality.

One *Hadīth* mentions, '*Whosoever lives in the open [the desert)] shall surely be hard-hearted.*' [261]

---

[261] Tirmidhī 2182, Nasāi 4235.

It was commonly known among Arabs that the Bedouins are very hard-hearted. With regards to communication, it is hard to explain to them the simplest of things. They are usually deprived of the education that generates understanding and common sense. We read that once a Bedouin sat down in one corner of Masjid un-Nabawī and began to urinate. The *Sahāba* were furious and shouted at him to stop. The Prophet 攁 said: 'Leave him, do not stop him.' When he relived himself, the Prophet 攁 instructed someone to get a bucket of water and pour it over the place the Bedouin had urinated. [262]

Once, after a war, the Prophet 攁 distributed the war-booty. He was walking when a few Bedouins came from the back and pulled his garment with such force that it left a bruise on his neck. They said, 'O Muhammad! Order for us some money from that which Allāh has given you, because you will not be giving from your own pocket, but from that which Allāh has let you keep.' The Prophet 攁 smiled and said: *'Give me back my sheet. I swear by He who holds my life, if I had wealth which would be in the number of the thorns of these trees, I would still distribute it amongst you, so that you would not think of me as a stingy person, a liar, or a coward.'* [263]

'Have they then not travelled...' This means that if you don't believe in Muhammad's Prophethood, you should just look around your city or your country, you will surely note the remains of the nations who came before you and rejected the prophets of Allāh 攁. You will be able to clearly understand what happens when people treat the prophets of Allāh 攁 in an evil manner.

'And surely the abode...' If you fear Allāh and refrain from rejecting His messenger, or rather if you obey him, love him, help him, treat him with respect and propagate his message, you may have to face some hardships in this world, but keep your sights on the hereafter. The Jannah that is being prepared for you which is going to be your abode, is much better than this worldly life.

---

[262] Bukhārī 213.
[263] Bukhārī 2609.

'Do you then not reflect?...' Do you not understand this simple thing? *Ākhirah,* the hereafter, is eternal, whereas this world is temporary. The Prophet ﷺ says, *'Wallāh! [I swear by God] This abode in relation to the Hereafter is nothing, but as if one of you would dip his finger in an ocean, then see how much water his finger brings back from the ocean.* [264] i.e. the amount of water that sticks to your finger is equivalent to your life in this world, whereas, the amount of water left in the ocean is like the life of the Hereafter. Furthermore, every *ni'mah* in this world is going to perish. Our health deteriorates day by day; our wealth is spent on our luxuries every day. We eat delicious food but the taste fades away and within a short time that food turns into urine and faeces. With this slow process, we are travelling towards our destiny. Therefore, a wise person should always bear in mind his eternal residence and should not engross himself into the pleasures of this world. It is for this reason, possibly, that Allāh ﷻ invites us to reflect, ponder and to try and understand what is being said to us.

Verse 110

حَتّىٰ إِذَا اسْتَيْـَٔسَ الرُّسُلُ وَظَنُّوٓا أَنَّهُمْ قَدْ كُذِبُوا جَآءَهُمْ نَصْرُنَا ٧ فَنُجِّيَ مَن نَّشَآءُ ۖ وَلَا يُرَدُّ بَأْسُنَا عَنِ الْقَوْمِ الْمُجْرِمِينَ ﴿١١٠﴾

"[Respite was given] until when the Messengers began to despair and began to think that they were told wrong, our help reached them and whosoever we willed, was saved. And our punishment can never be warded off from the sinning people."

In the aforementioned verse, Allāh ﷻ had questioned that, 'Did the people not travel around the world, so that they can see what was the ending of those who had rejected the Prophets?' in this verse, Allāh ﷻ also explains that we gave the disbelievers respite, and they went on to ill-treat the Prophets until such a time came that they began to taunt the Prophets by questioning them, 'Where is the punishment you had so often mentioned? Why is it still not coming down?'

---

[264] Tirmidhī 2245.

The matter came to such an extent that even the Prophets themselves had a feeling of desperation. They feared that they might have committed an act which caused the displeasure of Allāh ﷻ. Maybe Allāh ﷻ is displeased with them, and has decided not to send down any punishment while they are alive. He might give victory to their followers after their departure from this world. In some cases, this has happened, e.g. the Jews attained the promised land under the guidance of Yusha' ﷺ, after Mūsā ﷺ had passed away. Our Prophet, Hadhrat Muhammad Mustafā's ﷺ message was spread through the globe via his *Khulafā-e-Rāshidīn*. This is one interpretation of the verse.

Hakīm Tirmidhī ﷺ says, 'Our preferred explanation of this verse is that the Prophets feared, even though Allāh ﷻ had promised to help them, not because they doubted the promise of Allāh ﷻ. Rather, they feared for their own selves that they might have committed an act or deed which would deprive them from promises and assurances given to them by Allāh ﷻ.'

SECOND INTERPRETATION

They feared that they had misunderstood the promise of Allāh ﷻ. Allāh ﷻ had promised to help them, and they themselves estimated a time limit. The limit passed and no relief came. They thought that their estimate was wrong.

This does happen. Our Prophet ﷺ saw in a dream that he went to Makkah and performed *Umrah*. He related his dream to the Sahāba who were overjoyed, because the dreams of Prophets are also classed as revelations. They went to Makkah Mukarramah, but were refused entry, and made to return from Hudaibiah on the condition that they return the year after and perform *qadhā* of their *Umrah*. They thought that they would be performing *Umrah* in that very year, whereas Allāh ﷻ had destined it in the year coming. This type of misunderstanding is very rare with the Prophets. However, with regards to the *Ilhām* [inspirations] of the *Awliyā*, this is very common.

Hadhrat Maulānā Qāsim Nānōtwī ﷺ had a friend who was of a very simplistic nature. He used to ask Hadhrat a lot of questions. Hadhrat would reply according to his level of understanding. Once he asked, 'Molwīji, why is it that when the Prophets estimate something, they seldom made mistakes. Whereas in *ilhāms*, we see many mistakes?' Hadhrat was walking with him and asked him, 'Do you see that kothi [large house]?' He replied in the affirmative. Hadhrat asked, 'How far is it?' He replied, 'Maybe 300/ 400 yards.' Hadhrat kept walking and talking about other things until they came very near to the mansion. He asked, 'How far is it now?' 'Oh! Its only ten yards now', replied the friend. Hadhrat said, 'The *Awliyā* see things from the distance and thus misunderstand things. Whereas the Prophets see from very near and thus very rarely misunderstand.'

My beloved Shaykh, Hadhrat Maulānā Yūsuf Motālā *damat barakatahum* was asked regarding a Maulānā's estimation of *Qiyāmah*. The Maulānā says that *Qiyāmah* should come approximately around 2003, because in this year a double eclipse is predicted in the month of Ramadhān, which is among the signs of *Qiyāmah*. Hadhrat replied, 'how could you say for certain that it is this Ramadhān?'

He put forward an argument that Maulānā Badre-Ālam Mīrthi ؓ saw in *Kashf* that Imām Mahdī had been born. Hadhrat said: 'With due respect to Hadhrat Mīrthi, there can be misunderstandings in these types of things. When the Prophet was mistaken in the timing of his Umrah, then why can others not make a mistake? The time of *Qiyāmah* is fixed; only Allāh ﷻ knows that time. Our duty is to keep practicing and worry about our actions. These types of rumours scare people and drag their minds towards many general misconceptions.'

THIRD INTERPRETATION

Some Mufassireen say that the indication is towards the followers of the Prophets ﷺ, i.e. the followers of the Prophet ﷺ began to think that Prophets were sometimes told wrong. Shah Walīullāh ؓ has taken this meaning in his Tafsīr Fath ur-Rahmān.

Ibn Kathīr ؓ has also mentioned this. Hāfiz Ibn Kathīr ؓ narrates that a young man approached Sa'īd Ibn Jubair ؓ and asked, 'O Abū Abdullāh! Tell me the meaning of this verse, because whenever I come across it, I begin to wish that I had never started reading this sūrah, i.e. how can the Prophets despair, and how can they think that they have been told wrong?' Sa'īd ؓ replied, 'Yes, allow me to explain. The meaning is that when the Prophets ﷺ lost hope from their tribes, [that they are not going to believe now] and when the believers, those to whom the Prophets ﷺ were sent, began to think that the Prophets ﷺ were told wrong, that is when Allāh's ﷻ help arrived.'

Muslim Ibn Yasār asked the same question to Sa'īd Ibn Jubair ؓ and when he gave the answer, Muslims stood up and embraced Sa'īd saying, 'May Allāh relieve your anxieties as you have relieved mine.' Abdullāh Ibn Mas'ūd ؓ has also been reported to have taken the same meaning.

FOURTH INTERPRETATION

Hadhrat Ā'ishā ؓ would read '*Kuzzibū*' with *tashdīd*. She said the meaning is that: 'When the Prophets lost hope from those who had rejected them and began to think that those who have followed them have begun to doubt their promises, our help arrived at the eleventh hour.'

FIFTH INTERPRETATION

Hadhrat Maulānā Qāsim Nānōtwī ؓ says: 'The wording of the verse indicates that the Prophets themselves began to doubt, and eventually lost hope. Whereas in this sūrah itself we have read: '*Do not lose hope of the mercy of Allāh ﷻ. Only those lose hope from the mercy of Allāh ﷻ who are disbelievers.*'

Therefore, it is impossible that the Prophets would even think in that direction. They had the firmest belief that Allāh ﷻ is with them and will assist them. Just consider the story of Mūsā ﷺ: the ocean is in front of him, the huge army of Pharaoh is behind him. His people taunt him, yet he says, '*Nay, my Lord is with me! He will surely guide me.*' It is then, that Allāh ﷻ ordered him to hit his staff on the water, the sea divided itself, creating pathways and they were rescued. In the battle of Badr, the night preceding the battle is worthy of notice. Here is the Prophet of Allāh ﷺ weeping before his Lord Almighty saying, '*O my Lord. Send down your aid. My Lord, if this small group is defeated, then you will never be worshipped on this earth.*' He raised his hands and his garment fell down. Hadhrat Abū Bakr ؓ lifted it and returned it to his shoulders and said, 'O Prophet of Allāh, you have surely made enough plea to your Lord. He will never let you down.' The Prophet came out of his place of worship and was repeating the verse, '*Soon, will the multitude [of enemy] be put to flight. And they will show their backs [running away].*' He said, 'Here so and *so will be put down, and here, so and so will be lying dead.'* The companion ﷺ who narrates this *Hadīth* says, 'By Allāh! They [those whose name he had named] did not move a bit from the places he had indicated.'

Hadhrat Nānōtwī ﷺ says: 'They did not doubt the help of Allāh, nor did they complain or say anything that would incur Allāh's displeasure. Whatever desperation they may have felt, was due to the fact that they were human beings. It is only natural that we do sometimes get scared, like how Mūsā ﷺ threw his staff which turned into a python, and he himself was scared, until Allāh ﷻ comforted him and instructed him to take hold of it, and it returned to its original form.'

Hadhrat says, 'This fright has been depicted as desperation, and thinking that they had been told wrong. In other words, Allāh ﷻ is saying that they shouldn't have had this feeling, as I was always with them. My watchful eyes were watching them; my protection had never deserted them. It was only a matter of time before my aid had arrived.' [265]

In other words, one is 'Haal', the other is 'Qaal'. This verse is talking about their 'Haal' [apparent condition]. They had never uttered any words.

Allāh ﷻ says in another verse, *'Or do you think that ye shall enter the garden [of bliss] without such [trials] as came to those who passed away before you? They were inflicted with suffering and adversity, and were so shaken in spirit that even the messenger and those of faith who were with him cried, 'When [will come] the help of Allāh? Ah! Verily the help of Allāh is [always] near.'* [266]

Allāh ﷻ says: *'Alif Laam Meem. Do people think that they will be left alone on saying 'we believe' and that they will not be tested. Surely we did test those before them, and Allāh will certainly know those who are true from those who are liars.'* [267]

Allāh ﷻ also says: *'Be sure We shall test you with some form of fear and hunger and some loss in goods, lives and fruits. But give glad tidings to those who patiently persevere.'* [268]

Khabbāb Ibn Al-Arat ﷺ came to Rasūlullāh ﷺ, badly beaten and bruised. He requested him to supplicate to Allāh ﷻ. The Prophet ﷺ said: *'Those before you were often hacked into two pieces, and still, this did not cause them to deviate from*

---

[265] Ma'āriful Qur'ān Khāndlawī 75:4.

[266] Qur'ān 2:214.

[267] Qur'ān 2:1-3.

[268] Qur'ān 2:214.

their religion. Combs made from steel were brought and their flesh was torn out with the combs, still this did not change them. You are doing nothing but hastening things.' [269]

Allāmā Shabbīr Ahmed Uthmānī ﷺ sums up the *tafsīr* in very short and simple wording. He writes, 'Allāh is saying that do not be deceived by the delay in the chastisement. The past nations were also given respite, and the chastisement was delayed to the extent, that the the unbelievers became unflustered and increased in their mischief enormously. Whilst observing the disbelievers' condition, their [allocated] messengers lost hope in them accepting faith. On the one side, they were given such a lengthy respite that there were no signs of an impending punishment. The unbelievers rejoiced at this situation. They thought the promises of help to the Prophet ﷺ and the promises of annihilating the unbelievers were all absurd and wrong, and the warning of chastisement given to them was simply a farce to scare them, nothing more. Moreover, it is not inconceivable that, occasionally, Prophets were also bewildered at the observation of this impending situation, i.e. divine intervention did not occur in the manner we perceived. They might have thought that the reality of chastisement which they had warned off was less severe. Alternatively, they might have thought whether the promise of help and promises of annihilation would not be fulfilled as is said at another place in the Qur'ān: *'...And were so shaken in spirit that even the messenger and those of faith who were with him cried, when [will come] the help of Allāh...'* [270]

When the fearlessness of the criminals and the anxiety of the Prophets reached such a limit, divine help came, and God saved whomsoever He willed [the obedient and the believers], and eliminated the criminals.

Note: Despondency with the unlimited mercy and kindness of Allāh is *kufr*, but disappointment with external conditions and factors is not *kufr*. Thus, it is impossible for the Prophets to become despondent with Allāh.

When we ponder over the condition of the youth surrounding us, we look at their sorrowful state, and their indulgence in grave crimes. We could say that

---

[269] Bukhārī.
[270] Qur'ān 2:214.

it is a lost cause and a hopeless task in bringing them back to the right path. However, we also know that Allāh ﷻ has full control over everything, guidance is in His hands.

In the present case, ulamā have said disappointment of the messengers is based on the external factors, otherwise the Prophets can never become disappointed with the mercy of God.

Note 2: The flash of *kufr* is not *kufr*, nor in any degree against *imān* and *ismat*. Once the followers said to the Prophet ﷺ, 'O Messenger of God, we perceive such thoughts in our minds, that we feel it better to become cinders of coal, rather than utter those thoughts with our tongue.' The Holy Prophet of Allāh ﷺ said, 'Do you really get these thoughts?' 'Yes', they said. The Holy Prophet ﷺ replied, 'It is pure imān.' This response of the Prophet means that stray thoughts and whims which sometimes strike the heart and mind, should be totally ignored. One should get on with his duties and pay no attention to the bad thoughts that disturb him. A thief only enters the house in which there is something to steal. He does not go into a derelict building. Shaytān is a thief; if he whispers in your heart, it is because you have imān. He does not need to whisper into a *kāfir*, because the *kāfir* is already under his command.

Verse 111

$$ لَقَدْ كَانَ فِيْ قَصَصِهِمْ عِبْرَةٌ لِّأُولِي الْأَلْبَابِ ۗ مَا كَانَ حَدِيثًا يُّفْتَرَىٰ $$

$$ وَلٰكِنْ تَصْدِيْقَ الَّذِيْ بَيْنَ يَدَيْهِ وَتَفْصِيْلَ كُلِّ شَيْءٍ وَّهُدًى وَّرَحْمَةً لِّقَوْمٍ $$

$$ يُّؤْمِنُوْنَ ﴿١١١﴾ $$

There is in their stories, an admonition for those who have intellect. This is not an invented tale, rather a confirmation of what went before it, a detailed exposition of all things, and a guide and a mercy for people who believe.

This is the last verse of Sūrah Yūsuf. Allāh ﷻ makes a final closing comment in the sūrah, saying the stories of this Qur'ān are not fictional or from a novel that one would just read, take pleasure, and put away. Rather, they are narrated every now and then, so that the readers can contemplate, ponder, reflect and take heed from them. The wise people will surely draw lessons from them and gain immense benefit.

With regards to the story of Yūsuf 🕮, one could say that there are plenty of lessons to be learnt from this one *sūrah* alone. We have from time to time mentioned these lessons during the *tafsīr* of this *sūrah*. Therefore, we shall not repeat them here.

'*A confirmation of what went before...*' i.e. the books that were given to the Prophets were definitely true. They had the same message that the Qur'ān has. How can Allāh 🕮 give one message to one Prophet, and then give the other Prophet something that contradicts the first? That is why the Qur'ān says that all Prophets called towards the same God. Their message was to worship Him alone. The roots of the entire Prophetic calls were the same. The Qur'ān Sharīf confirms that the Tawrāh, Injīl and Zabūr were books given to different Prophets.

However, the claim of Hindus that the *Gita* is a religious book and was given to so and so person, and the claim of Buddhists that a certain book was given to their leader is untrue. The Qur'ān refutes these claims. On this earth, there are only two groups who could be classified as the people of the book: The Jews and the Christians. No other religion has a valid claim for receiving a book from God.

'*A detailed exposition of all things...*' i.e. regarding the beginning of this universe and its ending. The attributes of Allāh 🕮, His oneness, His wisdom, His power. Regarding the messengers, the hereafter, the *halāl*, the *harām*, the rules and regulations of *Sharī'ah*, what Allāh 🕮 likes and what He hates, how to please Him, and how to avoid His displeasure. The Qur'ān states all these important matters in details.

One should bear in mind that the Qur'ān is not a book of history, astronomy or geography. Although the Qur'ān hints and indicates towards the important facts of these sciences, it does not go into great detail about them, because there is no point into going into pinpoint detail of everything. The Qur'ān is a book of guidance and thus only relates those matters that have some kind of guidance in them. It can neither be compared with the encyclopaedias of our time, as their main aim is to provide information.

'*And guide and mercy for those who believe...*' One can only guide a person who believes in his guidance. If someone asks you a way to a street or a road, you guide him. If he does not believe you, then he will not take that route and will not reach his desired destination. He may go on to ask someone else to convince himself. Similarly, the Qur'ān can only guide those who believe that it is a book of God. As for those who have doubts about it, they shall never be guided by it. Rather, the Qur'ān itself will misguide them and lead them astray. '*By it He causes many to stray and many He leads unto the right path by it: But he causes not to stray except those who forsake [the path of Allāh]*'

May Allāh Almighty guide us towards the straight path and may He keep us steadfast upon whatever humble efforts we are putting forward to seek His pleasure. May He accept our humble deeds which are not even worthy of putting in His courtyard. May He forgive our misgivings as He has very much done so in the past. O Allāh! O my Master! I have very firm belief in You that You will not cause me to despair or go astray. O beholder of our hearts! Turn our hearts towards Thy obedience and do not put us in the trust of our *nafs*, because our *nafs* will only mislead us. [*Āmīn*]

THE BEST OF PLANNERS

BY SHAYKH IMRĀN MOGRĀ

Allāh ﷻ declares in the Qur'ān that He is the 'Doer of all that He intends.' [271]. In another verse, Allāh ﷻ contrasts the preferences of humankind saying that, *'It is possible that you dislike a thing which is good for you, and that you love a thing which is bad for you, but Allāh knows and you know not.'* [272]

It is this characteristic of Allāh's ﷻ doing, that makes it all the more intriguing to attempt to understand the meaning of Allāh ﷻ as being 'the best of planners'. Consider the following:

Have you ever fallen into a situation in which you felt confused and out of place, and then it turned out that you were precisely in the right place at the right time? Have you ever been ill-treated and felt that everything was going terribly wrong, only to find out that it all turned out to be good? It's great when that happens, isn't it? Suddenly it all begins to make sense and you whisper to yourself, 'That didn't just happen. It was meant to be. It wasn't just a coincidence.'

And that's true. It wasn't just an accident. In fact, there is no such thing as an accident. Everything that happens is part of a plan. This is true of those moments when things tick in a special way, and it is true at every other moment as well. Everything that happens, happens for a purpose.

Muslims have a word for this; *qadha'* and *qadar* [Divine will, decree, providence]. Hence, there is no such thing as coincidence. There is no such thing as luck; there is only Allāh's ﷻ plan. In the Qur'ān, Allāh ﷻ speaks of Himself as *'The doer [without let] of all that He intends.'* [273] And as One who is *'The*

---

[271] Qur'ān 85:16.

[272] Qur'ān 2:216.

[273] Qur'ān 85:10.

best to decide.' [274]. Allah's ﷻ plan includes everything, totally everything, even the insects creeping out of the cracks of rocks in springs, and the falling of leaves in Autumn.

Over and over again, Allāh's ﷻ plans are secret and we can't work out exactly how everything fits together. But even if the details are a secret, the results of the plan are not. The outcome is the definitive good of Allāh's ﷻ people [what does this mean?].

How do we know that? Because Allāh ﷻ, the Planner says so. In the Qur'ān, Allāh ﷻ says: *'Whoever does a righteous deed, whether male or female, and is a believer, such will enter the Garden [of bliss]: therein will they have abundance without measure.'* [275]

Do you believe in Allāh ﷻ? Do you have faith in Allāh ﷻ? Do you love Allāh ﷻ? Have you heard His invitation in the Qur'ān? Have you discovered His purpose for creating you? If so, you can be certain that Allāh ﷻ works all things for your good. You can celebrate on special occasions when everything falls into place, but even when you can't make sense of events, you can still draw strength from knowing about Allah's ﷻ decree. All things, even those that you don't understand come to you, not by chance, luck or accident but from Allāh's ﷻ benevolent 'hand'.

The Qur'ān states this as an indispensable yet simple teaching, and it also shows how this works out in the lives of living people.

In the twelfth *sūrah* of the Qur'ān, Allāh ﷻ narrates the most beautiful of stories, that of Yūsuf ﷺ. He began life as a privileged and well-treated child. His father, Yā'qūb ﷺ, loved him more than any of his other children and he didn't try to hide his love either. Was that 'inappropriate' parenting - to favour one child, and invite the hatred of the others? Even then Yā'qūb's ﷺ 'excessive love' was in some way a piece of Allāh's ﷻ good plan.

Young and handsome, Yūsuf ﷺ had an extraordinary sense of destiny from an early age. One night, he had a dream in which his dad, mum and his brothers were prostrating to him. Instead of keeping his dream to himself, Yūsuf ﷺ innocently told the dream to his brothers, and surprise, surprise, the brothers became all the more jealous and hateful. Yūsuf ﷺ was 'naive' in relating the dream to his brothers, and Yūsuf's ﷺ brothers were wrong to

---

[274] Qur'ān 10:109.
[275] Qur'ān 40:40.

hate him, and yet, in some way, Yūsuf's 🕮 'impulsiveness' and his brother's hatred were part of Allāh's 🕮 wise and good plan.

The brothers planned to get rid of him. But one of them said, 'Do not slay Yūsuf, but cast him into the bottom of a well.' Having thus plotted, they proceeded to Yā'qūb 🕮 and pleaded, 'Why don't you trust us with Yūsuf, let him come with us tomorrow so that he may refresh himself and play.' Yā'qūb 🕮 preferred not the slightest separation. Yet his plan was undoubtedly failing, Allāh's 🕮 plan was just beginning to take action.

When the brothers were at a distance from their home, they threw Yūsuf 🕮 down the bottom of the well and took his coat, smeared it with blood and returned home. Their plan had apparently succeeded.

So to ponder over this, some people are inclined to say that many things 'just seem to happen'. The caravan just happened to pass by. The caravan just happened to be heading for Egypt; and in Egypt an 'Azīz' just happened to be in the bazzar looking for a slave; and eventually there just happened to be a high official from the palace, the ruler of Egypt, Fir'aun.

In the palace of Fir'aun, Allāh 🕮 blessed Yūsuf 🕮 and he was very successful in everything he did. Before long, he was an important person, in charge of finance and agriculture. About that time, if you were Yūsuf 🕮, you might have thought 'at last things are falling to place'. But that's exactly when once again everything was torn apart.

Fir'aun's wife observed that Yūsuf 🕮 was a strong and attractive young man. She attempted to seduce him, but Yūsuf 🕮 told her, 'Allāh 🕮 forbid, surely the wrong-doers do not prosper.' And what did Yūsuf 🕮 get for standing firm against temptation and conforming to Allāh 🕮? He gets thrown into jail! The lady claimed that Yūsuf 🕮 had tried to rape her. She had lied, and she was responsible, and still her lust and lies were part of Allāh's 🕮 plan.

While this chaos prevailed over Yūsuf 🕮, the Qur'ān mentions that, Allāh 🕮 was 'hearing and knowing'. Then one day, two prisoners told him about their respective weird dreams that they didn't understand. Allāh 🕮 gave Yūsuf 🕮 the ability to interpret dreams. Good news and bad news. One dream prefigured death, but the other dream explained happier times. This man was Fir'aun's 'butler'. They were in prison because they had somehow incurred Fir'aun's wrath. Yūsuf ﷺ told the 'butler' he would soon be back in Fir'aun's service. Then Yūsuf ﷺ said, 'Mention me before your master.'

Well, no sooner was the 'butler' out of jail and back in Fir'aun's kindness that Satan made him forget all about Yūsuf ﷺ. So Yūsuf ﷺ spent some years in prison. Try to put yourself in Yūsuf's ﷺ place! This was the gratitude he received for doing a favour. And yet, though the 'butler' was wrong to forget Yūsuf ﷺ, Allāh ﷻ planned it this way.

Meanwhile, Fir'aun had a bizarre dream, and at last the 'butler' remembered Yūsuf ﷺ. He informed Fir'aun about how Yūsuf ﷺ had interpreted his dream. So Fir'aun instructed that Yūsuf ﷺ be brought to him. With Allāh's ﷻ assistance, Yūsuf ﷺ explained to Fir'aun that his dream meant that there would be seven years of massive harvests followed by seven dry years with little harvests. Yūsuf ﷺ advised Fir'aun to store up during the bumper years so that there would be food for the famine years.

Fir'aun accepted what Yūsuf ﷺ suggested. He thought Yūsuf ﷺ would be the right person to administer the entire crop program. Yūsuf's ﷺ interpretation came true. There were seven years of fantastic crops, followed by seven years of widespread famine. In the remote land, Yūsuf's ﷺ hungry family heard that there was food available in Egypt. When they arrived in Egypt, they encountered with none but Yūsuf ﷺ himself.

Yūsuf ﷺ recognised his brothers instantly, but they didn't recognise him. He could not identify himself. He confided to his full brother Binyāmīn and counselled him not to grieve over their doings. He also found out that they had changed little through a plan of the 'cup' deployed by Allāh ﷻ. Binyāmīn had to be retained in Egypt. However, the eldest brother volunteered to be a guarantor to save Binyāmīn. How baffling and agonising it must have been for all of them.

When they return from the devastated Yā'qūb ﷺ who had enjoined them not to despair of the mercy of Allāh ﷻ. Events had to turn. Verse 88 of the sūrah begins to unfold the emotional and penultimate scene, 'O Azīz! Distress has seized us and our family...be charitable to us...Allāh rewards the charitable,' The brothers mentioned Allāh ﷻ!!

Yūsuf ﷺ broke down in tears. He exposed himself, 'Remember what you did to Yūsuf ﷺ and his brother when you were ignorant.' It was almost as if he was 'excusing their nasty behaviour'. When asked by them if he was the one who they thought he was. 'Yes, I am Yūsuf' came the reply. 'Allāh has been gracious to us,' said he.

Amazingly there is no time to admonish but only reconciliation. He declares, 'There is no reproach for you today, may Allāh forgive you, and He is the Most Merciful of the merciful.' Then he throws his arms around his brother Binyāmīn and cries, and Binyāmīn embraces him, and cries. Then he kisses all his brothers and weeps over them. What a scene! Brothers crying, kissing and forgiving, filled with grief at past wrongs and yet seeing how even those wrongs had been part of Allāh's ﷻ secret plan for them.

Isn't Allah's ﷻ plan surprising? The dream of a young child was part of Allāh's ﷻ plan, and so was the dream of the most powerful ruler on earth. Yūsuf's ﷺ three coats were part of Allāh's ﷻ plan. The passing of the caravan, the bucket and the market were planned. Not forgetting the unsteady weather patterns, the good weather as well as the poor. No detail is too tiny for Allāh's ﷻ plan, and no person or power of nature is too great.

Remarkable as all this appears, the most remarkable and mysterious piece is that even the bad deeds of sinful people are part of Allāh's ﷻ plan and decree. Don't misunderstand. Allāh ﷻ doesn't like the evil. Allāh ﷻ is Holy and Pure. When people do sin they are responsible for it. And yet somehow in a way we can't possibly explain or understand, Allāh ﷻ using even evil deeds to accomplish his good purposes.

In the story of Yūsuf ﷺ, Allāh ﷻ didn't compel anybody to transgress. Allāh ﷻ didn't force Yūsuf's ﷺ father, Yā'qūb ﷺ, to pamper his son. That was Yā'qūb's ﷺ doing. Allāh ﷻ didn't make the brothers to envy and hate Yūsuf ﷺ. They were to blame for that. Allāh ﷻ didn't drive the lady to lust after Yūsuf ﷺ and then drive him into jail. She did that herself. Allāh ﷻ didn't make the 'butler' ungrateful and forgetful. That was the 'butler's' fault. And yet, although Allāh ﷻ does not like sinful actions, He somehow made these actions part of His plan and arranged them to suit His own purpose. All the sins that were committed against Yūsuf ﷺ ended up working together for the justice of all Allāh's ﷻ people in Egypt and for Allāh's ﷻ majesty. Indeed, Yā'qūb's ﷺ patience and his imploring Allāh's ﷻ help played a significant part. Then verse 91 is the crux of the matter: the brothers acknowledge their mistake, 'Verily Allāh has chosen thou above us, and we have been sinners indeed.'

Yūsuf ؑ is evidence that Allāh ﷻ can use apparently evil activities and unjust suffering to bring about something good. Muhammad ﷺ becomes even greater proof. There were more horrible sufferings that he had to tolerate. But although depraved people intended to harm Muhammad ﷺ, Allāh ﷻ intended it for the good of human kind, nay for all creation! So that humanity could be saved through faith in the oneness Allāh ﷻ.

The people who had a hand in the final event that led to the *Hijrah* of Muhammed ﷺ were responsible for their action. And yet, in spite of their bad intentions, they were bringing to fruition Allāh's ﷻ good plan. Or consider those who rejected him, bribed him, bullied him, persecuted him and poisoned him. These men and women were responsible for what they did, and yet Allāh ﷻ had decided and planned it all.

There are some striking parallels between Muhammad ﷺ and Yūsuf ؑ. Yūsuf's ؑ brothers thought he had misconceptions of greatness when he dreamt the sun, moon and stars. Some of Muhammad's ﷺ community thought he was crazy when he went around saying there was the only One, Allāh. Yūsuf ؑ was thrown into the well. Muhammad ﷺ was ostracised in the gorge of Abū Tālib. Yūsuf ؑ reached Egypt. Muhammad ﷺ reached Madīnah. Yūsuf ؑ was separated and Muhammad ﷺ was orphaned. Yūsuf ؑ was enslaved before Allāh ﷻ raised him. Muhammad ﷺ shed blood at Tā'if before Allāh ﷻ took him beyond *Sidrat ul Muntahā*. Yūsuf ؑ forgave his brothers; Muhammad ﷺ forgave his enemies. Allāh ﷻ guided Yūsuf ؑ down a road of sufferings in order to protect many people from hunger. Allāh ﷻ guided Muhammad ﷺ down a road of separation to protect people from *Shirk*. Yūsuf's ؑ brothers had to turn to Yūsuf ؑ in order to survive the famine. You and I must turn to the footsteps of Muhammad ﷺ so that we may dwell in peace.

Some parts of Allāh's ﷻ plan are still a secret, but it is no secret that Muhammad ﷺ is the final Messenger of Allāh ﷻ and Mercy to the world. It is no secret that the way to live forever is to repent of you sins and trust in the mercy of Allāh ﷻ and to depend on His pardon to give you eternal bliss. And it is no secret that in all things Allāh ﷻ works for the good of those who love Him. Once you become Allāh's ﷻ and belong to Him, you live each day by certitude and faith in the providence of Allāh ﷻ, knowing that all things come to us not by luck but from His generosity.

Some individuals imagine that if you believe everything is in Allāh's ﷻ plan, you will become inactive and detached. However is that what had happened with Yūsuf ﷺ? Not at all, his trust in Allāh's ﷻ plan didn't make him sit back. Yūsuf ﷺ was active in jail as well. Neither did Yā'qūb ﷺ do anything. It gave them the strength, the desire to keep hoping, praying and to keep doing their best even when everything seemed to be going wrong for them.

As for being detached from the temporal world, did Yūsuf's ﷺ faith in Allāh's ﷻ plan make him bitter, mechanistic and unemotional? In fact, it was quite the opposite. When Allāh's ﷻ plan finally became clear, Yūsuf ﷺ didn't coolly say, 'The jigsaw is now complete'. No, he cried and cried tears of pain he had undergone, and he cried and cried tears of happiness at what Allāh ﷻ had accomplished through those pains.

You see, Allāh's ﷻ providence is more than a keyboard in which Allāh ﷻ pushes the keys and the cursor starts blinking and the hard drive starts processing. It's a reality that's planned by a special Creator and directed by His Mercy, a reality that is lived out in the lives of people. Trusting in Allāh's ﷻ plan doesn't eliminate deep emotions or genuine tears. On the contrary, it has a stabilising result on you. It is a prescription for comforting broken hearts. It helps you to be patient in unpleasant times, thankful in pleasant times, and confident at all times.

Look at Yūsuf ﷺ again. His faith in Allāh's ﷻ plan helped him to be patient when things went wrong. His own brothers hated him and sold him as a slave. He was put into prison after doing the right thing. Someone whom he had helped and who could have freed him from prison forgot him. All this was a heavy burden on the shoulders of Yūsuf ﷺ but did he drown into self-pity, bitterness or anger? No, he continued trusting in Allāh ﷻ. At last, when he got a chance to get even with those who harmed him, what did he do? He forgave them. And he was helped to forgive by the knowledge that Allāh ﷻ uses even the bad actions of those who had hurt him to bring about plenty of good; for example, the admittance by his brothers of their sin.

Maybe something nasty has happened to you, or somebody has hurt you awfully. You don't have to like their *action*. You can cry about it. But do not give up when times are unfavourable, and do not seek revenge when people are nasty. Maybe Allāh ﷻ has an undisclosed plan to bring good even out of the bad, and your trust in His plan can help you to be a more patient and a more forgiving Muslim.

Trusting in Allah's ﷻ plan can also assist you to have a healthy attitude when things go well for you. When Yūsuf ﷺ eventually made it to the top, did he show off his own achievements? No, he gave Allāh ﷻ the credit. He said, 'My Lord! You have given me of the dominion, and have taught me the interpretation of discourse', and he went on further to say: 'Verily my Lord is subtle to whom He will. Verily He, only He, is the Knowing, the Wise.' Trusting in Allāh's ﷻ providence makes you thankful and humble, instead of letting success get to your head.

And whatever your circumstances, whether pleasing or difficult, you can always be confident about the future. No matter what you face, do not give up. Never ever give up on Allāh ﷻ. Yūsuf ﷺ stood up to all kinds of troubles, but never gave up. Why? Because he remembered the dream of the greatness that Allāh ﷻ had shown him, and he knew that somehow Allāh's ﷻ plan would bring him to that great destiny. Allāh ﷻ has also given us a vision, a vision perhaps even greater than Yūsuf's ﷺ. Someday we will be rulers over ourselves. The pious will have authority over the world. That's Allāh's ﷻ plan for each of His righteous people. Nothing should separate us from His love, and nothing should keep us from that destiny.

In the meantime, when you know about Allāh's ﷻ undisclosed plan, you relate all of your life to Allāh ﷻ, and you give Allāh ﷻ all the greatness. When Yūsuf ﷺ talked to his brothers about everything that happened, he kept talking again and again about Allāh ﷻ. 'This is part of why my Lord taught me...' '...That comes of the Grace of Allāh.' '...Unless my Lord do bestow His Mercy', '...Allah has indeed been gracious to us', '...Allāh will forgive you', '...Enter you Egypt in safety if it pleases Allāh', '...The fulfilment of my vision of old! Allāh has made it come true...' '...My Lord! Thou hast indeed bestowed on me some power, and taught me something of the interpretation of dreams.' Having directed all the credit to Allāh, ﷻ his supplication is captivating. He asks Allāh ﷻ to 'Unite him with the *Saliheen*.'

After all of Yūsuf's ﷺ up and downs, how did he relate to it and summarise it all? 'Allāh...Allāh...Allāh...'

That is what happens when you believe in Allāh's ﷻ decree. You look at your life, with all its highs and lows, and what it all boils down to is Allāh...Allāh...Allāh!

Undoubtedly, in Yūsuf and his brothers are signs for seekers after truth.

BIBLIOGRAPHY

1. Āp Bītī
An autobiography of Hadhrat Shaykh ul-Hadīth Maulānā Zakarīyā ﷺ [died 1402 AH].

2. Al-Jamāl Wa'l-Kamāl
By Qāzī Sayyid Sulaimān Mansūrpūrī ﷺ, a salafī scholar, originally a judge, turned towards writing during his retirement. His most famous work is 'Rahmat ul-lil-Ālamīn': Sīrah of the Prophet ﷺ.

3. Fadhā'il-e-Sadaqāt
By Shaykh ul-Hadīth Maulānā Zakarīyā ﷺ.

4. Hujjat-ullāh Al-Bāligha
By Shāh Wali-ullāh Muhaddith Dehlawī ﷺ.

5. Jāmi' Tirmidhī
A famous collection of Āhādith, by Abū Mūsā Mohammad Ibn Isa Ibn Sawrah Al-Tirmidhī ﷺ [died 279AH].

6. Ma'ālimul Irfān
By Sufī Abdul Hamīd Suwatī ﷺ.

7. Ma'ārif ul-Qur'ān
A lengthy but heart-warming and satisfying commentary of the Holy Qur'ān in the Urdu language. There are two tafsīr's with the same name, but different authors: (i) Muftī Shafī Sahib ﷺ, (ii) Maulānā Idrīs Kāndhlawī Sahib ﷺ. I have used that of Maulānā Idrīs Kāndhlawī because I found it more comprehensive and it was enough to quench my thirst. It consists of seven lengthy volumes.

8. Mazāhir-e-Haq

A commentary of Mishkāt ul-Masābīh, which is the famous collection of Hadīth. The author is Nawāb Muhammad Qutbuddīn Khān Dehlawī 🕮, who was among the students of Shāh Abdul Azīz Muhaddith Dehlawī 🕮.

9. Mishkāt ul-Masābīh

By Mohammad Ibn Abdullāh 🕮, who is better known as Khatīb Tabrezī 🕮. He gathered a fine compilation of 5495 Ahādīth. [died 740 AH].

10. Muhammad Rasūl-ullāh

A brief biography of the Final Messenger of Islam, by Maulānā Abul Hasan Alī Nadwī 🕮.

11. Muwattā of Imām Mālik

By Imām Mālik Ibn Anas Al-Isbahī 🕮 [died 179 AH], the great Imām, the head authority of the Mālikiyyah School of Fiqh, who was also a great Muhaddith. Imām Shāfi'ī is among his students. He says, 'Under the roof of this sky, there is no book [of Hadīth] more authentic than the Muwattā of Imām Mālik.' Note: Imām Bukhārī's work was produced after Imām Shāfi'ī 🕮.

12. Qasas ul-Qur'ān

By Maulānā Hifzur Rahmān Suyuhari 🕮.

13. Risalah Fit-Tawhīd

By Shaykh Walī Raslān 🕮.

14. Rūh ul-Ma'ānī

By Allāma Ālūsī Baghdādī 🕮. A very comprehensive tafsīr consisting of various topics, especially tasawwuf. He was a Hanafī scholar, thus supports the Hanafī research in masā'il.

15. Sahīh Al-Bukhārī

The famous Muhaddith, Muhammad Ibn Ismā'īl Al-Bukhārī 🕮, Amīr ul-Mu'minīn Fil-Hadīth, like my teacher Shaykh Yūnus Sahib 🕮 used to say whenever he would start the discourses of Sahīh Al-Bukhārī. He died in 194

AH. His book is well known for Sahīh Ahadīth, although this does not mean that all other Ahādīth are false, rather, it simply means that he has put forward a good collection of authentic Ahādīth.

16. Sahīh Muslim
Also a famous Muhaddith, Muslim Ibn Hajjāj Ibn Muslim Al Qushairī An-Naisāpūrī ﷺ [died 206 AH]. He followed in the footsteps of Imām Bukhārī ﷺ. He also acquired from Imām Bukhārī ﷺ a considerable amount of knowledge in the field of Asmā Wal-Rijāl [the science related to investigating the condition of each narrator in the chain of Ahādīth].

17. Sunan Abū Dāwūd
Another famous collection of Āhādīth, by Sulaimān Ibn Ashath Al-Sijistānī ﷺ. [Died 257 AH].

18. Sunan Ibn Mājah
By Abū Abdullāh Muhammad Ibn Yazīd Ibn Mājah Al-Qazwīnī ﷺ. [Died 257 AH].

19. Tafsīr Baidhāwī
By Abdullāh Ibn Umar Ibn Muhammad Ibn Alī Al-Shirāzī ﷺ [Died 641 AH]. He is known as Qādhī Baidhāwī. He authored many works, the most famous being his Tafsīr Anwār ut-Tanzīl Wa Asrār ut-Ta'wīl, which is known as Tafsīr Baidhāwī. Qādhī Baidhāwī has paid great importance to philosophy, theology, and Arabic grammar in this Tafsīr. Much of his Tafsīr has been taken from Imām Rāzī's Tafsīr Kabīr, Imām Zamaksharī's Tafsīr Kashshāf, and also from Tafsīr Rāghib.

20. Tafsīr Fat'h ur-Rahmān
By Shāh Wali-ullāh ﷺ. [Died 1176 AH].

21. Tafsīr Ibn Kathīr
By Hāfiz Imāduddīn Ismā'īl Ibn Umar Ibn Kathīr Ad-Dimashqhi ﷺ. I would say that without doubt, he is the number one commentator and no one can even come close to him. Tafsīr just flows from his pen like water gushing out

of a fountain. He is the most authentic commentator, in the sense the he only narrates the sound Ahādīth, and refrains from narrating any fabricated Ahādīth. Another beauty of his work is 'Tafsīr ul-Qur'ān b'il-Qur'ān', i.e he brings forth verses similar to the ones in connection, from different sūrahs of the Qur'ān.

Imām Suyūtī ؓ has said, 'No Tafsīr like it has been compiled.' Allāma Anwar Shāh Kashmīrī ؓ is said to have commented, that Ibn Kathīr ؓ has nothing but shortened the tafsīr of Ibn Jareer Tabarī. However, many other scholars say that this is not correct because Ibn Kathīr ؓ has increased with it many beneficial comments, which do not prevail in Ibn Jareer's version. Ibn Kathīr ؓ passed away on the 15th Shā'bān 774 AH. He was buried in the graveyard of the sūfiya, alongside Shaykh Imām Ibn Taymiyya ؓ.

22. Tafsīr Khāzin

The author of this tafsīr is known as Alī Ibn Muhammad Ibn Ibrāhīm Al-Baghdādī Al-Shafi'ī Al-Sūfī [died 741 AH], who is well known by the title 'Khāzin'. He completed his tafsīr on the 10th of Ramadhān 725 AH. The original name of the tafsīr is 'Lubāb ut-Ta'wīl Fī Ma'āni't-Tanzīl'. It is a very good compilation of prophetic narrations, fiq'hī masā'il, linguistics, and tasawwuf. However, one has to be cautious when taking narrations from it.

23. Tafsīr Mājidī

A commentary of the Holy Qur'ān compiled by Hadhrat Maulānā Abdul Mājid Daryābādī ؓ [died 1973]. Hadhrat Maulānā was educated in various universities of India. He has put a great effort in giving references from the gospels, due to his zeal to study comparative religion.

24. Tafsīr Nasafī [Madārik ut-tanzīl]

By Hāfizuddīn Abul Barakāt Abdullāh Ibn Ahmed Ibn Māhmūd An-Nasafī ؓ [died 701 AH]. A short tafsīr, but a marvellous collection of topics, especially the different Qirā'āt [dialects of the recital of the Holy Qur'ān], rhetoric of the Qur'ān and tasawwuf. Not very long, nor too short. When in a rush, I would quickly flick through it and find it sufficient.

25. Tafsīr Uthmānī
A footnote type commentary of the Holy Qur'ān by Allāma Shabbir Ahmed
Uthmānī ﷺ. Short, simple and informative.

26. Translation of the Holy Qur'ān
By Marmaduke Pickthall.

27. Translation of the Holy Qur'ān
By Abdullāh Yūsuf Alī, probably the most famous English translator and
commentator of the Holy Qur'ān. However, one has to be cautious in
narrating from him. He never mentions the names of any previous
commentators; sometimes he uses words which shock the reader. A book
called 'Errors of Abdullāh Yūsuf Alī' has been published in South Africa.

GLOSSARY

<u>A</u>

Abdiyyah: Total submission to the will of Allāh ﷻ

Adgāthu Ahlām: Disturbing dreams

Adhān: The call to *salāh* pronounced loudly, to indicate that the time of prayer has enetered

Āfiyat: Security

Ahl-ullāh: Saints

Ākhirah: Hereafter

Alayhas Salaam: Peace be upon her

Alhamdūlillāh: All praises are due to Allāh ﷻ

Alif: The first letter of the Arabic alphabet

Ālim: Islamic Scholar

Allāhū Akbar: Allāh ﷻ is the Greatest

Āmīn: O Allāh ﷻ, accept our invocation

Ansār: The companions of the Holy Prophet ﷺ, from the inhabitants of Madīnāh, who embraced Islam and supported it, who received and entertained the Muslim emigrants of Makkah and other places.

Ārif: One who has recognition of Allāh

Ashāb-e-Kahf: The people of the cave.

Assalāmū Alaikum: Peace be upon you.

Astaghfirullāh: I seek forgiveness from Allāh ﷻ

Āyat ul-Kursī: Qur'ānic verse no. 255 of Sūrah Baqarah

<u>B</u>

Bait ul-Maqdis: The famous mosque in Jerusalem, which is regarded as the third most sacred mosque in Islam.

Banū Isrā'īl: Israelites

Bāpū: An exorcist

Bārak-allāh Fīka: May Allāh ﷻ grant you prosperity

Basīrah: Foresight
Bāṭil: Falsehood
Bay'at: A form of taking an oath at the hands of a Shaykh
Bid'ah: Heresy for any innovated practice in religion
Burhān: Proof
Bushrā: Good news/Glad tidings

D

Dāmat Barakātuhum: May his blessing be eternal
Dajjāl: Pseudo Messiah/ The Antichrist
Dāwah: Invitation, propagation of dīn
Dīn: Religion/ Way of Life
Dhalāl: Astray
Du'ā: Supplication/ Invocation
Dunyā: World

F

Fāsiq: One who neglects or rejects a wājib injuction
Fiqh: The understanding and application of Islamic ideas, laws, rulings and commandments from original sources of *Sharī'ah.*
Firāq Dāllah: The misguided cults
Fitnah: Trial, tribulation
Fuqahā: [single: Faqīh] Jurist, one who has external knowledge and experience in the field of fiqh.

H

Hāsha Lillāh: I seek Allāh's 🕮 protection
Hadhrat: Respected
Hadīth: [Plural: Ahādīth] originally means a piece of news, tale, story, or a report relating to past or present events. In the technical meaning, it stands for the reports of the words and deeds, approval or disapproval of Rasūl-ullāh 🕮. In other words: the sayings, actions or consent of Rasūlullāh 🕮.
Hadīth un-Nafs: Conversation of the heart
Halāl: Lawful

Hanafī: A person who follows the school of fiqh related to the great Imām Abū Hanīfā ﷺ.

Haq: Truth

Harām: Unlawful, forbidden and punishable from the view point of religion

Haradah: Close to death

Hasanah: Reward, good

Hawā: Will, desire

Hīlā: Plan

Hidāyat: Guidance

Hikmat: Wisdom

Hunain: A valley between Makkah and Tā'if, where the battle took place between the Prophet ﷺ and the Makkan pagans.

Hurūf ul-Hijā: The alphabetical letters of the Arabic language.

I

Ibtilā: Test

Ihsān: Literally, to do good, to be kind. Thereafter, it is used for worshipping Allāh ﷻ with his constant remembrance and complete humbleness. Hadīth Jibrā'īl defines it thus, 'That you worship Allāh ﷻ as though you are looking at Him, and if you do not see Him, then He is watching you.'

Īmān: Faith, belief

Ijmā': Consensus

Ilhām: Divine Inspiration

Imām: The person who leads others in salāh/ Muslim caliph

Innā Lillāhī Wa Innā Ilayhī Rāji'ūn: Verily we belong to Allāh and to Him is our return.

Insān: Human being

Inshā'Allāh: If Allāh wills

Irfān: Recognition

Irshād: Direct

Ismat: Innocence

J

Jabr: Force

Jādū: Black magic

Jāhilīyyah: Pre-Islamic period of ignorance
Jā'iz: Permissible
Jalī: Open, disclosed
Janāzah: Funeral
Jannah: Paradise
Jihād: Sacrifice made for elevating the dīn of Allāh ﷻ
Jinn: A creation by Allāh ﷻ made from fire
Jumu'ah: Friday/Friday prayer

K

Kā'bā: A square stone building in Masjid Haram towards which all Muslims
turn their faces in *salāh*
Kaffārah: Compensation
Kāfir: Disbeliever
Kāmilīn: Saints, people who have rectified their souls and their actions and
have gained closeness to Allāh ﷻ.
Khafī: Concealed
Khalīfah: Caliph
Khalīl ullāh: Friend of Allāh ﷻ; also the name given to Sayyidunā Ibrāhīm
Khāti'īn: Wrong-doers
Khawārij: The people who dissented from the religion and disagreed with the
rest of the Muslims
Khulafā-e-Rāshidīn: The rightly guided Caliphs, namely, Abū Bakr, Umar,
Uthmān and Alī [May Allāh ﷻ be pleased with them all].
Khushū': Sincerity

L

Lāt and Uzzā: Well-known idols in Hijāz, which used to be worshipped in the
pre-Islamic period of ignorance.
Lailat ul-Qadr: The night of power, in the last 10 nights of Ramadhān

M

Mā'sūm: Innocent, free from sin
Madīnah: Second holiest city of Islām
Madrasah: School

Mahfūz: Protected

Makkah: The holiest city of Islam

Makr: Craft, plot

Masjid: Mosque

Masnūn: Sunnah of the Prophet ﷺ

Millat: Religion, path

Mu'min: Believer

Mu'tazilah: A cult born in the first Islamic century, which gained popularity among the Abbasid leaders. Their main difference with the Ahl us-Sunnah was to give preference to the Aql [logic] over Naql [Narrations]. They also had some differences in matters of Aqīdah [creed].

Mu'awwazatayn: Sūrah Falaq and Sūrah Naas, the last two Sūrahs of the Qur'ān

Muddathir: The one who is enveloped

Mufassirīn: Commentators of the Holy Qur'ān

Muftī Sāhib: A person who has studied the course of Iftā, and has developed in him the capacity to deliver legal opinions

Muhājirīn: Those Muslims who migrated to Madinah during the life of Prophet Muhammad ﷺ

Muharram: The first month of the Islamic calendar

Muhsinīn: Those who do good/ Those who practice ihsān

Muqām ul-Ihsān: The status of Ihsān

Mushrik: Polythiest, pagans, idolaters and those who associate partners with Allāh.

Mu'jizāt: Miracles, extraordinary events, which occured upon the hands of the Prophets of Allāh ﷺ.

Muzzammil: The one wrapped in garments

N

Nubuwwah: Prophethood

Nafs: Innerself

Nafs Ammārah: The inner self of a person that lures one towards sin

Nafs Lawwāmah: The inner self that reprimands oneself on committing sin

Nafs Mutma'innah: The inner self of a person reaches a stage that it fulfils Allāh's commandments with ease.

Nafsānī Khwāhishāt: Carnal Desires

Ni'mah: Blessing, bounty

P

Pīr: One's leader in the spiritual path, a master in tasawwuf

Pardah: Hijab or covering the parts of the body, which are essential to be hidden [for women]

Q

Qādariyyah: A cult in early Islām, which denied fate [Taqdīr].

Qamīs: Shirt or coat

Qibtī: A person from the tribe of Fir'awn [Pharaoh]

Qiyāmah: Day of Judgement

Qur'ān: The final word of Allāh Almighty, compiled and collected in the form of a book, in its original form upto this date

R

Radhi-allāhu Anhū: May Allāh be pleased with her

Rahmān: Merciful [one of the names of Allāh]

Rahmat-ullāhī Alayhī: May Allāh have mercy upon him

Rak'āh: One unit of salāh

Ramadhān: The ninth month of the Islamic calendar, the month of observing fasting

S

Sābirīn: Those who persevere and stay patient in hard times

Sādāt: Master [also used as a title name of the descendents of the Prophet ﷺ

Sadaqah: Charity, Alms giving

Sādiq: [Siddīq/Sādiqeen] Truthful

Sahābī: The noble companions of the Holy Prophet ﷺ, who saw him and believed him

Sajdah: Prostration

Salaf-e-Sālihīn: Pious predecessors

Salaf: Predecessors

Salāh: Prayer

Sālik: One who seeks connection with Allāh

Sharī'ah: Islamic code

Shaytān: Devil

Shirk: Polytheism, to worship other deity than Allāh

Shuhadā: Martyrs

Subhānallāh: Glorified is Allāh, Allāh is free from any blemish

Sūfī: Mystic, Ascetic

Sunnah: Way of the Prophet ﷺ

Sūrah: Chapter of the Holy Qur'ān

T

Tā'bīr: Interpretation of dreams

Tablīgh: Propagation

Tadbīr: To pre-plan, careful consideration

Tafsīr: Exegesis, most often used to describe the commentary of the Holy Qur'ān

Tahajjud: *Salāh* performed at night, the best time for which is the last portion of the night, between four to twelve rak'āt

Tajwīd: Intonation

Talāq: Divorce

Talbiyah: Saying Labbaik Allāhumma Labbaik [O Allāh ﷻ, I am obedient to your order, I respond to your call]

Tannoor: An oven especially made for baking Tanoori Naan [Generally people say Tandoori Roti, whereas it should be Tanoori Roti]

Taqwā: Piety, constant awareness of Allāh ﷻ

Tā'wīz: Amulet

Tawfīq: Ability, granted by Allāh

Tawhīd: To confirm the oneness of Allāh ﷻ

Tawriyah: Mis-direction [to say one word and take a meaning, while others are thinking of another meaning]

Thawāb: Reward

U

Ulamā: Scholars, Islamic Theologians

Ummah: Nation

Ummī: Unlettered, unschooled
Umm ul-Mu'mineen: Mother of the believers
Ustādh: Teacher

W
Waḥī: Revelation
Wājib: Obligatory
Walī: A friend of Allāh ﷻ
Wilāyat: Friendship of Allāh ﷻ
Wallāh: By God!

Y
Yā Ayyuha'n-Nabī: O Prophet!
Yā Ayūha'r-Rasūl: O Messenger
Yamāmah: A place in Saudi Arabia towards Najd
Yaqīn: Perfect absolute faith

Z
Zakāh: Charity, 2.5% of surplus wealth, which a Muslim should give to the poor, once in the whole year.
Zikr-ullāh: Remembrance of Allāh ﷻ
Zinā: Adultery
Zuhd: Abstinence
Zul Qarnain: Name of a great leader mentioned in the Qur'ān in Sūrah Kahf